CHAMP FERGUSON
Confederate Guerilla

CHAMP FERGUSON AND GUARD

Champ Ferguson

Confederate Guerilla

THURMAN
SENSING

VANDERBILT UNIVERSITY PRESS

THIS BOOK IS AFFECTIONATELY DEDICATED TO MY SON,

THURMAN SENSING, JR.

MAY HIS ENTHUSIASTIC INTEREST IN THE HISTORY OF
HIS COUNTRY ABIDE WITH HIM THROUGH THE YEARS TO
COME.

Preface

CHAMP FERGUSON was a man strong in purpose and strong in body. Fighting throughout four years of civil strife as a Confederate guerilla, he was too clever to be caught, too strong to be subdued—and possibly too lucky to be killed. All the while he was destroying his enemies. In some manner captured after the War was over, he was formally accused and brought to trial for the murder of the amazing number of fifty-three persons. Testimony revealed that he killed others not mentioned in the charges and specifications. He may have killed still others.

The story of Champ Ferguson's career, as developed from his trial, is unique in the annals of crime and in the annals of trials. It deals with a phase of the War Between the States that has not been developed to any extent; in fact, that has been largely ignored by historians of the period. It deals with a people—the people of the Cumberland Mountains along the Kentucky-Tennessee border —who are of a type unto themselves in our land. They are marked by a stubbornness of spirit, an independence of action, a fixity of purpose, an Indian-like stoicism.

The prowess of Champ Ferguson was respected by his enemies. By the time of his trial, his captors had reason to know that to reckon lightly with him might be disastrous. He was kept in a prison cell built in solid stone, the only ventilation being a grating at the top of a door opening on to the corridor. He was carefully guarded throughout the trial by a detail of Federal soldiers, and his rescue or possible attempt at escape at one time being rumored, he was thereafter kept heavily ironed. (The handcuffs used on Ferguson at the time are still on display in the Tennessee State Historical Museum at Nashville.) Transported to and from prison to the courtroom by his guards each day, they were at one time on the way surrounded by a howling rabble, crying, "Lynch him.

Kill him." The lion was tied and the jackals could howl! But the trial dragged on to its bitter end and the acts related by the witnesses affected the lives of many persons—persons whose descendants still live throughout the length and breadth of the Cumberlands.

So far as I am aware, I first came upon the name "Champ Ferguson" while reading *Morgan's Cavalry,* by General Basil W. Duke, brother-in-law of General John H. Morgan. In this book, published in 1906, the author stated that in June, 1862, at Sparta, Tennessee, Morgan's Men, on their first Kentucky raid, were joined by Champ Ferguson, who reported as a guide, and that he there saw for the first time a man of whom he had heard much, one who had the reputation of never giving quarter, and one who, at the close of the War, probably did not know himself how many men he had killed. According to Duke, Morgan's cavalrymen crowded around Ferguson, anxious to see in the flesh this man who had become even thus early in the War almost a legend in that section.

It occurred to me that a man who could so interest Morgan's Men must be an interesting character indeed. I therefore decided to find out what more I could about Champ Ferguson, having no idea a great deal of information would be available. At the time, I was not aware that Ferguson had been on trial before a military court in Nashville during the summer of 1865, charged with the murder of fifty-three persons, and that the local newspapers had carried very full accounts of the trial.

The search for information led me in many directions—to the War Department at Washington, to the *Official Records of the Union and Confederate Armies,* to various memoirs and books of history, even to personal conversations and correspondence in connection with visits to his birthplace, the scenes of his activities, and his final resting place. The largest volume of information, however, came from the accounts of his trial in the Nashville newspapers of 1865, the *Dispatch,* the *Daily Union,* and the *Daily Press and Times.*

An astonishing and unexpected amount of materials was thus

discovered, and the story contained therein seemed well worth recording. The account of the trial of Champ Ferguson becomes, in its completed form, a history of guerilla warfare in the Upper Cumberlands during the War Between the States. Ferguson's constant participation in these activities from the beginning to the end of the War makes an account of his own record almost a chronicling of all guerilla activities in that region.

The very name "Champ Ferguson" seems to carry with it the flavor of Caledonian strength in combat. Champ Ferguson lived at a time and in a region where physical strength was both necessary and admired. This Tennessee-Kentucky mountain region has produced men of great courage, intense personal convictions, and conspicuous ability. Sergeant Alvin York, of Fentress County, named by General Pershing as the outstanding individual soldier of the World War, and Cordell Hull, of Overton (now Pickett) County, Secretary of State, are men of this type. Both were born, and Sergeant York still lives, in the immediate neighborhood of the birthplace and of the scenes participated in by Champ Ferguson during his colorful but unfortunately not so glorious career.

This is a region where feuds among the mountain clans have caused bloodshed and death for generations. Only lately have these practices been curbed by the laws of the commonwealth. It is a land where not many of the active men "lived until they died." The nature of the people and the almost inaccessible territory in which they lived made it possible for them to be a law unto themselves for a century or more. What law was there was usually on the side of the clan having the most members or the straightest shooters.

Division of opinion and resultant feuds along the Kentucky-Tennessee border did not start with the War Between the States. Divided sentiment was bitter—on politics, on family matters, on individual rights, on slavery, on state's rights, even on religion—so bitter that, in accordance with the nature of the people, it was often committed into action. Such was the state of affairs long before the War started and these feuds were to linger long after the War had ended. The War simply gave the factions concerned a military cloak under which to conceal their private struggles.

Guerilla warfare was nothing new to the people of the Cumberland Mountains. Their forebears had been trained to such fighting by Indian warfare and had continued the custom in their personal feuds. It was only natural that this would be the accepted method of battle in this region during the War Between the States. The customs and habits of this people must be understood to secure an accurate picture of the deeds of Champ Ferguson. Champ Ferguson was, by nature and desire, a hunter, as his Grandfather Champion Ferguson had been, and as the men who were his grandfather's contemporaries, Daniel Boone, James Harrod, Benjamin Logan, and others, had been. Known to the Indians as the Long Knives, or the Long Hunters, they had conquered the Dark and Bloody Ground. History does not record men of greater bravery or greater physical stamina than these men, and in this respect at least Champ Ferguson was a worthy descendant.

In addition to more than forty references to Ferguson in the *Official Records of the Union and Confederate Armies,* a surprising number for a Confederate guerilla soldier, some account of his career is given by a good many writers of this period. Some of these relations, I found to be largely true but some of them are true to only a limited extent and others completely incorrect. Rumor and legend have colored many, even those written by Ferguson's contemporaries. Some of the facts will never be known, but we now have enough to separate in large part the true from the false. Indeed, truth is sometimes stranger than fiction, and Champ Ferguson's actual career was as strange and spectacular as the most vivid imagination might have created.

CONTENTS

CHAPTER ONE

The Camp Meetin' Fight

CHAMP FERGUSON was seized at his home near Sparta, in White County, Tennessee, on May 26, 1865, one month and seventeen days after Lee had surrendered to Grant at Appomattox. He was brought to Nashville and placed in the Military Prison on May 29th. His trial, which was to last throughout the summer and into the fall, began on July 11th.

"Ferguson," stated the Nashville *Daily Press and Times,* on May 12, 1865, two weeks before his capture, "is one of the blackest scoundrels in the guerilla calendar, and we sincerely hope that his bloody career may be speedily brought to an ignominious close." . . . . The people of Nashville were to have brought out in public trial the details of an amazing number of exploits, about which much had been heard. Truth was to reveal them as stranger than hearsay, unbelievable as some of these reports had been.

On July 7th, four days before the trial opened, the *Daily Press and Times* again reported:

"Communications are pouring in upon the authorities, detailing either new atrocities or reciting additional particulars relative to those already known. Also names of more witnesses are constantly being forwarded who stand ready to testify to the wretch's cold-blooded murders. The testimony is accumulating mountains high on the head of this monstrous criminal."

The newspapers of this period were published by Northern sympathizers since with the fall of Fort Donelson in 1862 the city had been occupied by Federal troops. None of them would have dared come out openly with Rebel sentiment even had they wished. Comments by the papers upon Champ Ferguson and his trial were not calculated to encourage sympathy on the part of the reader. They did serve, however, by their very bitterness to increase an already heightened interest in Champ and in everything connected with the trial.

The newspaper reports led Champ to suspect that his case was being prejudiced and naturally he felt unkindly toward the newspapers. One reporter, however, a Mr. Rogers, of the *Dispatch,* succeeded in getting himself in Champ's good graces by securing permission from the authorities to furnish the prisoner daily with a copy of his paper. In return for this favor, and perhaps some few others, Rogers obtained during the summer two or three "scoop" interviews. It is from his "stories" that we get certain personal items of information not available elsewhere. These will be alluded to later.

Champ Ferguson was born on the 29th day of November in the year 1821, on a branch of Spring Creek about a mile and a half from Elliotts Crossroads near Albany, Clinton County, Kentucky. His birthplace was just over the Kentucky line, north of Pickett County, Tennessee, formerly part of Fentress and Overton. He was named, so he tells us, after his grandfather, "who was sometimes called Champion."

Champ was the eldest of ten children, of whom seven were living, as was his mother, at the time of his trial.

"I never had much schooling," said Champ, "but I recollect of going to school about three months, during which time I learned to read, write, and cipher right smart."

He was married at the age of twenty-two, in 1843, to Ann Eliza Smith, who bore him one child, a boy. Both his wife and child died about three years after the marriage. In 1848 Champ was married again. His second wife, Martha Owens, also bore him one child, a daughter, who was in her sixteenth year at the close of the War, and who, with her mother, visited Champ during the summer of 1865 while he was being held prisoner in Nashville. His deep affection for his wife and daughter was most noticeable to those associated with him during that summer and was, by some, considered a redeeming trait in his character.

Aside from these items of information, we know little about Ferguson's life before the War. He no doubt led the usual life of the mountaineer farmer, depending a great deal on his skill at hunting to provide a large part of the needed food supplies. We can guess, with good reason, that he ranged far and wide through the Cumberland Mountains on his hunting expeditions, for he knew the country like a book, knowledge which served him well as a guide and a scout, and aided him to seek out, and to escape from, his enemies as occasion might require.

Champ was well known along the Kentucky-Tennessee border by the opening of the War. He was forty years of age, in the prime of life, and was adept in the use of the gun and the knife and in horsemanship, and could take care of himself in a rough and tumble engagement. It was a common practice in that day and time for young men to engage in feats of skill and strength, and we can be sure that Champ lived up to his name along these lines. There is nothing on record indicating Champ's ability at singing, but we do know he was fond of his liquor, loved a fine horse, and was probably of more than average attraction to the women of his neighborhood.

"For twenty years he has borne a loose character," said the reporter for the *Daily Press and Times*. "He has been known as a gambling, rowdyish, drinking, fighting, quarrelsome man. He seemed to always be in hot water." . . . . It should be pointed out again, however, that this statement is far from impartial, as this reporter, in particular, was bitter in his denunciation of Champ Ferguson as the trial opened.

During his first interview with Champ Ferguson, Rogers, the *Nashville Dispatch* reporter, asked him about the killing of a constable named Read before the War commenced. Champ, of course, was not being tried for this act at the time, but the deed had apparently attracted considerable interest, as well it might from the reporter's account of the happening as told him by Champ:

"Sometime before the War, there were two brothers named Evans, who lived in Fentress County, Tennessee. They came over to Clinton County and purchased a large number of hogs from my brothers, Ben, Jim, and myself, and in fact from all in that neighborhood who had hogs to sell. Floyd Evans gave his note for the payment. At the time appointed by him to meet at Albany, we went down to get our pay. On the road we met Alexander Evans, one of the brothers, and a number of others, who appeared to be in a big flurry about something. When we rode up, they told us that Floyd had run off with all the money, and they were hunting for him. Alexander Evans had done this to mislead his brother's creditors, and Floyd in the meantime had left on the boat.

"Mr. Riter and I proceeded to Livingston, and brought suit against Floyd Evans and got judgment. When we would catch Alex Evans in Kentucky, we invariably attached his horse, and this is the way the horse was taken that I have been charged with stealing. After awhile, Floyd Evans returned, and sent to Riter to have the suit withdrawn, giving security for the payment of the debts.

"Sometime after this, my brother, Jim, and Bill Jones went over to Fentress County and brought back the mare to Kentucky and had her attached. A few days after this I went to a Camp Meeting in Fentress County, at Lick Creek, with a friend, and was entirely ignorant of the taking of the mare by Jim and Bill Jones. However, they got the idea in their heads that I was the author of it, and after we were on the ground a short time, a friend came to me, and called my attention to a crowd, who were with the Evans boys plotting some mischief. He advised me to leave the ground, for he had overheard them talking in groups and that they intended to kill me or give me a severe thrashing. I told him that I did not fear them, and would not leave the ground until I got good and ready. By this time, I noticed them talking in little squads and looking toward me.

"Finally, I concluded that rather than have any trouble with them, I would leave. Accordingly, I started for my horse when the mob commenced picking up stones and shouting 'kill him,' and at the same time sending a shower of rocks at me. There were about twenty of them, and I had nothing but a small pocket knife about me. However, it was brand new, and sharp as a razor. I succeeded in mounting my mare, and 'lit out,' with the whole pack in pursuit like so many wolves that had got a taste of blood. They took all the horses they could find on the ground, and the race was for life with me.

"I had a fleet little mare, but she was in foal. At a gulley or two my mare fell in making the jump, and hurt herself, so that I had to dismount and trust to my legs. They overtook me, and Floyd Evans came up first. I tried to reason with him, and said, 'Floyd, what do you mean?' He made no answer, and came at me, throwing rocks. I then gathered up a few, and sent them back at him, and by this time Jim Read and some of the others had me surrounded. A furious battle ensued with rocks. I struck Floyd Evans with one in the stomach, and he doubled up and got out of the fight.

"Read, who was a large man, and would weigh fully two hundred pounds, closed on me. I suppose he was acting as constable. When he got within a few feet of me, I clinched him, and had my pocket knife out and open. We had a scuffle, and I kept cutting him all the time, until he fell, and I stabbed him once or twice. I then turned my attention to Huddleston, and chased him down a hill to a fence, which he leaped and got away from me.

"The Evans boys came running down the hill after me, followed by the gang. I stood, and Floyd Evans and I came together. I had my knife in my hand, but it got twisted some way, and split my thumb open. We had a desperate struggle for the top, and finally I got my knife in play, and commenced sticking him until I threw him and he fell with me astraddle of him. I drew him up by the collar, and had my arm raised to plunge the knife in his bosom, when he looked piteously in my face. I spared his life and threw him away from me.

"The others closed on me, and I had to run for dear life. I jumped several fences in crossing fields and left them far behind me. I never knew how fast I could run until that time, but a man can make a big race when his life is at stake. I ran into a house, and got upstairs. I found a heavy, old-fashioned bed wrench, and stood waiting for the next attack. They soon came to the house, and cried out, 'Where is he?' at the same time searching for me. I shouted to them, 'Here I am, and I dare any of you to come after me.' A dispute then arose about who would take the lead in ascending the stairs to take me. After a great deal of blustering and cursing, every one of them backed out. By this time, all the women from the camp ground were in and around the house, screaming and crying, some of them fearing they would kill me and others afraid that I would kill some of their relatives.

"Matters stood this way for some time, until the sheriff arrived, and I was called upon to surrender. I refused, unless they could give me some assurance that my life would be protected against the mob. After about two hours threatening, Jim Wright wanted me to throw down my knife, but I refused until a sacred promise was made that I would have a fair trial. I then came down and gave up, after which they tied me hand and foot and carried me to jail. Shortly afterwards, I was let out on bail, and when the War broke out I was induced to join the army on the promise that all prosecution in that case would be abandoned. This is how I came to take up arms."

The history of the times records that camp meetings were used for other purposes than praying and preaching, and this one apparently was no exception. We gather that having the Evans boys' horses attached became almost a habit with their creditors. As a matter of fact, we might almost assume that the "attachment" of the mare, which got Champ into so much trouble, probably took place after dark, and at other times and in other places would be called by a different name. As to whether Champ knew that his brother, Jim, and Bill Jones had brought the mare back into Kentucky, we have his statement that he did not, but in any case he got the blame. Champ says that he was blamed for many happenings during the War for which he was not responsible, and if this is true, this particular occurrence may have been only a forerunner of what was to come. This incident was also probably the beginning of that bitter strife between Champ and his brother, Jim, which naturally made a Rebel of the one and a Yankee of the other.

The story of the Camp Meeting probably bringing it to mind, the *Dispatch* reporter at another point during his first interview questioned Champ with reference to his religious views. His account of the answer to this question follows:

"We asked Champ if he had ever embraced any religion, or whether he had any religious faith. He raised his head, and a smile crinkled in his expressive eyes. He looked at us a moment, in doubt, and asked if we were only joking, or really in earnest. In order to assure him that we were not joking, we put the question in a more comprehensive and broader light. We asked him if he believed in God Almighty, and a future world, and if he ever had any inclination or preference for one religious denomination over another. Champ fully understood us now, but he could not refrain from smiling at the novelty of our asking him if he was a religious man. He made the following statement, which shows that he is at least a believer in Christianity, if he has not practiced it:

" 'Well, I believe that there is a God, who governs and rules the universe, and that we are all held responsible for our acts in this world. I think, in fact, that the "Old Man" has been on my side this far in life, and I believe He will stay with me and bring me out of this trouble all right. I have been mighty lucky through life, and I always thought that God favored me. I place all my hope in Him, and I don't believe the "Old Man" will throw me now.

" 'You asked me about my religious choice. I always thought that the Campbellites were just as good as any of them, and maybe a little better.' "

The newspaper accounts of the interviews with Champ Ferguson during the summer of 1865 are hardly as satisfactory as they might have been, because of the method of reporting which seems to have been in vogue at the time. It is difficult to tell, for instance, whether certain parts of the reports are actually Champ's own statements or whether they are the opinions of the reporter. Champ probably had difficulty in expressing himself, hence the reporter was constrained to give what seemed to him the gist of the conversation in his own words.

Even as Morgan's Men, themselves seasoned soldiers by the time, crowded around Champ Ferguson, anxious to see in the flesh this man of blood of whom they had often heard, so naturally one of the first interests of the newspaper reporters as the trial opened was to present to the public a word picture of his appearance.

What manner of physical man was Champ Ferguson? What did he look like? What did he wear? How did he act? All these questions, and more, the people were asking, and for those who were unable to visit the courtroom and see the notorious character in person, the newspapers were quick to supply the answer by drawing, by photograph, and by printed word.

The *Nashville Daily Union* on July 12th, the day after the trial opened, gave the following description:

Ferguson is a tall, well-built man, of about forty-five years of age. His hair is black and tolerably short, and seems from long habit to have grown in one direction, at an angle of forty-five degrees backward from the surface of his head. This gives him a somewhat fierce appearance. His forehead is large, white, and well proportioned. Beneath it are two penetrating eyes which look as though they were little accustomed to tears. His cheek bones are rather prominent, suggesting to one's mind a well-formed, half-breed Indian.

Added to these features, is a well formed nose, prominent and slightly aquiline. Beneath this is a large bulging lip, covered with black bristles of about two weeks growth. The lower lip is small, and when the mouth is shut gives the latter a compressed and somewhat puckered appearance. The small chin aside from its knottiness does not indicate great firmness, but the whole face betokens an immense amount of it. His beard is short and seems to be about a fortnight old. Its blackness renders the small space of clear skin upon the upper portion of the cheeks doubly transparent. If we mistake not, there are signs of pretty free drinking in little bloodshot network resembling the hectic flush of a consumptive.

A coarse, heavy, rusty sack coat covers his broad shoulders while a checked flannel shirt and dark blue pants, with his half heavy boots, all well worn, make up the balance of his wardrobe.

Interest in Ferguson's trial was not confined to Nashville. A framed page from Frank Leslie's *Illustrated Newspaper* of September 23, 1865, hangs on the wall of Andrew Johnson's tailor shop in Greeneville, Tenn. The copy on the page is mainly about Andrew Johnson, but it also contains a photograph purported to be of

Champ Ferguson, labeled "Photo by C. C. Hughes, Nashville, Tennessee." At the bottom of the page are two or three paragraphs reading as follows:

CHAMP FERGUSON

This noted guerilla, the Mosby of the West, is now on trial in Nashville, Tennessee, for the many horrible atrocities perpetrated by him during the War. It was this man who boasted that he had, with his own hands, put to death 100 Union Prisoners.

Champ Ferguson appears to be about forty years of age or upwards. He stands erect, is fully six feet high, and weighs about two hundred pounds. He is built solid and is evidently a man of great muscular strength. He has a full round face, which is bright and intelligent looking. His large, black eyes fairly glitter and almost look through a person. His face is covered with a stiff black beard. His hair is jet black, very thick, and cut rather short. He brushes it back from a high forehead. He is certainly a very intelligent looking man and nothing vicious is portrayed in his face. His countenance is, on the contrary, pleasing and one would readily take him for an honest farmer as he appears. His face is beginning to reveal the footprints of age and wrinkles can be traced on his forehead and under his eyes.

He dresses in shabby style. A pair of coarse gray homespun pants and a faded gray Rebel uniform coat, over which he wears a very old and greasy black heavy cloth coat, a coarse factory shirt and a faded black slouch hat, with good heavy boots, completes his attire.

His voice is firm and it is evident that he is a man of iron nerve.

The *Nashville Dispatch* of October 3, 1865, not without a bit of gratuitous editoralizing on the *Illustrated's* ethics, denies the authenticity of the photograph reproduced:

Frank Leslie's Illustrated Newspaper of September 23rd gives its readers and the world a cut purporting to be a correct likeness of Champ Ferguson, taken from a photograph by C. C. Hughes of this place. It is simply no likeness of Champ at all and is in all probability an old cut of some person which has lain in the office for years and was used for convenience. That kind of enterprise is about played out and Frank Leslie ought to be the last person to pawn off such deceptions.

Two authentic photographs of Champ Ferguson are in existence, one in the private collection of an individual residing in Nashville and the other reproduced in General Bromfield L. Ridley's *Battles and Sketches of the Army of Tennessee.* Comparison of these photographs, both of which were undoubtedly made during the summer of 1865, although the photographer is unknown, with the reproduction in Leslie's *Illustrated Newspaper* would indicate that the *Dispatch* is probably right in its contention. It is rather difficult to be positive about this, however, as the two authentic photographs are both full-face while Leslie's is side-view; also the photographs are naturally somewhat faded with age.

Ridley's photograph shows Ferguson standing, with one of his guards by his side, the guard holding his musket with bayonet affixed in one hand, the other hand resting on Ferguson's shoulder. The privately owned photograph shows Ferguson in a sitting position. The similarity of background in the two photographs would indicate that the two were taken by the same photographer, probably at the same time. Both show Champ Ferguson to have been not unpleasing of feature. His countenance, in fact, shows rather strongly in these old photographs, comparing most favorably in this respect with that of Tinker Dave Beatty, whose photograph is also contained in Ridley's journal. The photograph of Ferguson standing by his guard shows him a full head taller than the guard and his loose-fitting, shabby clothes do not entirely conceal a well-formed body evidencing the great muscular strength and agility which enabled him to perform the many feats attributed to him during the course of the War.

Many years afterwards, General Basil W. Duke, in his *Reminiscences,* said of Ferguson:

He was a rough-looking man but of striking and rather prepossessing appearance, more than six feet in height and very powerfully built. His complexion was florid, and his hair jet-black, crowning his head with thick curls. He had one peculiarity of feature which I remember to have seen in only two or three other men, and each of these was, like himself, a man of despotic will and fearless, ferocious temper. The pupil and iris of the eye were of nearly the same color and, except to the closest inspection, seemed perfectly blended. His personal adventures, combats, and encounters were innumerable. Some of his escapes, when assailed by great odds, were almost incredible and could be explained only by his great bodily strength, activities, adroitness in the use of his weapons, and savage energy.

Such was the man Champ Ferguson, mountaineer, rebel, guerilla-fighter, facing trial before a United States Military Court, charged with the murder of fifty-three persons. For more than four years he had carried on his activities amid a hot-bed of his enemies, much of the time in Federal territory, always successfully evading capture. Seven weeks after the close of the War found him in prison, awaiting trial.

In view of all these unusual physical attributes assigned to Champ Ferguson by those who saw him and knew him, and in view of his successful evasion of his many enemies throughout the long course of the War, how, it will be asked, could he have been captured or why should he have surrendered? These are pertinent questions. Although the complete story of Champ Ferguson's seizure after the close of the War belongs later in our story, it would seem desirable that these facts be set forth at this point before proceeding with an account of his deeds during the War.

CHAPTER II

The Capture of Champ Ferguson

GENERAL ULYSSES S. GRANT sat on a log in the Virginia woods on April 7, 1865, and, while the ashes from his cigar fell on his unbuttoned blouse, wrote out a message to General Robert E. Lee. Two days later, April 9, 1865, in the home of Mr. Wilmer McLean, at Appomattox Court-house, Va., General Grant, bluff and untidy, but a gentleman withal, met General Lee, a gentleman always, both in appearance and demeanor, and agreed on honorable peace terms, as might two brothers who, in honor of a common mother, patch up a quarrel. The general terms of surrender as laid down by General Grant and accepted by General Lee were:

Roll of all officers and men be made in duplicate, and one copy be given to an officer to be designated by me and the other to be retained by such officers as you may designate; the officers to give their individual parole not to take up arms against the Government of the United States until properly exchanged, and each company or regimental commander sign a like parole for the men of their commands. The arms, artillery, and public property to be packed and stacked and turned over by me to officers appointed to receive them. This will not embrace the side-arms of the officers, nor their private horses or baggage.

This done, each officer and man will be allowed to return to their homes, not to be disturbed by United States authority so long as they observe their parole and the laws in force where they may reside.

Thus were set forth the terms that were to end a long and bitterly fought war. These terms were so clear in purpose and so simple in execution that any misconstruction or difficulty in carrying them out was an exception. The outstanding exception was the case of Champ Ferguson.

For some time before the end of the War it had been determined by the Federal authorities that Champ Ferguson would not be allowed to surrender. Of this, there can be no doubt, and whether or not "Yankee trickery" brought about his capture it is difficult to say. But we can also be certain that Champ Ferguson was not aware of this decision by the Federals; else he would never have allowed himself to be captured. He could easily have withdrawn into the fastnesses of the Cumberlands, where his capture would have been practically impossible, or he could have vanished into the hinterlands of the West, where so many of his compatriots went at the close of the War.

The reporter for the *Nashville Dispatch* quotes Champ on this point:

"When I surrendered I never dreamed of being arrested. I did suppose, however, that they would make me take all the oaths in existence, but that I was willing to do, and live up to them. Why, I could have kept out of their hands for ten years and never left White County, and might have left as Hughes did, had I been disposed to do so. As an evidence of this, Hughes returned to his home quite a time before I did, and left without any trouble for parts unknown, and who doubts but that I could have done the same. But I have set forth all the facts concerning my surrender in the affidavits and pleas filed at the beginning of the trial."

Regardless of all the arguments on both sides, as they shall be set forth, two points seem to be perfectly clear: first, that the Federal authorities had definitely made up their minds that Champ Ferguson's surrender would not be accepted on the basis of parole; and second, that Champ Ferguson, if he did surrender, would never have done so had he known that he would not be paroled.

From the *Official Records,* we take the following dispatch from Major-General Burbridge, at Lexington, Kentucky, to Brig.-General B. W. Duke, of the Confederate Army, on February 24, 1865:

General: Your information that I propose to hold your command responsible for the murder of negro soldiers under my command at Saltville in October, 1864, is incorrect. I have ascertained what troops are responsible for the outrages referred to, and should an opportunity occur I shall hold them to a strict accountability. The murder of Lieutenant Smith at Emory and Henry Hospital by Champ Ferguson was one of the most diabolical acts committed during the War, and I am surprised at its being passed over without notice by Confederate authorities. Should he or any of the band that accompanied him on that occasion fall into the hands of the U. S. forces they will not be treated as prisoners.

General Burbridge did not know that Ferguson had been arrested by the Confederate authorities and received at Wytheville, Virginia, on February 8, 1865. His name appears on a list of prisoners in the guard house at that place on February 20, 1865, charged with killing Federal prisoners. Opposite his name on this list, which is now part of the official records of the War in the Adjutant General's office in Washington, appear the words "on parole." Champ Ferguson himself, later on, told the reporter for the *Nashville Dispatch* of this arrest, and said that he was released because proof of his guilt could not be produced.

Proof may have been lacking; certainly in the harassed last days of the Confederacy there was little time for collecting evidence or for holding trials. Again, it may be that the Confederate authorities felt that there was justification for Ferguson's action. Whatever the reason, they did not press charges against him.

Three months later, after Appomattox, the Federal authorities had no intention of being so lenient. The following dispatch from the *Official Records* indicates that Ferguson had been given an opportunity to surrender but that he had not done so. Of this nothing further is known. It makes clear how Ferguson was thenceforth to be regarded:

From Captain H. C. Whittemore, Acting Assistant Adjutant General, at Nashville, to Major-General Milroy, on May 16, 1865:

In accordance with orders heretofore published of the Major-General commanding the Department of the Cumberland, Champ Ferguson and his gang of cut-throats having refused to surrender are denounced as outlaws, and the military forces of this district will deal with and treat them accordingly.

By command of Major-General Rousseau.

This order was passed on under date of May 19th from John O. Cravens, Assistant Adjutant-General at Tullahoma, Tennessee, to Capt. Henry Shook, at McMinnville, Tennessee:

Sir: Your letter of this date reporting the fact that a number of bush-whackers had surrendered to you has been received. Your action in the matter has been approved by the Major-General commanding. All other bands may be received in the same way. Champ Ferguson and his band have been declared outlaws by Major-General Rousseau. The Major-General commanding therefore directs that you do not accept the surrender of Ferguson, or any member of his band, and that you treat them as outlaws. You will immediately make a list or roll of all those who have surrendered to you, giving name, to what band they belong, how long in service, age, rank, and when and where surrendered, to whom surrendered, and where they live.

A dispatch, from Wm. D. Whipple, Brigadier-General and Chief of Staff, to General George H. Thomas, under date of May 30th, indicates that at least in the opinion of the Headquarters of the Federal Army, Champ Ferguson's apprehension had been by capture, not by voluntary surrender:

The capture of Champ Ferguson and surrender of his guerillas has restored complete quiet to Overton and Fentress counties. I have directed General Rousseau's expedition not to move. General Stoneman will go on.

As these dispatches make clear, Champ Ferguson was accorded the thoroughly doubtful honor by the Federal commanders of being singled out as one partisan of the Confederacy whose surrender would not be accepted in accordance with the terms granted General Lee by General Grant at Appomattox. Thus, rather strangely, was the War's most notorious guerilla soldier accorded the same treatment as Jefferson Davis, the President of the Confederacy, the latter, of course, under quite different circumstances and for quite different reasons,—but the two of them standing apart from all others in this respect. As will be seen, it was finally decided that the other members of Ferguson's band might be allowed their paroles, but for Champ it was "unconditional surrender."

When Ferguson's trial opened, attorneys for the defense tried desperately to secure a discontinuance on the plea that the prisoner came under the provisions of these terms and therefore was not subject to prosecution by the United States Government. The plea was presented on July 13th, the third day of the trial:

THE PLEA FOR DISCONTINUANCE

And the defendant in proper person comes before the Commission, and for plea to the charges and specifications read against him, says that he ought not further be prosecuted upon them nor made further to answer unto them. Because, he says, that in the year 1861, a war commenced and existed between the United States and the States of the South, called the Confederate States; that the war was recognized by both governments, and each acknowledged belligerance, not only by each other, but by the various governments of the world. That the defendant was regularly commissioned as a Captain by the authorities of the so-called Confederate States on the —— day of ——, 1862. Previous thereto, he volunteered and was a regular private of Captain Bledsoe's company, attached to the Confederate States.

He further avers that all acts done and performed during the existence of said war were in conformity to the laws of war, and not in violation thereof, and which were recognized and approved of by the Confederate States that he was serving. He further avers that Gen. Robert Lee surrendered his army to General Grant, and by the terms of capitulation, the officers and men of his army were paroled, and permitted to return to their homes to remain peaceable citizens, and not to be molested by the authorities of the United States, but to be protected by them so long as they observed in good faith their paroles. That General Johnston surrendered on the same terms of capitulation granted to General Lee and his army.

And defendant further avers that Col. Joseph Blackburn, commanding the 5th Regiment of Tennessee Mounted Infantry, a part of the army of the United States commanded by General Thomas, did on the 15th day of May, 1865, address a letter and cause it to be placed in the hands of James Walker, of White County, in Tennessee, where the defendant and his company were located, with directions that the same should be submitted and read to the defendant, which letter asked the surrender of the defendant and his command, and gave him the assurance if he and his command would surrender that they should be entitled to the same terms of capitulation granted to Generals Lee and Johnston and their armies. And the defendant avers that he submitted this proposal to his command and urged them to accept the same, advising them to go in and make the surrender, lay down their arms, be paroled, and return to their homes to live as peaceable citizens.

That according to said article of capitulation, he, the defendant, and his command agreed to surrender upon the terms proposed by Col. Blackburn, representing the Government of the United States, and in pursuance of said terms he and his command did, on the 23rd of May, 1865, surrender themselves to the said Col. Blackburn and were paroled, excepting the prisoner, whom Col. Blackburn said he could not parole until seeing or consulting with General Thomas at Nashville. That the defendant was, however, permitted to return to his home, keeping his side arms, and that the defendant did return to his home in White County, peaceably and in good faith, to be a loyal citizen to the Government of the United States to await further word from Col. Blackburn.

While engaged at work on his farm on the 26th day of May, 1865, Col. Blackburn sent for the defendant, who readily reported at his headquarters in accordance with their agreement, but that instead of being paroled he was seized, brought under heavy guard to Nashville, and lodged in the Military Prison. That the defendant now claims the protection of the Government of the United States due to a prisoner of war; that he should be discharged from the prosecution and should not be compelled to make any further answer to the same. All of which he is ready to verify, wherefore he prays the judgment of this Military Commission that he be discharged.

After the plea had been presented, the Judge Advocate announced that the Commission would render a decision the following morning. This decision will be referred to later on in the account of the trial; it suffices to say at this point that the plea was not granted by the Commission.

This plea, of course, sets forth a very important point. If Champ Ferguson surrendered in good faith as a Confederate officer and on the promise of a representative of the U. S. Government that his parole would be accepted in accordance with the terms of General Grant to General Lee, which the defense insisted was the case, then by all that was honorable he should have been allowed to go in peace.

The plea differs importantly, however, from a statement of the capture made by Col. Blackburn, who was called on to testify during the trial. His testimony was given late in the trial, on August 24th, but will be presented at this point.

Colonel Joseph Blackburn, the person responsible for Ferguson's actual seizure, being sworn, gave the following version of how the capture came about:

"I saw by the papers that there was an order for the guerilla bands to come in and surrender and lay down their arms, and knowing the character of those bands in that country up there, I came here to Nashville to see about it myself. I came and saw General Thomas, and saw General Rousseau the same day, and I talked to them about it, and told them that there were several bands there belonging to different regiments and different companies, and they all had concentrated under Capt. Walker. Before I came down here, I had received a letter from Capt. Walker, stating that he wanted to surrender, with all the men.

"When I consulted with General Rousseau, he referred me to the order that was issued by General Thomas, and I returned. When I got to Gallatin that night, I received a telegram from General Rousseau that they all could surrender but Ferguson. When I returned back to my command at Alexandria, several notes were there from Capt. Walker and also citizens of that country, wanting me to go up and accept the surrender. I started up, I think about the 24th of May, and met Walker on the Calfkiller, along with some major, I think it was Bledsoe. Walker was introduced to me and we all had a long chat. He wanted to see the orders I had, and I showed him those I received from General Rousseau, the telegram I spoke of among them, and they all found out that Ferguson couldn't come in.

"Walker and the citizens seemed very anxious to have Ferguson come in, and while we were talking about it, Walker said that Ferguson was in the woods near there, so I told Walker to have him come and see me. Captain Walker remarked that Ferguson was afraid to come down where I and my men were, and I told him I was not afraid to go to him if he would tell me where he was. Myself and Captain Vanatta, of my regiment, got on our horses and went into the woods with Captain Walker about a quarter of a mile, where Ferguson was, at the end of a lane, in a grove of timber. We found Ferguson and the rest of the men, some twenty-nine, I believe, all there together. When we got there, I think Captain Walker asked me if I could pick Ferguson out, and I picked him the first time.

"We were then introduced, and I told Ferguson the order that I had,— that it was against him coming in, but all the rest were allowed to come in. Ferguson then said he wanted to have a private conversation with me, and we went off down the side of the fence and had a conversation. I told him about the order, and he said that if he couldn't come in and be treated the same as the others, he wouldn't come in. I begged of him to come in, told him that if he stayed up there he couldn't escape; that he would be captured, and the court authorities would take hold of him, and that it looked like it was death for him either way, and that it would be easier for him if he would come in and give up. He swore he would be d—d if he would go and give up unless he had some assurance,— those are about the words he said.

"We then walked back up to where the rest of them were, and Ferguson remarked to me if I would let him be harmed if he went out to where the boys were. I had told him before that Capt. Dowdy was there, and he said he would like to see them all if I wouldn't have him interfered with. We went out there, and I begged him again, and the citizens did, to come in, but he refused coming, and the rest of them surrendered. This was at Mrs. Bradley's house, where my men were.

"When I went to leave, Ferguson wanted to know if I would go and try to get an order for his surrender. I told him I would go and try, but didn't believe it could be done.

"After I had returned to my headquarters at Alexandria, some two days after that, I detailed five men and started them up there after Ferguson. It was a very bad looking night, and I thought it would be a very good time. It was some forty miles and I started them in the evening, and I told them to go all the way that night and get near the house and watch for him to come in to breakfast. They reported, when they came back, that they got lost in the night and didn't get there until some twelve o'clock the day after they started. They told me they found him in the stable, and his arms in the house. Two of the boys went to the house and got his arms.

"I had given them orders not to kill him unless he began at them. I think they said his arms were not loaded, and that they gave his arms to him and let him keep them until they had got out a piece this side of the house, when they disarmed him and tied him to his horse, and brought him on to me, getting in the next morning about eleven or twelve o'clock. I brought him on here to Nashville and turned him over to the Provost Marshall General. The men said Ferguson didn't make any attempt to escape."

The facts as set forth in the plea and those set forth in the testimony of Col. Blackburn are directly contradictory, and cannot be reconciled. It is certain that Champ Ferguson never "readily reported" anywhere, disarmed and tied to his horse!

Colonel Blackburn was then placed on cross-examination by counsel for the defense:

Question—Look at the letter, now shown you, of May 15, 1865. Was that one of the letters addressed to Capt. Walker?

Answer—Yes, sir, I think it is. It was written by Dr. Shields and signed by me.

Question—Was the surrender made in pursuance of that letter?

Answer—Yes, sir, I think it is the same letter. I wrote him several letters and had several from him.

Question—You speak of Walker and guerillas generally, without exception. Did not they and Ferguson come in that day without previously being apprized that there would be any exceptions made in the surrender?

Answer—I don't think I wrote him any other letter about Ferguson, or that he could not come in. I told Walker, though, that morning that Ferguson couldn't come in. That was before I saw Ferguson or any of the men.

Question—Do I correctly understand you that Ferguson did not get information from you that he would not be permitted to surrender until the day of the surrender, as you have stated?

Answer—I can't know as I did.

Question—Are you not satisfied that Ferguson came in with his men to surrender under the order of General Thomas and your letter, and was very anxious to surrender and comply with the terms?

Answer—Well, it don't look as if he was. I don't know how he came there. When I told Capt. Walker that Ferguson would not be allowed to surrender, he said that Ferguson would like to see me. When he asked me to go and see Ferguson, he didn't tell me that the other men were with him.

Question—Did you understand from Ferguson that he came in that day with his men to surrender, relying upon the protection promised him in your letter?

Answer—No, sir. When I went out there and commenced talking to him, he told me he would not surrender unless I had a written order from General Thomas, or the commander of this post, for him to surrender and receive protection. When I got to Mrs. Bradley's and met Walker and told him I would like to see Ferguson, and he said that Ferguson would not come to see me, that he was afraid to come where I and my men were, from that I supposed he had heard that he could not surrender. I told Walker that I was not afraid to go where he was and I went and saw him, as I have stated, about a quarter of a mile from the place where the surrender took place.

Question—When you got to where Ferguson and his men were, did you alight from your horse, and were you kindly treated by them?

Answer—Yes, sir, I got down off my horse when Ferguson told me he wanted a private conversation with me, and we went down by the fence together. I wasn't interfering with any of them at that time.

Question—Did you understand from Ferguson and the men that they were anxious to surrender?

Answer—Yes; well, that was the understanding with the men. As to Ferguson, when I told him what my orders were, he told me that if he couldn't be treated the same as all other Confederate soldiers, he would be G-d d—d if he would surrender. I begged him to surrender and come in, that it would be easier for him, and I told him that day that it wouldn't be long before I would catch him.

Counsel for the defense then asked this very significant and pertinent question:

Question—Did you not tell Ferguson to go home and go to work, and that you would do what you could to have him protected, and when you wanted him you would send for him?

Answer—Yes, sir; I told him if I could get an order I would send for him, and he said he would go home and go to work,—that he wasn't afraid of me nor my men, that he wouldn't run from us. I told him it was not safe to trust us too far, and he said he wasn't going to fight any more soldiers unless some of those home guards came there and got after him.

Question—Did not the prisoner, that day, propose to surrender his arms to you, and did not you tell him that he was an officer and entitled to keep them?

Answer—No, sir; he wanted to know of me if he would be allowed to keep them. He asked me, in place of my telling him. I would have taken his arms and been very glad to have got them, if he had offered them.

The testimony of other witnesses as to the negotiations and other details of the meeting at the Widow Bradley's will be presented later in our story, but here we have set forth the main contentions of each side as to how Champ Ferguson finally came to be lodged in the Military Prison at Nashville.

It was quite apparent that letters had been written by Colonel Blackburn to certain influential citizens in the Upper Cumberlands, asking all guerilla bands to come in and surrender under the terms of General Thomas' promise of amnesty and parole. It was also apparent, however, that Champ Ferguson had heard he would not be allowed to surrender, and it was agreed by both sides that Col. Blackburn told Champ Ferguson at their first meeting that he would not be allowed to surrender on parole as the others were doing. Furthermore, both sides agreed that, having no promise of parole, Champ Ferguson refused to surrender but did exact a promise from Col. Blackburn to endeavor to secure from General Thomas an order allowing him to come in under the same terms granted all the others, and that he thereupon returned to his home to wait the result of this intercession.

So far as the testimony shows, Col. Blackburn made no attempt to secure another ruling from General Thomas on the matter but, after waiting for two days at his headquarters in Alexandria, dispatched a detail of five soldiers, under what he considered favorable conditions, to effect the actual capture of Ferguson.

It would be most interesting, therefore, to know just what the five soldiers sent by Col. Blackburn to Ferguson's house told him when they got there. It is unfortunate that at least one of the five soldiers could not have been placed on the witness stand. Did they actually surprise Champ Ferguson at his home and capture him before he had a chance to escape or defend himself or, in order to seize him, did they tell him that General Thomas had now countermanded previous orders and had issued the permit necessary in order to enable him to surrender as the others had done?

It seems reasonable to assume, to say the least, that Champ had no inkling of Colonel Blackburn's purpose to take him to Nashville to be placed in a military prison, else Colonel Blackburn would not have been able to make the statement: "The men said Ferguson didn't make any attempt to escape." It simply would have been contrary to all of Champ's previous record not to have made such an attempt between the time the five soldiers found him in his stable and the time they reached Colonel Blackburn's headquarters forty miles away. He had escaped from more difficult situations before.

It is also quite improbable that Champ was caught without his weapons, as they had become a part of his dress almost during the past four years and times were still too troublous to lay them aside. Then, too, is it likely that these five soldiers informed Champ when they found him at his home that he was to be taken to prison, at the same time allowing him to wear his arms as they started back to headquarters? Why did they let him wear his arms as they started away, only to disarm him a "piece this side of his home" and tie him to his horse? It was also generally agreed that Champ had positively stated he would not surrender without some assurance that he would be treated like other soldiers.

In view of these discrepancies, illogical and contrary to human nature, we are inclined to the conclusion that something more than force was used in effecting the capture of Champ Ferguson. His instinct not to give himself up at the Widow Bradley's had been correct; his rage must have been terrible when he found that he was to be imprisoned and treated like a common criminal.

Champ Ferguson's rage, however, was probably no more complete than the satisfaction of the Federal authorities in having finally in their power a long sought, greatly feared, and much hated adversary.

CHAPTER III

Murder Charges

THE trial of Champ Ferguson lasted from July 11th until mid-September, 1865. Throughout its inordinate length tremendous interest was maintained by the citizens of Nashville, both in the main character himself and in the events related by those who testified against him.

The court room, which was located on High Street (now Seventh Avenue) near Broad Street, was daily thronged by the curious, those interested in the legal battle being waged, those interested in the testimony presented, and those interested in Ferguson himself. As late as August 23rd, almost six weeks after the trial had opened, the *Dispatch* carried the following item indicating the sustained interest of the local citizenry in the noted guerilla:

A number of persons visit the court room daily to see this noted prisoner, and great curiosity is manifested by the visitors. They frequently ask the guards to point out Champ to them. Yesterday, a man asked the guards to show him Ferguson, while the prisoner was sitting next to them in the hallway, waiting for the Court to convene. The guard pointed to our friend, Judge Advocate Blackman, who was sitting at the table in the court room, intently reading a paper. The curious visitor surveyed the Judge from every standpoint, while Ferguson and the guards sat behind him enjoying the joke. After he had taken a good long look, he turned to the guards and remarked: "Well, he does look ferocious, and I expect he is a very bad man." The man, then, with an air of satisfaction, went on, while the guards took a hearty laugh, and none seemed to have enjoyed the joke more than Champ.

Almost from the beginning of the War report after report had come to Nashville of the amazing feats of personal combat per-

formed by Champ and the bloody and cruel methods he used in
disposing of his enemies. His name had become a by-word of
strength and ruthlessness and courage and vindictiveness throughout
the Tennessee and Kentucky mountains, a section where the War
was decidedly personal, where as a rule no quarter was given and
none was expected. It was legendary in this section that Champ
had sworn to kill no less than one hundred of the enemy and that
he had more than made good his oath. It was related that he
killed his enemies with knife and pistol after they had surrendered
and thrown down their arms, while they were lying in bed asleep,
even while they were lying sick and wounded in the hospital.

At the same time, there were scores of tales of his own remarkable
personal courage in encounters with sworn enemies, and his almost
miraculous escapes when assailed by great odds. It is ironic that
Ferguson was not captured until after the War was ended. One
may well wonder whether Champ Ferguson was as well equipped
for peace as for war.

Many persons in Nashville were interested in Champ Ferguson's
case and anxious to help him if it became possible to do so, some
who would always take the side of anyone who fought for the
South, and others who considered he had been wrongly treated.
Possibly it was this interest on the part of Nashville citizens that
prolonged the trial throughout that dry, hot summer of 1865 when
everything was crushed in the South except the spirit of the Southern
people. The city of Nashville had been occupied by the Federals
since February, 1862, but the people of Nashville had never surrendered. True, some of her prominent citizens had been sent to
prison in the North, while others had gone further South rather
than live under the Federal rule. True, also, many of the inhabitants
had taken the oath of allegiance rather than undertake either of
these alternatives; but many Nashville citizens, especially the
women, whatever they appeared on the surface, remained staunchly
Southern at heart and never overlooked an opportunity to render
service to the Confederate forces. However, those who sympathized

with Champ Ferguson represented a lost cause, were practically without authority, and had to be very circumspect in their efforts to aid his case.

The trial of Champ Ferguson, though, gave these "Rebels" one last chance to express their sentiments, and while there was little they could do other than maintain a sustained interest in the proceedings, this they did to the end of the trial. During the latter part of the trial, at least, the women of Nashville were allowed to furnish Champ with certain comforts in the way of clothes and special articles of food. These acts were rather irritating to the Federal authorities. We may wonder even now why they allowed the imprisonment and trial to be dragged out for five weary months, when trials by a military court are usually more summarily dealt with.

One thing, certainly, in which Champ Ferguson was fortunate was in the character of legal counsel which came to his defense. Probably more than any other single factor that caused the trial to extend over an inordinate period of time for a trial of this character was the courage, devotion, and legal ability of this counsel.

Chief counsel for the defense was one of the ablest lawyers in the Tennessee country at that time, Judge Jo Conn Guild.

Born of pioneer parentage, young Guild lived the typical life of a pioneer boy, with all its hardships, and throughout his long life he had no use for the unnecessary luxuries and folderols of living. His parents died on successive weeks of a strange malady, then known as milk poison, and as a ten year old boy, alone with his father the evening he died, he rode a horse twenty miles in the dark through a blinding storm and pathless woods to his uncle's house for help. His home at the time was near the headwaters of Bledsoe's Creek, in Sumner County, Tennessee. His uncle, Major Josephus H. Conn, made available to the boy what schooling the neighborhood afforded, limited, no doubt, but thorough.

In the year 1821, the year Champ Ferguson was born, Guild, then nineteen years of age, walked from Gallatin to Nashville and secured a job in the law office of Col. Ephraim H. Foster one of Nashville's leading lawyers. In exchange for making the fires, sweeping out the office, bringing drinking water from the spring, and acting as messenger boy in general, he was allowed to read Col. Foster's law books. During the next eighteen months, he says, he read Blackstone ten times and then, upon examination by Judge John Haywood, was granted a license for the practice of law.

During the forty years before the War Between the States broke out, he was intimately acquainted with most of the leaders of this section, Henry Clay, Felix Grundy, Andrew Jackson, Sam Houston, James K. Polk, among others. Refusing to take the oath of allegiance after the occupation of Nashville, he was sent to Federal prison at Fort Mackinaw, Michigan, where he was kept about six months before being allowed to return to his native city. During his stay there, he voluntarily defended in court a young Indian who had killed his rival in love and secured an acquittal, much to the disgust of the prosecution and the delight of the Indians.

Steadfast in his convictions and never lacking the courage to uphold what he believed to be right, we find him now after the close of the War staunchly defending Champ Ferguson, a Confederate guerilla whose reputation left much to be desired, but a Southerner withal in need of help. The record of the trial shows that Judge Guild put just as much energy into the case as he might had he been defending Jeff Davis himself.

Even three years later, in 1868, Judge Guild made a bitter speech against the election of Grant, when carpetbag rule made this a dangerous thing to do. He lived, however, to see the South again enfranchised and reconciled to remaining in the Union.

Associated with Judge Guild in the defense of Champ Ferguson was Capt. R. M. Goodwin, a young Confederate officer lately returned from the army, and while his reputation was yet to be made, Capt. Goodwin made up in zeal and energy what he lacked in experience. As a matter of fact, by the end of the trial he had so impressed everyone concerned with his honesty and his earnestness that he was entrusted with the important duty of making the final appeal for the defense.

The Military Court appointed by the Commanding General to conduct the trial was composed of Major Collin Ford, 100th U.S.C.I., Captain E. C. Hatton, A.A.G.Vols., Captain Thos. H. Osborn, 4th Ohio Volunteer Cavalry, Second Lieut. William O. Bateman, 7th Penn. Volunteer Cavalry, Second Lieut. E. P. Leiter, 15th Ohio Volunteer Infantry, and Captain H. C. Blackman, 42nd U.S.C. Infantry. On July 11th, the Court was sworn in by Capt. Blackman, who was in turn sworn as Judge Advocate by Major Ford. Thereupon Captain Blackman, as Judge Advocate, became the prosecuting attorney in the case; while Major Ford served as President of the Military Commission. Later, on July 18th, Capt. Thos. H. Osborn was mustered out, and on July 22nd Capt. O. B. Simmons, U.S.C.I. and Capt. Martin B. Thompson, 154th Illinois Infantry, were sworn in as new members.

The stage was now set, and on July 11, 1865, the indictment was read in court. Champ Ferguson was indicted on two charges: first, of being a guerilla; second, murder. There were twenty-three specifications of the latter, charging murder of fifty-three persons, as follows:

1. Lieut. Smith, 13th Ky. Cavalry; shot in the head while a prisoner, and lying sick in the hospital at Emory, Va.
2. Twelve soldiers, whose names are unknown, at Saltville, Va.
3. Two negro soldiers, names unknown, while lying wounded in prison, at Saltville, in Oct., 1864.
4. Nineteen soldiers of the 5th Tenn. Cavalry, names unknown, on Feb. 22, 1865.
5. Reuben Wood, near Albany, Ky., in 1861.
6. Wm. Frogg, while sick in bed, in 1861.
7. Jos. Stover, private 1st Ky. Calvary, in Clinton County, Ky., in April, 1862.
8. Wm. Johnson, in Clinton County, Ky., in 1862.
9. Louis Pierce, in Clinton County, Ky., in 1862.

10. A lad named Fount Zachery, near Spring Creek, 1862.
11. Elijah Kogier, in Clinton County, Ky., in 1862. His little daughter was clinging to her father after Champ shot him, pleading for his life, but he fired several shots, killing him.
12. James Zachery, in Fentress County, Tenn., in May, 1862.
13. Alex Huff, in Fentress County, in 1862.
14. Joseph Beck, near Poplar Mountain, Clinton County, Ky., in summer of 1862.
15. Wm. McGlasson, in Cumberland County, Ky., November, 1862. Told him to run, then shot him.
16. Elam Huddleston, shooting him through the head, in the back, in January, 1863.
17. Peter Zachery, while lying sick in bed, at Rufus Dowdy's house, near Russell County, Ky., in January, 1863.
18. Allan Zachery, same time and place.
19. John Williams, by torturing him with knives and sharp sticks, afterwards cutting him to pieces.
20. David Delk, by chopping and cutting him to pieces, at the house of Mrs. Alex Huff, in Fentress County, in 1863.
21. John Crabtree, a prisoner, near the house of Mrs. Piles, in Fentress County, in 1863.
22. A negro man, name unknown.
23. Mr. Tabor, in Albany, Clinton County, Ky., in 1862.

The charges and specifications were prepared and signed by Major G. P. Thruston, Acting Judge Advocate of the Military Division of Tennessee, who was to settle in Nashville and become a prominent citizen of the city.

The charges were formidable. No wonder the trial created excitement and Champ Ferguson attracted interest. And even then the specifications were not complete! While some of those included in the charge were not to be supported by testimony, yet a number of other murders were laid at the door of Champ Ferguson by witnesses before the trial was over.

To many concerned, it seemed that the commencement of the trial had been delayed interminably. Ferguson had been captured at his home on May 26th. On May 29th, upon arriving at Nashville, he was placed in the old Tennessee State Penitentiary (located at Church and Stonewell Streets, now Church Street between Fourteenth and Sixteenth Avenues) which had been used as a military prison since the Federals had taken possession of the city. It was now July 11th and the trial was just getting under way. In the meantime, the prisoner had been held practically incommunicado, and according to the claims of his defense did not know the charges against him until a few days before the trial. This caused the defense attorneys to at once set up claims for a continuance of the trial to a later date, on the plea that the prisoner was on trial for his life and was therefore due a reasonable time in which to secure his witnesses.

During the bitter legal battle that ensued and the discussion of the technicalities involved, Champ Ferguson sat intently regarding the proceedings. As he sat there in the little, crowded court room, we can imagine his bewilderment at the procedure in whose web he had become entangled. Here was a situation where physical strength availed nothing, and while he might not understand the legal aspect of the points discussed, his association with men instinctively told him that here under the trappings and formality of law were as dangerous enemies as any he ever confronted in his bloody encounters in the Cumberland Mountains.

CHAPTER IV

The Reasons Why

REPORTERS for the Nashville newspapers at the time of the trial of Champ Ferguson quite often went beyond the mere factual reporting to which we are accustomed today. They editorialized, they philosophized, they speculated on cause and effect. Said the reporter for the *Daily Union* in his report of the first day of the trial:

When we first saw him (Ferguson), he was in the court room, with his two guards, and evidently did not observe that we were watching him with interest. He was thinking, no doubt, of very unpleasant things, and was uneasy from causes other than weariness of body from long sitting. We were not displeased to notice that occasionally he heaved a deep sigh. What memories of other days—days of peace, days of young manhood, days when the homes of Tennessee were quiet, and the annals of crime were yet unfilled with the pictures of blood, rapine, murder, and arson, now so familiar to us—were filling his soul, who can say? We will not undertake to fathom the depth of feeling—of agony, of despair, in the human heart, whose pulsations are at the mercy of offended justice.

This reporter was undoubtedly assigning to Champ Ferguson an imaginative temperament to which he was not entitled. Whatever sighs Champ heaved may have been in remorse, but they were much more likely to have been in remorse for having allowed himself to be captured than for anything he had done before he was captured. At no time in the trial did Champ exhibit regret over the events of the preceding four and a half years. There is no shred of evidence that he ever felt any real compunction concerning his actions. Instead he stoutly claimed justification, maintaining always that he killed only in self-defense, that he killed only those who, had they had the chance, would have killed him.

It was not unnatural, of course, that Champ Ferguson's contemporaries, as well as commentators of later days, should attempt to discover some motive, other than that of ordinary warfare, for his deeds. A man who had reportedly sworn to kill at least one hundred of the enemy and who had so nearly made good his oath must have been actuated by an extraordinarily impelling force.

At various times, different persons in their memoirs or conversations have attempted to give reason for, if not to justify, Champ's actions. The first of the two reasons that have usually been assigned is set forth as follows by Bromfield L. Ridley, in his *Battles and Sketches of the Army of Tennessee,* published in 1906:

A typical mountaineer—such was Champ Ferguson. The times in which he lived called forth physical energy, egged on by passion. The acts of his adversaries prompted his course, and raging war made his career in the strife of 1861-65 one of blood.

Champ was a citizen at his home when the tocsin was sounded, and stayed there until his own precincts were invaded. A rabid fire eater passed his house with a troop of Blues. You ask why he was so desperate. It was told in camp that Champ Ferguson's little three-year-old child came out onto the porch waving a Confederate flag. One of the men in blue leveled his gun at Champ and killed the child. O, anguish! how that father's heart bled! His spirit welled up like the indomitable will of the primitive Norseman. In a moment of frenzy he said that the death of his baby would cost the "blue coats" a hundred lives. And it did. One hundred and twenty is believed to be the number he put to death. (Comrade S. H. Mitchell got this from Champ himself.)

He took to the woods and for four years his war upon them was unrelenting, and vengeance was never appeased. It increased like the raging torrent, as his family and friends were vilified and abused. In the Cumberland Mountains, clans formed and terrorized the section by petty warfare, until the caldron of fear and apprehension invaded every home. The hunger for vengeance grew with the years, and Champ became the terror of the Northern side, while Huddleston and Tinker Dave Beatty were the same to the Southern. The acts of the latter, because they belonged to the victorious side, are buried in the tomb and the government perhaps honors their memory; but the acts of Champ Ferguson, because of the misfortunes of war, are bruited as the most terrible in history.

If the sea could give up its dead, and the secrets of men became known, Champ Ferguson's actions as bushwhacker, in comparison, would excite only a passive and not an active interest. Champ was a mountaineer; rude and untrained in the refinements of moral life; he had entertained that strict idea of right that belongs to the mountain character. Nature had instilled into him a consuming passion for vengeance for a wrong. His method was indiscreet, his warfare contemptible; but, in palliation, how was it compared to the open murder of starving out our women and children, burning our houses, and pillaging our homes? Champ Ferguson was well to do in this world's goods when the war began. Had he been let alone, a career of good citizenship would have been his portion. Had he lived in the days of the Scottish Chiefs, the clans would no doubt have crowned his efforts; but now, since his flag has fallen, history marks his career as more awful than that of John A. Murrell. . . . . The times in which he lived must be considered, the provocation, the surroundings, and then let history record Champ's actions.

In his zeal for the South to win, he became hardened; and the more steeped in blood the more his recklessness increased until irritability occasioned by treatment of his home folk drove him to maniacal desperation.

Captain Bromfield Lewis Ridley, the author of these comments on Champ Ferguson, became an enlisted soldier in General John Morgan's cavalry at the age of seventeen, and was later attached to the staff of General A. P. Stewart, of the Army of Tennessee. His father, Judge Bromfield Lewis Ridley, was a prominent lawyer in the Upper Cumberlands when the War broke out and was an ardent secessionist, having five sons in the Confederate Army. Judge Ridley had been one of the founders of the Law School at Lebanon, Tennessee, later to become Cumberland University, and for twenty years before the beginning of the War had been Chancellor of the Fourth Chancery Division of the State, comprising the whole mountain district where lay the scenes of most of Champ Ferguson's activities during the War.

Captain Ridley's early life, up to the time he enlisted in the army, therefore, was spent in the Upper Cumberlands, and he was amply equipped to write at first hand of the temperaments and customs of the mountain people. In his comments on Champ Ferguson, he recognizes Champ's failings but leaves no doubt as to where his sympathies lie. Rather strangely, however, he is completely wrong as to the reason behind Champ's actions. His memoirs, which it will be noted were written forty years after the close of the War, still assign as the main reason for Ferguson's start on his career of crime, the killing of his three year old child by Union men. This story seems to have had considerable credence during the War, and is even yet given some credit in the folk traditions of the country in which he resided. We, of course, know that it is not true; that Ferguson's first wife and three year old boy had died some sixteen years before the War started, and that the only child from his second marriage, a daughter, was twelve years old at the beginning of the War.

The second reason usually assigned for the career of death and vengeance upon which Champ Ferguson entered at the beginning of the War was often referred to during the War and is still given more general credence than any other among the descendants of the people with whom Ferguson lived. There may be good grounds for this tradition, although an incidental questioning of Champ regarding it by the reporter for the Nashville *Dispatch* during his first interview brought a denial. The deadly vengeance with which Champ pursued a certain number of men throughout the length of the War, however, is naturally a good basis for the belief that there was some strong, underlying motive beyond the mere strife of warfare to account for the relentlessness of his pursuit, so far as this particular group is concerned.

As the story goes, most of Ferguson's neighbors in Clinton County, Kentucky, including his own family, were Union advocates and had deeply resented his taking up the Southern cause. A more elemental code prevailed in the mountains than in the Blue Grass country. When a man took sides in the mountains, all ties were cut loose and all on the other side became enemies. In the Blue Grass, a father might give each of his two sons a thoroughbred horse and a slave as retainer, one to ride off with the Gray and one with the Blue, blessing each one equally and receiving both gladly should they return. There was a different code in the mountains. If one be against you, how can he be for you was a question they must always answer negatively, and nothing short of death, at least pending conclusion of the War, could change the answer.

It is related, further, that a certain group of eleven men in Champ Ferguson's neighborhood, seeking vengeance for what they considered his betrayal, and possibly taking advantage of the cloak of warfare to avenge themselves of other wrongs, real or fancied, at his hands, forced their way into his home while he was away, shortly after the War began, forced his wife and daughter to undress and cook a meal before them in this manner, and then drove them down the public road thus unclad. It is said that Ferguson's anger, when he heard of this, knew no bounds, that he swore he would kill every one of the men involved with his own hands, and that he accomplished this vow in full when he killed the last of the group as he lay wounded in a Southern military hospital. Tradition asserts, further, that Champ went at once to Southern authorities, told what he had done and why he had set himself to this task, that he was not held for his actions, and in fact was praised by many for his stand.

There is enough reasonableness in this folk-tradition to give it some semblance of truth, though the *Dispatch* reporter, after his first interview with Champ, gave the following account of his incidental questioning concerning the Emory episode:

We have repeatedly heard it stated that Lieut. Smith, who was killed at Saltville in the hospital, went to Ferguson's house with his company, and offered Mrs. Ferguson and her young daughter the most outrageous insults. This, it was said, led Champ to kill him. We asked him if it was so. He said that the story was absurd, that Lieut. Smith was a relative of his first wife, and that his family were never insulted or mistreated by Federals during the war; but they robbed her, like everybody else, of all she had to eat, which was a slight failing on both sides. He says that Lieut. Smith came to his house one night with his men, killed an old gentleman named Pierce, who was stopping there. Champ denies the killing of Smith or the massacre at Saltville, and claimed alibi.

We cannot afford to give this statement too much weight. As will be learned, Champ Ferguson actually did kill Lieut. Smith, and if his statement is wrong on this point, it could be also wrong on the other.

If one were inclined to support with arguments this second of the two main reasons assigned for Champ's war of vengeance, he might point out that by insulting Champ's wife and daughter in the manner described, his enemies selected that form of revenge which they knew would hurt him most and make him most angry. Knowing Champ as they did, however, it can be surmised they must have well fortified themselves with "pop skull" whiskey before incurring his anger to such extent.

One might also point out that it would be contrary to mountaineer code or custom either to admit that such a thing had happened or to discuss it after it happened. We do know that Champ was forced to move his family shortly after the War started from Clinton County, Kentucky, to White County, Tennessee. Malicious gossip directed against Champ Ferguson's wife, Martha, and his daughter, Ann, along with impotent shame on their part, it may be, could have had as much to do with this move as danger to Champ Ferguson himself. It would be nothing at which to be astonished that the matter should never again be voluntarily referred to by Champ Ferguson or admitted when referred to by another.

From that time on, Champ Ferguson and his wife and daughter were to live among strangers and were never to return to live in the land where they had heretofore spent their lives. Champ himself, however, was to go back many times during the next four years,— and many were those who would fear his coming and many were those who would live to see him come but would not live to see him go again.

As has been intimated, we shall have occasion later in this account to refer to a further statement by Champ with reference to the killing of Lieut. Smith, a statement directly contradicting part of that quoted above, but since it sheds no further light on the motive behind the killing, we shall reserve it for another point in our story. It might be well worth remarking at this point, however, that at no time during the trial nor in any of the records of the case as compiled from other sources does the given name of Lieut. Smith appear. This is rather strange, to say the least, because it was the killing of Lieut. Smith, apparently, that rankled most in the hearts of the Federal authorities.

Was the name "Lieut. Smith" a convenient alias? Could he have been Champ's brother, Jim, who took the opposite side at the beginning of the War? Reading between the lines, we can surmise that before the War a blood feud had started between the brothers, brought about by the events leading up to the "Camp Meeting" fight. Champ's only reference to his brother, at any time after his capture, was that Jim had driven him "fairly to desperation" during the War. Had Jim evaded his brother's vengeance throughout the War, only to be killed shortly before the close while lying wounded in the hospital? Was this another case of the Dillon twins, in John Fox's *Little Shepherd of Kingdom Come?*

There is no factual basis at all for these rhetorical questions, and the idea is probably only a wild suspicion. There is no mention made during the trial of any member of Champ's own family,— not one comes to his defense, not one even comes to see him,—but we do know that Jim was alive at the beginning of the War, that he was a Union man, and that he was not alive at the end of the War. Further than that, the records do not show.

The logical reason for Champ Ferguson's deeds during the War, as is so often the case, is probably the most natural one. Rather than seek out any strange or unusual reasons as to why Champ should kill so many people during the War, we might simply accept the statement used by his defense and by himself,—that he was killing in self-defense, that he only killed those who would have killed him had they had the chance. He simply beat them to the draw. The feud in the mountains between the Yankees and Rebels was deadly, and it was a case of kill first or be killed. It was "an eye for an eye and a tooth for a tooth." In carrying out this law, Champ was most effective, and the fact that he was able to kill so many persons could simply be attributed to his unusual physical capabilities and native cunning.

CHAPTER V

The Trial---Nashville

THE lines of battle for the prosecution and defense formed rapidly. The prosecution had been careful to place two charges against Champ Ferguson: that of being a guerilla; and that of murder, the specifications in the latter charge covering fifty-three cases of homicide.

Since it would be difficult to prove a charge of murder against a regularly enlisted soldier, the strategy adopted by the prosecution was to make assurance doubly sure by first proving that the accused was a guerilla, that he was not a soldier acting under orders from his superiors and was therefore alone responsible for all his acts during the War.

The case was called before the Military Commission on Tuesday morning, July 11, 1865, at eight o'clock. The counsel for the defense immediately gave notice that they would file an affidavit for a continuance. The Court accordingly adjourned until two o'clock that afternoon, at which time it was again convened, and the affidavit for continuance was submitted by Captain Goodwin.

The affidavit set forth as grounds for continuance the plea that Ferguson had not had sufficient opportunity to procure the attendance of his witnesses, who were numerous, widely scattered, and resident at a distance from the seat of the court. It stated that the defendant expected to prove by a number of witnesses that he was not guilty of the first fifteen specifications, and that he could prove himself innocent of the rest if a continuance were granted and he were given a reasonable time to get additional witnesses before the court. The affidavit further set forth the defense counsel's claim that the accused had held a regular Captain's commission in the Confederate service, the certificate of which had been taken from his home in 1862 by Federal soldiers, and that he had surrendered to Colonel Blackburn under promise that he would be accorded the terms under which Lee had surrendered to Grant.

Thus were the issues joined. The prosecution were ready to prove Champ Ferguson a guerilla fighter who had used his irregular connection with the Confederate forces as an opportunity to commit brutal private murder. The defense, on the other hand, claimed that he was a regularly commissioned Confederate officer, subject to parole, and that he was guiltless of the murders with which he had been charged. They prayed for an opportunity to procure witnesses whose testimony would establish the truth of their claims.

In reply to the affidavit, Judge Advocate Blackman stated that it contained one vital error and until this was corrected, the Court could not even consider the affidavit; namely, that there was no time specified in which the accused expected to get his witnesses and he had fixed no date to which he desired a continuance. Furthermore, the defendant had not shown that he had reasonable grounds for believing that he could get the witnesses or that he had not had ample time to get them there.

Judge Guild replied that the affidavit stated the names and residences of the witnesses and that they could be produced there in a reasonable time, considering their number and the distances at which they lived. He further pointed out that the affidavit was specific and showed what the defense expected to prove by the witnesses.

To conform with Army Regulations, however, as set forth by the Judge Advocate, counsel for the defense altered the affidavit so as to read that the witnesses were within the jurisdiction of the Court and asked to the first day of September, 1865, as a reasonable time in which to procure their attendance.

The Court then adjourned until the following morning, at which time, the Judge Advocate announced, he would reply to this affidavit for continuance.

On Wednesday morning, July 12th, the Court assembling at eight o'clock, the Judge Advocate's argument with reference to the affi-davit for continuance was read. It stated that the Commission had not the power to grant the prayer of the accused, that on the 30th day of June, 1865, Major-General George H. Thomas, commanding the Department of the Tennessee, ordered General Rousseau, com-manding the District of Middle Tennessee, to have the prisoner tried on the charges and specifications in this case at as early a day as practicable, and that on the 3rd day of July, 1865, General Rous-seau ordered this Commission to try this case.

"Wherefore," said the Judge Advocate, "this Commission has no power to entertain this question."

The Judge Advocate went on further to point out that the affidavit did not state to what command Ferguson belonged or under whose orders he was acting when the crimes with which he was charged were committed.

In answer to this opinion, Captain Goodwin stated that the affidavit plainly showed that Champ Ferguson was regularly com-missioned and that he and his command only obeyed the orders of superior officers, and that the affidavit should be accepted at its face value.

"It is true we are unable to designate the command to which he be-longed or produce his commission," said Captain Goodwin, "and it is for this very reason we ask a continuance in order to procure oral testi-mony to prove the existence of lost written testimony."

When Captain Goodwin had concluded, Judge Guild got to his feet, and stated that the accused not only had a moral right to con-tinuance of the trial but a legal right as well; that on principles known to the English law for five hundred years no one could be brought to trial when fifty or sixty cases of murder were combined in a single indictment unless he had proper time to secure the attendance of witnesses whose testimony might save his neck. He stated that if the prisoner were charged with committing crimes in only one locality, even then he would be entitled to a postponement to secure the presence of important witnesses, but in this case the charges were numerous and the places were many.

Judge Guild further pointed out that Champ had been confined to military prison since May 29th without any opportunity to procure evidence on his behalf, not even knowing the charges against him until the past few days, and that Captain Goodwin, the first person allowed to confer with him, had done so only about a week beforehand. Judge Guild stated further that the affidavit as presented complied with Army Regulations with reference to postponement of trial, namely, showing that the witnesses were material, that he had used more than due diligence to secure their attendance, and that he believed them necessary to acquittal.

"Therefore," said Judge Guild, "if you wish justice done in this case, you must give us time. We presume you want the accused to have a fair trial. Then don't force him into it in the absence of all his witnesses."

The Court then adjourned until the following morning, at which time a decision on the affidavit was to be rendered.

The Court opened on Thursday morning, July 13th, with the reading by Major Ford, President of the Commission, of the decision of the Commission on the question of continuance:

. . . . If the prisoner can prove his parole, as he alleges, it would be a bar to further proceedings against him for his acts of legitimate warfare, but not for his acts in violation of the rules of war.

If this plea be made out, the case, so far as his legitimate acts of war are concerned, must be dismissed. But his parole, if he has one, cannot be made a bar to trial to unlawful acts, or acts in violation of the laws of war.

But again, the affidavit claims that witnesses material to his defense on other special pleas which he may introduce, or on the general plea of *not guilty,* are scattered and at a great distance and he has not had

time to produce them, and therefore asks a continuance on his case. . . . .
Our opinion is that by due diligence on the part of the defense, the
attendance of his witnesses may be procured by the time the Commission
will be ready to hear their testimony.

We therefore decide not to refer the record to the authority convening
the Court, for a continuance of the case.

After reading the decision of the Commission, denying the plea
for continuance, Major Ford added that the Commission would not
take advantage of its rulings to the injury of the prisoner's cause,
but would give him every reasonable opportunity for the procurement of evidence.

Judge Guild then addressed the Court again, setting forth once
more the conditions of the surrender of the prisoner, and proposed
to present an affidavit as a special plea asking for a continuance of
ten days, in order to procure the attendance of twelve material
witnesses to prove the terms of the surrender and to prove that the
defendant was regularly commissioned as an officer in the so-called
Confederate States Army.

After he had finished, Judge Advocate Blackman proceeded to
make the following comments:

"This continuous argument for postponement of the trial is trifling
with the Court. As yet no issue is joined before the Court. File your
pleas, then replications will follow, and something will be before us for
our action."

The delaying tactics of the defense were becoming an aggravation
to the prosecution. Judge Guild immediately arose to make the
following reply:

"I am too old to trifle, and I have too much respect for this Court for
such a dereliction of duty. Justice demands this step at our hands. If
we file our plea now, we must go to trial on it now, and are cut off from
applying for a postponement. By our parole, we could introduce testimony that would stay further proceedings and save time. We need ten
days in which to secure evidence proving that the parole was granted."

"Why are the gentlemen afraid to file their plea?" asked Blackman. "Let it be filed now, and the issues made."

"If you will put it on record," interposed Judge Guild, "that you waive any objections to a postponement of the trial we will consider the plea filed. Then our rights will not be prejudiced by the filing of the plea."

"I will state," answered Blackman, "that paragraph 886 of the Revised Army Regulations will not exclude the filing of an affidavit when issue is made up."

Whereupon, the accused withdrew the affidavit for the present, and the plea was filed. This plea, which has been presented in the account of Ferguson's capture, was accepted by the Court, which advised it would render a decision the following morning.

As the Court met on Friday morning, July 14th, the fourth day of the trial, counsel for the defense stated they wished to file another plea, in addition to the one of the previous day. Permission was granted by the Court.

This plea, after reciting the facts and terms of Lee's surrender, set up the order of Major-General George H. Thomas, issued May 1, 1865, to General Lovell H. Rousseau, as covering the entire case of the prisoner. That order read as follows:

Headquarters Department of Cumberland
    Nashville, Tenn., May 1, 1865.
To Major-General Rousseau:
Send a summons under a flag of truce to all and every band of armed men in your vicinity or of which you may know, who are operating nearer to yours than any other command, and call upon them to surrender to you or any officer you may name for that purpose, upon the same terms as Lee surrendered to Grant.
If they disregard your summons and continue acts of hostility, they will hereafter be regarded as outlaws, and be proceeded against, pursued, and when captured, treated as outlaws.

                        Geo. H. Thomas,
                        Maj.-Gen., U.S.A.

The remainder of the plea set forth the conditions surrounding Ferguson's surrender, with which we are already familiar, claiming that he was induced solely under this order to give himself up. The plea was made, said the counsel for the defense, in bar of all further proceedings in the case.

The Judge Advocate said he needed only a short time in which to prepare answer to this plea, and after a short recess, the Court again convened and the following opinion was read:

. . . . The fact that General Thomas has ordered his trial on these charges is prima facie evidence that he has been refused a parole as a prisoner of war, and this Court is bound by that refusal. . . . . General Thomas has ordered General Rousseau to cause this man to be tried as a guerilla and on the charge of murder. . . . . General Thomas, in the exercise of his right, chose to except this man from pardon. . . . . Is this Court reviewing the authority of General Thomas? He has fixed the status of the prisoner, and ordered his trial, and we have only to obey our orders.

I therefore overrule the claim set forth in the plea.

"The Judge Advocate," said Judge Guild, "makes the most extraordinary proposition to come from a Judge Advocate that I ever heard. Because our client has been arrested and thrown into prison, is that any reason to refuse him a fair trial? Does this military commission sit here merely to sentence a prisoner to be hung? Is he to have no show at all? Even has General Thomas examined the facts of this case? No, he simply ordered the trial which is to determine guilt or innocence by investigation. General Thomas does not propose to adjudicate this case but has reposed this duty in your hands.

"Does General Thomas' order for the trial of this defendant tell you that you shall find him guilty of being a guerilla or murderer before any evidence is adduced? That order does not instruct you to convict the prisoner. I have already suffered the judgment of this Court once, but thank God, the prisoner has got men in his defense who will see that justice is done him. All we desire is a fair and impartial trial. And I boldly assert that when we do get a fair hearing on this plea, there is no power on earth that can legally try the prisoner on these charges.

"But the Judge Advocate says the order of General Thomas adjudicates this case. Would General Thomas adjudicate it without any proof? The truth is, General Thomas knows nothing of the case. All he knows is that Ferguson was brought to the military prison, and he ordered his trial. As for a written parole, we care not for any such document. We look to the substance of things. When we present, in the second plea, that the defendant surrendered to Col. Blackburn, does the Judge Advocate controvert this? If he cannot controvert it, there is no use of his prosecuting the case any further. How can we form an issue of law unless a principle of law is asserted by one side and denied by the other?

"A word more. I verily believe that the order of General Thomas, issued on the 1st of May, was one of the best ever promulgated. Under the generous terms embodied in it, the army of the South melted like snow under a mid-summer sun, and peace dawned brightly over the entire country, causing every loyal heart to rejoice. There were scattering bands of armed men in rebellion, and General Thomas by his far-seeing wisdom issued this order and gave peace to the land, stopped the flow of blood. It announced a principle. It was sent out to stop the further effusion of blood and restore peace. It implored every armed band of guerillas to come in and lay down their arms. It promised a pardon to those men, and the subordinate officers were instructed to send forth the messengers of peace to these bands, offering them the magnanimous terms of General Grant to Lee.

"The order embracing all the facts is in our plea. Ferguson had faith in the plighted honor of the Government. He never once thought that such a proposition would be made by our Government in bad faith. The terms of the order were offered him and he accepted them, and has faithfully abided by its provisions.

"I say this plea shows that it was a bona fide surrender. This order is of itself a parole. It is very important to bring these pleas to an issue. We will prove every fact alleged in them. I maintain that the prisoner cannot be lawfully tried on these charges. If any of the allegations in either of the pleas are controverted, we then have the right to a continuance for the time asked."

"Answering the senior counsel for the defense," said Judge Black-man, "all I desire to say is that I will not reply to the argument of the gentleman at length, for nine-tenths of what he said has no application to the case. As to the claim set up in the plea that the defendant is a prisoner of war, I say General Thomas has fixed the status of this man, and he is the proper judge of his action."

Apparently about to reach the end of his patience, the junior counsel for the defense, Captain Goodwin, answered this statement with the following impassioned remarks:

"General Thomas has simply ordered the trial of the prisoner. The Judge Advocate seems determined to rule out every legal point advanced. He says the prisoner has only a right to trial, without the benefit of the incidents thereto. Under this ruling, the prisoner comes here as a sheep to the slaughter. He cannot file a plea or an affidavit. Is this Court simply a tool? Has it no discretion lodged in its hands at all? Are you babies on the question of trial and giants on the question of condemnation?

"The Judge Advocate says the Court has no power to decide these questions. Then let him send them to the Commanding General for his decision. If we are not allowed the benefit of a single point of law, then this trial is simply a mockery and it will go out to the world that a Military Court is nothing but a slaughter pen. If we are not allowed to set forth the facts, and all plain principles of law are ignored, then the sentence might as well be rendered without the mockery of a trial. If this be treason, I say boldly, I am a traitor!

"I say it is for this Court to determine whether or not the defendant is a prisoner of war, and not for General Thomas. He is not the Court, and he supposes that he has legal gentlemen here able to conduct the case for the Government."

These were bold and stirring words, but Judge Advocate Black-man was not to be moved or swerved from his position:

"I am very sorry," he answered, sarcastically, "that I cannot conduct this case to meet the views of the defense, but it is simply a difference of opinion which I cannot help. The question is, whether or not the defendant is a prisoner of war. That is, as I said before, for General Thomas to decide and not this Court. When General Thomas ordered his trial, he decided this question. But just observe how inconsistent the counsel are. They admit that the prisoner has no written parole, yet they set up the claim that he surrendered under Grant's terms to Lee, which explicitly stipulates that the parole must be in writing.

"General Thomas has decided the status of this man, and from it there is no appeal this side of General Grant or the President of the United States."

By this time, apparently, the counsel for the defense were pretty will convinced that they would be able to secure no respite from the Military Court conducting the trial. Captain Goodwin thereupon announced to the Court that he wished to submit the following petition, through the Court, to the General commanding the District of Middle Tennessee:

NASHVILLE, JULY 13th, 1865—MAJOR SMITH, A.A.A.G., DISTRICT MIDDLE TENNESSEE: We have the honor to appeal to the General commanding the District of Middle Tennessee for relief and justice before the Military Commission appointed by the General commanding the District, in the case of Champ Ferguson, under charges of the nature of a capital offense, which are now before said Military Commission. The cause for making this appeal, we beg to state briefly:

On the 11th day of this month, we as Attorneys for the defendant, made the affidavit that the witnesses for the accused were not present, that no time had been granted for the purpose of issuing subpoenas for them—that they were important and material, and that we believed they could be procured in a reasonable time, and designated the time as the 1st day of September, 1865, and set forth the names of the witnesses, etc., in sixteen of the counts or specifications against the defendant. (We herewith file a true copy of said affidavit, as exhibit A, which will show for itself its completeness and validity.)

Yet in the face of this, and contrary to the law of Tennessee, which reads as follows: "Any case may be continued by consent of each of the parties, or on sufficient cause shown by affidavit," and contrary to all laws and statutes of the separate States of the United States at large, and the laws of Great Britain, both common and statutory—acknowledged as precedents in our own country—this application under oath was refused to be granted by the Honorable Commission, and the prisoner, although on trial for his life, was compelled to go to trial wholly unprepared and so remains. The impossibility of the immediate attendance of the witnesses is fully shown in the affidavit, and a compulsion to immediate trial will necessarily do the prisoner great injustice.

We, therefore, ask and pray for the sake of humanity, and that our unstained history may not be tarnished, that the proceedings in the case may be arrested, and that the prisoner may be allowed due time to prepare for his trial. We, therefore, pray that the General who organized this Commission (or his successor) and has full power over the same, will so direct it to act that the accused, Champ Ferguson, may have justice according to law and custom and should it so occur, that after a fair, pure, just and untrammeled trial, he is found guilty, no complaint can be made but all the world will say he has had an investigation according to law, and in compliance with reason. Wherefore, we humbly pray that the Court may be so directed as to continue this case until the witnesses may be procured for proper defense.

This communication we have been made bold to submit by reason of the Magna Charta, the Constitution of this, our beloved country, and Article 34 of the Articles of War, all of which allow a respectful petition, even from the lowest subject.

We have the honor to be very respectfully,

Your obedient servants,

GUILD & GOODWIN
Attorneys for Defendant.

The President of the Commission then announced an adjournment until Monday morning, in order to give the Court due time to consider the pleas.

CHAPTER VI

Judge Guild's Argument

WHEN the Court convened on Monday morning, July 17th, the counsel for the defense notified the Court that they had still another plea to submit. After considerable discussion, the plea was admitted.

In this plea, the third to be presented by counsel for the defense, the defense denied the legality of a military court to try a citizen, and in this case the plea set forth that the Court had no jurisdiction to try the prisoner, he being a citizen and not belonging to either the land or naval forces of the United States. It stated that no war existed in either Kentucky or Tennessee, where these crimes were alleged to have been committed; that the criminal courts of the different counties named in the specifications were in full operation, and that, therefore, he should be tried in the counties where the deeds charged were committed. Further, the defense desired to argue the questions involved in these pleas.

The Judge Advocate stated that it was understood by both sides, on Friday, that the argument on the pleas was closed.

Judge Guild replied that it was, of course, a mere matter of courtesy whether or not the Court would hear the argument of the defense, but that this was the first time in the history of the Government that such questions had ever been brought before a Court and they deserved full consideration.

"The proceedings," replied Judge Blackman, "are getting very irregular. Here are three pleas in three days, all of the same substance. The Court is aware of the fact, unofficially, that this very plea was on the table last Friday. Why was it not presented then? This disposition to delay the Court cannot be tolerated."

After some further discussion, however, it was decided to hear the argument of the defense on the questions involved in the pleas, which argument was presented by Judge Guild in a speech that must have reverberated through the crowded courtroom and overflowed into the streets outside. It was a speech that must have gladdened the hearts of devotees of old-time oratory and raised the spirits of those sympathetic to the cause of Champ Ferguson. At the same time, it was probably merely an aggravation to the Court and to those not sympathetic to the defendant's cause.

Judge Guild probably realized that in legality there was not so much he could say in support of the pleas presented by the defense, but in actuality there was a great deal he would say. He proceeded forthwith to say it,—and at length. For two hours or more he held forth eloquently on the privileges of mankind in general and the rights of Champ Ferguson in particular.

Not for nothing had he read Blackstone's *Commentaries* ten times while studying law as a young man in the office of Colonel Foster. Now, some forty years later, in arguing the case of Champ Ferguson before the Military Court, he made good use of the opportunity to delineate the tortuous growth of the legal safeguards that had been thrown around the rights of the individual as developed through the centuries past. Champ Ferguson was in grave danger of his life and no one knew it better than counsel for the defense.

"In presenting the great questions involved in the special pleas filed and relied upon," said Judge Guild, in opening his argument, "I need not invoke the matured and well-considered judgment of the Commission or impress upon you the high responsibilities of your position,—the greatest that ever rested upon man,—a responsibility upon your part of depriving the prisoner of his liberty, and it may be, of his life.

". . . . The Commission will perceive that those three special pleas raised three important questions which are of importance to every citizen of the country, and vitally so to the accused:

1st. That this Commission has not jurisdiction to try and punish the accused.

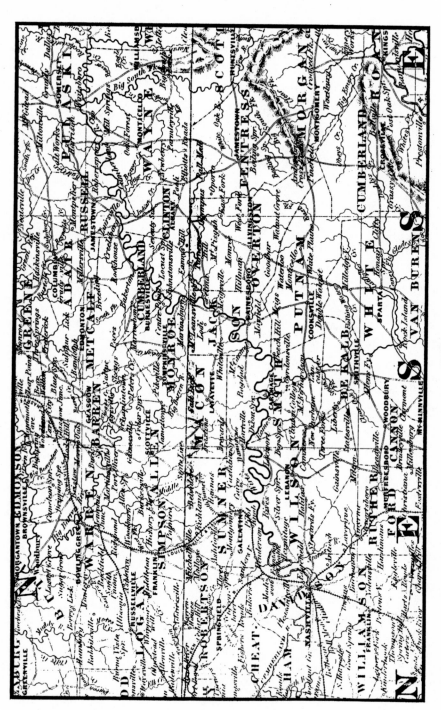

SECTION OF KENTUCKY-TENNESSEE, 1865, CHAMP FERGUSON'S "COUNTRY"

2nd. He was a Confederate Captain, and surrendered to Colonel Blackburn, of the United States Army, upon the same terms granted to General Lee's army, and is entitled to the protection of the Government.

3rd. That General Thomas issued his order of the 1st of May, 1865; sent abroad messengers asking the surrender of all independent bands, which includes guerillas,—announcing that they shall be received upon the same terms granted to General Lee's army,— and those availing themselves of that Order, it is insisted, are entitled to the protection of the Government.

"Although those pleas are different in form and substance, they point to the same result,—a bar to a further prosecution of the prisoner by the military arm of the Government. They deny the jurisdiction of this Commission to force the prisoner to the general issue upon the charges and specifications made against him. They deny the legal and constitutional power of this Commission to convict and take the life of the prisoner.

". . . . The fifty-three distinct charges of murder, alleged to have been committed in Virginia, Tennessee, and Kentucky, are common law and statutory offenses of those states. By law, those states have organized civil courts with juries to try and punish persons committing this crime; and these courts, by the Constitution and laws of those states, have original and exclusive jurisdiction."

After these preliminary remarks, Judge Guild went into an extended discussion of the various developments in history which tended to safeguard the life and liberty of the individual. He went back to the laws of the Romans. He came on down through English history to the Petition of Rights, the Bill of Rights, and the Magna Charta, and showed what brought them about. He showed how these principles had been brought to the Colonies of America by the first settlers and how they were incorporated into the Declaration of Independence, the Constitution of the United States, and the constitution of each individual state. He quoted at length from such legal authorities as Mr. Story, Mr. DeHart, and Mr. Blackstone. He ventured to say that if the voice of Daniel Webster could be heard from the tomb, it would be raised against the jurisdiction and punishment of the prisoner at trial in that his constitutional rights were being violated thereby.

"I maintain," said Judge Guild, "that those constitutional guarantees remain the same in the time of war as well as peace, and it is more important and essential to the citizen that they should be observed and adhered to in times of war than in peace. In times of peace they would scarcely ever be invaded or trampled upon. If they should, an outraged people would have the constitutional remedy applied, but in times of war and such a war as we have lately had, where States and people shall have become divided—where a great civil war with all its carnage and desolations shall have swept over the land; when men's passions have become frenzied and they are utterly disqualified to judge impartially of each other's actions—the citizen stands most in need of the shield thrown around him by the Constitution. In such wars, the people on either side, as well as those in power, are less restrained by Constitutional limitations and are apt, naturally, to fall into the heresy of being authorized to do anything irrespective of the laws and Constitution which, in their opinion, might save the Republic. The history of the world has shown that the greatest wrongs have been committed and every principle of freedom has been violated by adhering to and acting upon this heresy. It is in such times of public danger and a disposition to disregard and trample upon the rights of the citizen that he needs most the enforcement of his constitutional rights; and they are claimed and insisted upon in behalf of the prisoner."

The assembling of a military court by order of the president or his commanding general, Judge Guild went on to say, had not been heard of in the history of the United States until the great civil war which had just ceased to exist, and then only in the case of a person connected with the land or naval forces of the country. He thundered that trial by jury of the vicinage in which the alleged crime is committed is guaranteed the accused by the Constitution and that no power on earth could legally or justly deprive him of it; that Champ Ferguson was a private citizen and due all the constitutional guarantees of a private citizen; that Congress, which alone had power to make laws, had never intended that the Articles of War should be extended to include anyone who was not a member of the military forces of the land.

He then explained how the three branches of government, the legislative, the executive, and the judiciary had been carefully developed with checks and balances so that no one branch could of its own volition work to the detriment of the individual. He stated it as his considered opinion that the prerogatives of the executive were being extended beyond warrant in this particular case and that Champ Ferguson was being brought to trial without proper authority.

"Upon all questions," said Judge Guild, "involving the life of a citizen, it is a human principle of the criminal law, as is maintained by the eminent jurists of every country, that our minds must be fully convinced, beyond a reasonable doubt, before life is taken; that the tribunal having in charge the prisoner has the legal and constitutional jurisdiction to try the prisoner and pronounce judgment of death upon him. If our minds doubt or vacillate upon this question of jurisdiction, it is your duty to discharge the prisoner; for it is better for the country that a great criminal should escape punishment than that a dangerous precedent should be set involving the liberty and life of every citizen of the land.

". . . . Upon these grounds, respectfully urged, I maintain that this Commission has not the jurisdiction to try and condemn the prisoner; therefore ask for his discharge and that he shall be compelled to make no further answer to this prosecution."

Judge Guild then went on to discuss his second and third propositions, namely, that Champ Ferguson was a commissioned Captain of the Confederate States, that he and his company were a part of the Army of the Confederacy, that he acted upon and obeyed the orders of his superiors, that after the surrender of the armies of Generals Lee and Johnston the defendant had surrendered himself and his command to Colonel Blackburn, commanding the 4th

Tennessee Mounted Infantry of the United States, which surrender was accepted, and that he was entitled to the protection of the Government of the United States.

"It is true," said Judge Guild, "that Colonel Backburn did not give him a written parole. But it is insisted that such a parole is not necessary, because the prisoner was assured by Colonel Blackburn if he would come in and surrender to him, he would be entitled to the same terms granted Generals Lee and Johnston—the protection of the Government. The contract was fully performed on the part of the prisoner, and the Government was bound to perform its part. We look to the substance of things and are not controlled by shadows.

"After the prisoner had surrendered himself and men, had unarmed and placed themselves within the power of the forces of the United States, it was then too late for the Government to refuse to grant them the same terms given to General Lee. Every principle of good faith on the part of the Government demands that this contract shall be carried into effect; that he is not subject to arrest and trial by the military arm of the Government upon the many charges now preferred against him."

He stated that he did not consider tenable the Judge Advocate's position that a paroled prisoner was not exempt from a prosecution for murder before a military commission—that it was the promise of the Government that those who surrendered would remain unmolested so far as the Army of the United States or its military courts were concerned. He pointed out that several of the generals of the Confederacy who had surrendered and who had lately returned to Nashville had stood indicted in the Circuit Court of the United States for treason, but that the United States District Attorney had written to Washington for instructions and had received a reply from the Secretary of State saying that they were not subject either to arrest or trial.

Judge Guild then made the further statement that the second plea was even stronger than the first, in that it avoided the argument of the Judge Advocate that the prisoner could be tried for an offense committed contrary to the laws of war,—that it did not state he was a Confederate Captain or that he and his command were a part of the Confederate Army, but simply that he was a Captain commanding an armed band that took sides with the Confederate States and that he had surrendered himself and his company under the order of General Thomas and the assurance of Colonel Blackburn and that he was therefore entitled to the protection of the United States Government.

"Why," asked Judge Guild, "did General Thomas issue his order of May 1st? The interest of the Government and the safety of the people demanded it. The country had been dislocated by a war of great magnitude and vast proportions. The best of American blood had gallantly and freely flown upon a thousand battlefields, displaying an endurance and courage on both sides never before shown. General Lee's army had surrendered on the 9th of April, liberal terms being granted by the Government. Shortly afterwards, General Johnston and his forces, east of the Mississippi, surrendered on the same terms. Then followed General Forrest, General Roddy, and shortly afterwards General Kirby-Smith, west of the Mississippi.

"But still there were scattered bands in various counties in Tennessee, chiefly independent or guerilla bands and bushwhackers, and the question arises as to what course should now be taken by our remaining Generals to restore safety and repose to the country. Major-General Thomas, who was and is in command of the Department of the Cumberland—a man of strong, practical intellect, a man whose courage and skill as a soldier, displayed upon many a hard-fought battlefield, has made his name illustrious as well as the army he commanded—determined this important question.

"In determining it, there were important matters to be considered. The patriotic object was to close this war, give repose to the country, and stop the further flow of blood. Shall these independent or guerilla bands be cut off from all chances of amnesty and pardon by pursuing them to the death, in which onset many must die on either side and desolation shall still mark the earth and inflict the people with all the horrors and woes of war; or shall I, as a representative of the Government, flushed with victories that have saved the integrity of the nation, and proud of

her magnanimity to a beaten and fallen foe, offer to these independent or
guerilla bands amnesty and pardon by inviting them to come in, lay
down their arms, and surrender themselves to the authorities of the
United States and return to their allegiance to the Government? By so
doing, they should receive the same terms granted to General Lee's army—
the protection of the Government.

"That far-seeing and magnanimous course was adopted by General
Thomas, and hence the promulgation of the Order of the 1st of May,
1865, which was the olive branch of peace, and protection extended to all.
It was accepted by Captain Ferguson. He urged his command to accept
it. They did voluntarily come in by the promises enunciated in that
order, and the assurances given by Colonel Blackburn, and made the
surrender. His officers and men received the protection of the Government and they remained unmolested at home; but their Captain, who
urged their surrender and made it in good faith, is now arraigned by
the Government before a Military Commission upon charges involving
his life. Is not the plighted faith of the Government pledged that this
thing shall not be done? . . . .

"All others have received the protection of the Government. Shall the
prisoner alone be excepted? He placed his life upon the assurance given
him. He had a just expectation that those assurances would be carried
out, and in good faith enforced. Does not every principle of justice and
public faith pledge the man that they should be enforced, and an end
put to a prosecution involving the life of a prisoner? If the plighted
faith of the Government shall not be extended to him; if he shall not
receive the protection of the Government which he believed that he was
entitled to and would receive upon his surrender, then does not good
faith and justice require that he should be placed in the position in which
he was found? Let him be permitted to return to his distressed wife
and helpless daughter, who have been driven to the woods for shelter,
and assurances are here given that he will become a peaceful, loyal citizen to the Government. And if the civil authorities shall see proper to
take steps for an investigation upon any of the matters here charged,
let it be done in the civil courts of the country where the witnesses are,
and where all the constitutional rights of the prisoner will be extended
to him. . . . .

"Let us be fully convinced that we have the constitutional right to take the prisoner's life before we extinguish it. Let us be fully assured that we stand upon impregnable ground and let us be certain that we do nothing that shall in after times, when the passions of men have subsided, disquiet our own consciences, or place a blot upon the escutcheon of our own Government!"

Counsel for the defense well knew that the hates of war were still hot. Counsel for the defense knew that any delay would allow these hates to cool and the longer the delay the less likelihood of retributive vengeance. If they could not prevent the trial, perhaps they could postpone it. If they could not postpone the trial, they could at least delay it as much as possible by whatever means were at their command.

It is fairly apparent, by this time, that it was the tactics of the counsel for the defense simply to out-talk the opposition if possible, to introduce as many confusing pleas and issues as possible, and to delay proceedings in general. There was certainly nothing to lose by delay.

CHAPTER VII

No Legal Quarter

COUNSEL for the defense had now exhausted their legal resources and used all the ingenuity at their command, in efforts both to delay and to quash the action. The pleas of the defense had been filed and the arguments supporting them, presented by Judge Guild with all the skill derived from long years of experience in court procedure, had been heard. A full week had been used in this procedure. Debate had been acrimonious and tempers had become frayed.

The legal tangle and the questions involved were common subjects of discussion wherever men gathered in Nashville during that first week of the trial, and differences of opinion must have been just as pronounced and just as bitter, and probably just as impossible of reconciliation, as were those which brought about the War in the first place.

The reporter for the *Dispatch* had said, on Friday, July 14th:

This trial involves some very important points of law, and the noted character of the prisoner together with the unprecedented number of murders charged against him, has excited a deep interest not only among the legal fraternity but all classes of our citizens.

The reporter for the *Daily Union,* as usual, was quite bitter in his denunciation of the delay being effected by the defense, and on Saturday, the 15th of July, had gone so far as to set forth his own opinion on the matter:

Our readers will recollect the charges and specifications against Ferguson are very strong, the latter embracing no less than fifty-three distinct murders. To what extent he is guilty is not for us, now that he is on trial, to judge. The people of those counties through which his band roved are deeply interested in the result of his trial. Nor does the interest cease there. The limits of the effect of General Thomas' Order are to be defined. If the fact that Generals Grant and Lee agreed upon certain terms by which large and regular armies were to be surrendered, paroled, and exempted from molestation by the authorities of the United States makes it competent for every officer subordinate to General Grant to offer the same terms to notorious outlaws, and thereby estop the government from all proceedings against them for violations of the rules of civilized warfare, the people wish to know it.

We make bold to say if the Order of General Thomas, above referred to, is to be thus interpreted, its wisdom is at best exceedingly questionable. After the surrender of Lee, Johnston, Taylor, and Smith, was the peace of the country so endangered that it must be preserved at the price of literally compounding the most atrocious felonies? We cannot believe it. General Thomas' Order cannot act as an estoppel to the investigation of such a case as Champ Ferguson's. If so, we deprecate that it was ever made. We pass no opinion upon the prisoner's guilt or innocence, but we do say that there ought to be no legal bar to a trial of his case. The country cannot afford to smother it up in a mist of legal quibbles.

Apparently, however, someone called the hand of this reporter overnight, to a certain extent at least, so that on Sunday, the 16th, he qualified his statement of the previous day somewhat:

It was not our intention to say anything which would in the least damage the defense in this case. The Commission will not be influenced by any newspaper article to decide for or against the prisoner. We only meant to say that where persons charged publicly with such fearful crimes as are alleged to have been perpetrated by Ferguson cannot be tried upon the merits of the case because of some bar to the proceedings, then must there be a great compensation to society in some respect.

Is it not possible that our military commanders, in their eagerness to secure the entire pacification of the country after the great success of our arms which caused the surrender of the main Confederate forces, overstepped the bounds of good policy in extending to noted freebooters the same terms as were granted to the regular soldiers? There was not, in our estimation, a condition of things requiring such a general extension of clemency. These guerillas were at the mercy of the government. With our troops released from watching large armies, any number of them could at once have been sent against the remaining bands who were robbing and murdering without stint upon their own hook, and they would all have been speedily captured or dispersed.

If, however, the government through its agents has plighted its faith to these men, wisely or unwisely, let that faith be kept. Though Champ Ferguson be steeped in crimes too horrible for recital, if he was induced by a promise of the Government of the United States not to molest him afterwards to surrender his person into its hands, we would blush at the Nation's dishonor were that pledge to be broken. The question now is, is the Government in fact so pledged to him? We shall soon know.

Thus was presented the viewpoint of the prosecution in general, as represented in Nashville that summer by the "third estate." Nor were Nashville newspapers alone in criticizing the Federal military commanders for their actions at the close of the War and in demanding harsher terms than those laid down by these commanders. The South was conquered, Lincoln was dead, and the vengeful had not been appeased.

After Judge Guild's lengthy argument in behalf of the pleas had been filed, Judge Advocate Blackman stated that he had already answered the arguments relating to the first two pleas in bar and that, as to the argument on the third, the question of jurisdiction, he did not consider it an improvement in any way upon those he had already read in the reports of numerous military trials. Apparently, Judge Guild's waves of oratory had broken themselves futilely against the stone wall of military court procedure and the fixed determination of the Federal military authorities comprising the court to try Champ Ferguson upon the charges made.

Major Ford, President of the Commission, thereupon read the following opinion of the Commission, overruling all the pleas:

The first part of the plea in bar filed by defendant's counsel is based upon the ground that the prisoner had been an officer in the so-called

Confederate States Army, and surrendered on conditions of parole, and is therefore not subject to prosecution for the offenses alleged against him in the charges and specifications. But it is not stated in the plea that the prisoner himself was in fact paroled. He only states that the officers and men under his command were paroled, and sent to their homes; and that the prisoner was permitted to go to his home, there to remain until Colonel Blackburn, to whom he had surrendered, could confer with the General commanding in reference to the accused. It further appears that when Colonel Backburn had so conferred with the General commanding, he sent for the defendant and placed him in arrest, hence this part of the plea shows no parole, and affords the prisoner no protection.

The second part of the plea avers that the prisoner surrendered to Colonel Blackburn on the terms of an order issued by Major-General Thomas to Major-General Rousseau, dated May 1, 1865, requiring the latter officer to send a summons under a flag of truce to all and every band of armed men in his vicinity, of which he might know, who were operating nearer to his than to any other command, and call upon them to surrender to him or any officer he might name for that purpose, upon the same terms as Lee surrendered to Grant. Also notifying them that if they disregarded this summons and continued acts of hostility, they would thereafter be regarded as outlaws, and be proceeded against, pursued, and when captured, treated as outlaws.

The plea avers that the prisoner surrendered, but it does not aver that he was paroled as the cartel between Grant and Lee required.

Why the General commanding allowed all the officers and men under Ferguson parole, and refused to parole him, is not a matter of this Court to adjudicate.

It is sufficient for the purpose of this case, for this Court to know that the General commanding did except this prisoner from the cartel and that he had authority for doing so.

General Order No. 100, dated War Department, Adjutant General's Office, Washington, April 24, 1863, Section VII, page 133, reads as follows:

"No prisoner of war can be forced by the hostile Government to parole himself, and no Government is obliged to parole prisoners of war, or to parole all captured officers, if it paroles any. As the pledging of the parole is an individual act, so is paroling, on the other hand, an act of choice on the part of the belligerent."

It is urged in argument by the defendant's counsel that even the most important matters are acted upon by Staff Officers without consulting their General, and that the Order to try Champ Ferguson is not the Order of General Thomas, but that of his Judge Advocate. This is simply an imputation upon the integrity of high minded and honorable officers, which refutes itself, and can have no weight or bearing whatsoever in this case. But, again, this Court does not conceive that the cartel between Grant and Lee bars proceedings even against a regularly paroled officer or soldier for criminal offenses or acts committed in violation of the established laws of war; and such are the acts here charged against the prisoner, hence the Court overrules the plea in bar.

This Court does not consider itself so far bound by law forms of procedure as to defeat a hearing of this case on its merits.

But when the Court comes to hear testimony on the part of the defense, the accused may adduce evidence as to any parole he claims to have had extended to him, so that the reviewing authority, at the proper time, may consider its force.

The plea to the jurisdiction of the Court is overruled, but the plea will be made a part of the record, so that the accused may have all the benefits before the reviewing authority.

The Court no doubt felt it was being lenient with the accused in permitting the pleas to become a part of the record of the trial, while it denied at the same time that there had been any grounds for the filing of the pleas. The preliminary skirmishes were about over and the real battle was now to commence.

Judge Guild and Captain Goodwin had made a brave effort in three directions: first, to seek postponement of the trial; second, to claim exemption from prosecution under the terms of Lee's surrender to Grant; and third, to question the jurisdiction of a military court to try one who, since the War was now ended, was a private citizen. The decision of the Court made it clear, and the counsel for the defense no doubt saw it thus, that the attack had failed along all three fronts. It was the decision of the Court that there was no need for a postponement of the trial; that even had the prisoner been paroled, which he had not, he would still be subject to prosecution for the crimes with which he was charged; that the Commanding General had ordered the Commission to try the case and that it was their duty to do so.

Before adjourning for the day, the Court took occasion to reprimand the counsel for the defense for presenting the petition to the General Commanding the District of Middle Tennessee:

"As to the paper addressed to General Johnson," said the Court, "read before the Court on the 14th and published in the city papers on the 15th inst., we have authority to say that it is a direct reflection on the integrity of the members of the Court as men and their character as officers—we hope not intentionally so—but it admits of no other interpretation. We cannot, therefore, take any further notice of it, than to return it to the counsel, with the assurance that such papers will not in the least influence our conduct, and expressing the hope that no more such papers will be submitted to us.

"It is noticed by this Court as a startling fact that fifteen days have elapsed since the charges and specifications were read to the prisoner and a copy furnished his counsel, and as yet not a witness has been summoned for the defense, nor a subpoena asked for. Such dereliction of duty on the part of the counsel will no longer be tolerated by the Court, and if persisted in longer, the Court directs that the Judge Advocate summon the material witnesses of the accused without delay."

Very evidently, the Court had not taken kindly to the petition addressed, over their heads, to the Commanding General; and probably the "authority" referred to in their comment was a message from the Commanding General expressing no intention of calling a halt to the proceedings! There was nothing left for Champ Ferguson to do but answer the charges.

In rebuking the counsel for the defense for lack of diligence in summoning witnesses, the Judge Advocate did not know, and neither at the time did the counsel for the defense know, that these witnesses were never to be secured. It is one of the startling and almost incredible facts of this trial that whereas about fifty witnesses were presented by the prosecution, only four were procured for the defense. One of these four, it is true, was a General of the Confederate Army; yet the fact that the defense was never able to produce witnesses to refute statements made by witnesses for the prosecution made their case immeasurably more difficult.

The strong contention of the defense for postponement in order that certain witnesses might be secured, who, it was asserted, would easily be able to prove the guiltlessness of the prisoner, was to look exceedingly weak before the trial was over. Though on the next day, Tuesday, July 18th, the defense secured upwards of eighty subpoenas for defense witnesses, only four were ever to appear.

There are, of course, a number of good reasons which might be advanced for the defense's failure to secure witnesses. On the face of it, though, it looked as if there actually were no such witnesses as the defense claimed, and for all we shall ever know this may have been the case.

On the other hand, the witnesses that the defense might have presented were on the losing side at the end of the War, and this fact may have intimidated them to such an extent that they were hesitant to appear. If Champ Ferguson were in danger of losing his freedom and, mayhap, his life, they too were in danger.

Then, again, in those days the almost inaccessible country in which most of the acts charged were committed made it both difficult to get word to these witnesses that they were wanted and difficult for them to find satisfactory traveling facilities for coming out of the mountains down to Nashville. To these people, the journey of more than one hundred miles to Nashville was a tedious one and not to be undertaken lightly, and to go that far to testify in public trial before a hostile court was a fearsome thing. Moreover, unlike the government witnesses, it was probably quite difficult to provide any possible witnesses for Champ Ferguson with funds for the trip—a most important factor.

Whatever may have been the reason, the stark fact remains that either there were no such witnesses, or if there were, none of them had the courage or were sufficiently interested in Champ Ferguson's welfare to make the effort necessary to come to his aid.

Two more days were to elapse before the examination of witnesses for the prosecution could begin. Capt. Thos. H. Osborn, a member of the Court, had been mustered out of service on July 15th, and the Court did not wish to proceed until his place was filled; authority for this action had to come from the Commanding General of the District of Middle Tennessee, at Murfreesboro. An order was received from General Johnson on July 19th, authorizing Captain O. B. Simmons and Captain Martin B. Thompson to take their places on the Court, and the trial was scheduled to begin in earnest the next day.

But when the Court convened on Thursday morning, July 20th, nine days after the trial had opened, Judge Guild had thought of one other possible loophole by which his client might escape: the defendant ought not to be prosecuted upon several of the specifications of the charge of murder because more than two years had intervened between the alleged commission of said offenses and the order of the Commanding General assembling the Commission. He thereupon filed a general plea, signed by Champ Ferguson, praying discharge from prosecution upon these specifications on the grounds that they were barred by the lapse of time.

Judge Advocate Blackman quickly disposed of this plea, however, with the statement that Champ Ferguson had not been amenable to justice during the intervening period, having been in arms and resisting the charges of the United States, so that he could not be arrested until on or about the 26th of May, 1865, which fact excluded him from the benefit of such a plea.

The Judge Advocate then read the charges and specifications, to each of which the prisoner pled, in a clear and firm voice, "Not Guilty."

The first charge, that of being a guerilla, was the first to be investigated, and the first witness to be presented by the Government was the most notable, probably, of all Champ's adversaries, "Tinker Dave" Beatty.

CHAPTER VIII

Tinker Dave Beatty

T HE first witness called for the Government in this case," wrote the *Dispatch* reporter, "was the celebrated Union Scout, 'Tinker Dave,' who was at the head of a company of home guards, and who has fought Champ Ferguson from the beginning to the end of his career. It would almost seem that both of these men bear charmed lives. They have shot at each other innumerable times, and each has received ugly wounds. They were deadly enemies, and hunted each other down with savage ferocity.

"The real name of 'Tinker Dave' is David Beatty. He is a man about forty-five years of age, medium size, but of iron mould and great courage. He is covered with scars received in battle, and many a Rebel and bushwhacker has bit the dust from his unerring aim. They feared Dave on account of his cunning and courage."

It would be interesting to know where David Beatty got his nickname. Whether he was a tinsmith or a peddler, or adept at fixing things that wouldn't run, we do not know. Tinker Dave was undoubtedly no match for Champ Ferguson physically, but he made up in cunning what he lacked in strength. It was the old feud between the fox and the lion.

A. V. and W. H. Goodpasture's *Life of Jefferson Dillard Goodpasture,* printed in 1897, contains the following illuminating comments on Tinker Dave Beatty:

The most desperate set of Federal guerillas in the Mountain District was the company commanded by Tinker Dave Beatty, of Fentress County. Before the War, Judge Goodpasture had defended Beatty in the Circuit Court at Jamestown, on an indictment for a very grave offense. This circumstance gained him immunity from the bloody raids of his men during the War, as it also gave him a sort of protection during the equally dangerous time just succeeding that demoralizing struggle. About the close of the War, Judge Goodpasture met Tinker Dave for the first time after hostilities had commenced. He was somewhat embarrassed as he did not know how he would be received. After passing the compliments of the day, he enquired for the news. "Nothing new," said Tinker, but after a moment he added, "Well, I believe our men did kill a lot of the Hammock gang this morning." In the course of the conversation, Judge Goodpasture observed that Beatty had never been at his house. "No, sir," he replied, "I had no business with you."

This last statement he took as an assurance that Tinker still remembered his former services, and with his characteristic ability to turn an advantage to account, he determined to make Tinker's friendship useful to him. When the War closed, there was a great accumulation of business awaiting the opening of the courts. He had a number of bills ready when the first court met at Jamestown, which he determined to file. It was considered as much as his life was worth to attend this court, and would be if he failed to receive Tinker Dave Beatty's protection. No other lawyer ventured to appear. The evening before the court met, Judge Goodpasture rode directly to Beatty's house, about twenty-five miles over the rough mountain roads, where he was received in a friendly spirit, and spent the night. In the morning Beatty rode with him into Jamestown, and after he had dispatched the business in hand, brought him back to his house. Next day, when Judge Goodpasture was ready to depart, Beatty told him it would not be safe for him to go alone, and sent his brother, Flem, with him as far as old man Hill's, at the foot of the mountain, whence he reached home in safety.

Thus was the law afforded protection in a curious way, but Judge Goodpasture had lived in the Mountain District all his life, having been born in Overton County in 1824, and he knew the type and temperament of the people with whom he had to deal.

Judge Goodpasture had espoused the cause of the Confederacy when the War broke out, although he never entered the army. Some twenty years before the War, he had decided to practice law and had borrowed from Judge Alvin Cullom, of Livingston,

Tennessee, who will be mentioned later in this account, Blackstone's *Commentaries.* Having mastered the contents of those famous volumes, he entered the law office of Judge E. L. Gardenhire, at Livingston, in 1845, and for more than thirty years before moving to Nashville, practiced law in the Mountain District with great success.

Judge Goodpasture was a shrewd trader all his life; he accepted the results of the conflict between the States as a *fait accompli,* and was ready to go ahead with his law practice, making use of the most noted guerilla on the Union side to his own profit. His brother, Winburn W. Goodpasture, was to be an important witness during the latter part of the trial of Champ Ferguson.

In his *History of Morgan's Cavalry,* General Duke states:

The great opponent of Champ Ferguson in the bushwhacking business was Tinker Dave Beatty. The relentless ferocity of all that section made that of Bluebeard and the Welch giants, in comparison, sink into insignificance. Sometimes, Champ Ferguson with his band, would enter the cove, carry off Dave's stock and drive him to his retreat in the mountains, to which no man ever followed him. Then, when he was strong enough, he would lead his henchmen against Champ and slay all who did not escape. He did not confine his hostilities to Champ Ferguson. There were not related of Beatty, however, so many stories illustrative of his personal courage as of Ferguson.

Champ and Tinker Dave seem to have had a healthy respect for each other, and neither bore particular personal resentment against the other. Perhaps the fact that they were open and avowed enemies from the beginning accounts for this mutual respect. One of the tragic and deadly features of the War, especially in the region wherein lies the scene of our story, was the fact that neighbor could not trust neighbor and brother could not rely on brother.

Almost a month after Tinker Dave took the witness stand, the *Dispatch* reporter had his first interview with Champ Ferguson. During this interview, he asked Champ what he thought of his

mortal enemy, David Beatty, expecting, he said, to hear a tirade
of imprecations concerning him, since it was to be remembered
that they had fought singly and with their companies, giving no
quarter. He was surprised, therefore, to receive the following
answer:

"Well, there are meaner men than Tinker Dave. He fought me
bravely and gave me some heavy licks, but I always gave him as good
as he sent. I have nothing against Tinker Dave. He spoke to me very
kindly at the court room when he was giving his testimony against me.
We both tried to get each other during the War, but we always proved
too cunning for each other. There are meaner men than Dave."

There is an element of pathos as well as admiration of one strong
man for another in Champ's comment: "There are meaner men
than Dave." This was probably as near a compliment as Champ
would likely come in speaking of an adversary. So far as these two
men were concerned, at least, there was no hypocrisy; they were
sworn enemies, without quarter, and it was clearly understood on
both sides.

General Duke again says:

We find references to both Champ Ferguson and David Beatty in a
little book "Mountaineers," by Reverend John Wesley Smith:

"Among these people you will find the elements of strong manhood.
They are brave, fearless people but not savage, as they have sometimes
been pictured by their traducers. Such men as Pleas Taylor of Fentress
County and Lee Taylor of White County were not only living examples
of good morals and good citizenship, but their very names were a terror
to evil doers. The noted bandits, Champ Ferguson and Tinker Dave
Beatty, who kept up a regular guerilla warfare from 1860 to 1865 on the
Cumberland Mountains between Kentucky and Tennessee, both feared
and respected the Taylors."

The Reverend Mr. Smith adds a sentence that is more startling than
his assertion that there were as many as two men on earth who could
overawe Ferguson and Beatty: "The writer knew 'Tinker Dave' Beatty,

the famous outlaw, and was at a religious service some years after the
War where the bandit knelt, weeping, at the altar of prayers."

It is interesting to note that Mr. Smith uses the adjectives "bandit" and "outlaw" in describing Tinker Dave. Had the fortunes
of war been reversed, it is easy to believe that the positions of
Ferguson and Beatty would also have been reversed after the
war had ended.

This feud between the two leading guerilla tacticians was, of
course, well rumored in Nashville by the time the trial opened on
July 11th, and now, nine days later, since Tinker Dave was to be
the first witness for the prosecution, there was naturally a great
deal of interest in what he would have to say.

The testimony of Tinker Dave occupied the better part of two
days, July 20th and 21st. Questioning by the prosecution and cross-
examination by the defense brought forth the following account
of his experiences with Ferguson during the War:

"I live in a cove in Fentress County, surrounded by high hills. I have
known Champ Ferguson for eighteen or twenty years and I saw him
a number of times during the War, sometimes accompanied by only a
few men, sometimes with quite a large company. Some of the men I
saw him with at the beginning of the War were Scott Bledsoe, Bob
Bledsoe, John Simpson, Hans McGinnis, John Hughes, Abe Bledsoe,
Jobe Simpson, John Lee, Henry Sublett, Bob Brown, and Ben Barton.
During the early part of the War, he was usually with Capt. Bledsoe's
men, who were conscripting, killing, and shooting at Union men in
general, including myself."

At this point, Judge Guild objected to the legality of the evidence
furnished by the witness on the ground that it was not confined
to the distinct charge made; that the defendant was not charged
with shooting at the witness; that the proof should be confined to
what the defendant did; that what others may have done should
not affect the defendant.

The Judge Advocate stated that the proof was legitimate; that the defendant was charged with being a guerilla, the specifications being that he had been a common robber, freebooter, and murderer during the years 1861 to 1864 inclusive and up to May, 1865.

"The testimony does not show," replied Captain Goodwin, "that these acts did not take place in a skirmish of regular warfare."

The court room was then cleared for the deliberation of the Court on the question raised. On reopening the doors, the following decision was read:

The Court overrules the objection and holds to the principle that any acts showing the accused was practicing guerilla warfare may be shown in evidence, though not distinctly and severally set forth in the specifications of the charge. The Court thinks no injustice can be done the prisoner by this ruling, for he can meet this kind of proof by showing he was a peaceable and quiet man.

One does not have to look hard to detect sarcasm in this decision. Beatty then went ahead with his story:

"About ten or twelve days after the Mill Springs fight (about the 1st of February, 1862), several of Bledsoe's men came to my house and told my wife to tell me I must take sides in the war or leave the country. They took some of my property, some saddles and other things belonging to me, when they left and as they were going down to cross the creek I fired on them, wounding one man and a horse. I was in the field at the time, a short distance from the house, with my two sons and a neighbor.

"After this they kept running in on us every few weeks, Ferguson, Bledsoe, and others, killing and driving people off. I told my boys that before I would leave home or run away I would fight them to Doomsday and if they killed me, let them kill me. So I took my sons and raised a company of men to fight them. Sometimes I had as many as 60 men, sometimes as low as 5. Things went on this way until General Burnside went into East Tennessee, whence he wrote me a letter saying that he wanted me to go out in the mountain forks and bushwhack the Rebels and keep the roads open, saying that I could accomplish much good for our cause in this way. I have the letter at home now. We were not getting any pay but the Government furnished us with all the ammunition we needed. I don't know how many men we bushwhacked and killed but I suppose we killed 25 or more during the War."

The "Mill Springs fight" mentioned by Tinker Dave, known variously as the Battle of Mill Springs, of Fishing Creek, of Somerset, and of Logan's Crossroads, was fought on January 19 and 20, 1862.

The Federals were under the command of General George H. Thomas, who was to figure very prominently later in the destiny of Champ Ferguson, while the Confederates were commanded by Generals George B. Crittenden and Felix K. Zollicoffer, the latter being killed in the battle. General Zollicoffer's body was sent to Nashville, where it lay in state for two days in the State Capitol, being viewed by thousands, and was then buried in the Old City Cemetery.

The battle is of particular interest at this point, since it was fought near the headwaters of the Cumberland River, not a great distance from Champ Ferguson's birthplace and the scene of most of his activities; and since General Crittenden, in making his official report of the battle, stated that the independent cavalry company of Captain Bledsoe was part of his command.

"Many officers and men," said General Crittenden in his report, "frightened by the false rumor of the movement of the enemy, shamelessly deserted and stealing horses and mules to ride, fled to Knoxville, Nashville, and other places in Tennessee."

From testimony given during the trial, we learn that Champ Ferguson was not in this battle, but we do know that the first organized band with which he was associated was that of Captain Scott Bledsoe. The victory was a very important one for the Federals, as it opened the gateway for them into the eastern half of Tennessee through Cumberland Gap; it was a forerunner to the evacuation of Kentucky and Tennessee by the Confederate armies.

"About three weeks after the Battle of Mill Springs," Beatty continued, "Ferguson came to my house along with about 20 other men, some of whom wore our uniform, some had on citizens clothes, and some wore the Rebel uniform. They also had a Union flag with them. I was in a field at the time, which was on the opposite bank of the Obed River about 150 yards from the house. The only ones I recognized were John McGee and Ferguson. I hollered over and asked them what they wanted. One of them replied 'We want Captain Beatty to help us drive off the d—d Rebels, who are now coming in on us.' I told them he was down at George Wolsey's at a log rolling but that I would go for him, which I did and forgot to come back. After that they all rode off.

"During the next few weeks, I shot at Ferguson and his men four or five times, I guess, and they shot at us. Bledsoe, Hughes, and Ferguson and their men never came into Fentress County without trying to kill us. When the guerillas would run in after us, we had to lie out from them and shoot at them whenever we got a good chance. We had to live out in the bushes in times like those and take all the advantages of them we could.

"Some time in March, 1862, I got sight of Ferguson and Hughes with some citizens of Fentress County in their custody, namely, Woods, Edwards, and Sells. This was in Overton County. The night before, my men and I had had a scrap with Hughes and some of his men. The second day after that I saw the bodies of Woods and Edwards as they were being taken back home. I didn't know at the time what had become of Sells but I know I haven't seen him since. I did not examine the bodies but looked at them as they were lying in the wagon and saw the wounds on them. Edwards had been in the regular service of the United States and was home on furlough. Woods had been away in Kentucky but was generally at home. Edwards had been with me before he joined the regular army, but none of the others had ever joined up with me. I don't know of my own personal knowledge that Ferguson killed these men but I saw him along as they went down. I don't know that any of Morgan's men were along when these men were killed. It was my understanding that Hughes and Ferguson took the men.

"I saw Ferguson at various times after that—once about two years ago [July, 1863] not far from Monroe in Overton County with a group of men driving some horses and mules; and again about a year ago [July, 1864] with a big drove of horses and mules and with a band of about 75 men. They were driving them up in the coves and I was at Bowden's Still House about ten o'clock in the morning when I saw them. These guerillas often came into our country during the War and waylaid us, watching our houses. We would lie in wait for them whenever we could and quite often shot at them while we were lying concealed in the bushes. At one time I wounded one of their men and took him up home without killing him. We never took any prisoners except that one. This wounded man escaped, though we told him we were not going to kill him.

"The last time I saw Ferguson before seeing him here on trial was at Jimtown [the local name for Jamestown, Tennessee], in Fentress County, about three weeks after the surrender at Richmond, as I recall. [This would have been about May 1st.] He and five more men came to a house where I was eating supper, and demanded my arms. After giving them up, they gruffly ordered me to get on my horse and direct them to the Taylor place [the home of Pleas Taylor, a resident of Fentress County, and "a terror to evildoers"].

"After I mounted, they filed three on each side of me. I knew that Champ Ferguson knew where the Taylor place was as well as I did, and that his design was to shoot me after we got away from the house. Champ rode on my left, and I watched him closely. It occurred to me that if I could turn my horse suddenly and slip out, they would not dare shoot for fear of shooting each other, and before they could turn around, I could get a start.

"I resolved to try it, for it was life or death for me, and this was my only hope. I wheeled my horse like a flash, and one of them instantly snapped a cap at me. They then turned and fired about twenty shots at me as I dashed down the road. Three of the shots took effect, one in the back, one in the shoulder, and one in the hip. I, however, got away from them, and did not show them the Taylor place."

At this point, reported the *Daily Press and Times,* the witness showed the Court the hole from which the ball lodged in his breast had been extracted and where another had passed through his shoulder below the blade, ranging upward, making very ugly wounds.

"I have no personal knowledge of the killing of Lieut. Smith, or any of the others mentioned," said Beatty. "I only know what I have heard."

Tinker Dave's testimony related only in barest outline his various encounters with Champ. We can almost believe that while he thought it was all right for Champ and himself to fight each other, he felt it hardly the proper thing for a third party, even a Federal military court, to inquire into the matter. We can also imagine that the prosecution may have hesitated to have Tinker Dave talk too much, for fear it would be realized by the general public that he was just as bad on his side of the fence as Champ was on the other side. These Yankee and Rebel guerillas unquestionably fought each other in the mountains practically without quarter, as the defense attempted to bring out in cross-examination. The defense also attempted to show that the three men, Woods, Edwards, and Sells, with whose killing Ferguson was implicated, (although they are not included, it will be noted, in the specifications), were part of Beatty's command; also, that Ferguson was connected with General Morgan's troops while carrying out the action described by Beatty.

In addition to these things, the defense also endeavored to show that Tinker Dave and his men were not regularly enlisted soldiers in the Union Army, to which admission was practically made by Beatty when he said they served without pay, and that he had simply been requested by General Burnside to operate as bushwhackers in the mountains.

All in all, the prosecution was probably entirely willing for Tinker Dave to step down from the stand. This he did after two days testimony, the Court adjourning until Monday morning, July 24th, at eight o'clock.

CHAPTER IX

The Killings Begin

THERE was no chronological order in the charges of murder with which Champ Ferguson was accused. As a matter of fact, the first specification concerns the murder of Lieutenant Smith, who was the last person, in point of time, with whose murder Champ was charged.

Also, during the examination of the witnesses who were to testify during the weeks following Tinker Dave Beatty's appearance on the stand, there was no particular order followed, either with reference to the chronological order of the murders or the order in which they were listed in the specifications. In reviewing their testimony, therefore, we shall not follow the apparently haphazard order in which they were introduced but arrange their stories chronologically in accordance with the events they relate. By so doing, we may reconstruct in some detail the picture of Champ Ferguson's life and activities throughout the War.

The indictment, it will be remembered, charged Champ Ferguson with the murder of 53 persons. The first of these in point of time was the sick-bed killing of William Frogg, which occurred on November 1, 1861.

This was shortly before the abortive attempt by a rump convention at Russellville, Kentucky, to bring about secession of that state from the Union.

The political division between the North and South was the Kentucky-Tennessee line, although both Kentucky and Tennessee were families greatly divided within themselves. The Confederates were in the minority in Kentucky, while the Federals were in the minority in Tennessee, but these minorities were very strong in each state and made life very uncertain during the early years of the

War, especially along the border where sentiment was most evenly divided. Early in 1861, Tennessee had voted to remain within the Union but Lincoln's call for troops so changed sentiment in the State that by June the vote was changed to secession. However, as in Kentucky, but for the opposite purpose, there was also an attempt made by a meeting held at Knoxville either to keep the State within the Union or form a separate state that would remain loyal to the Union, which attempt also failed.

In the meantime, Kentucky was trying to remain neutral. Early in 1861, the legislature adopted resolutions of neutrality and in June the commander of the Kentucky State forces, Maj.-Gen. Simon Bolivar Buckner, a very conscientious gentleman and later to be the "goat" at Fort Donelson, entered into neutrality agreements with General Geo. H. McClellan, stationed at Cincinnati, for the Union, and Governor Isham G. Harris, of Tennessee, for the Confederacy. The neutrality of the State of Kentucky during that summer, however, was actually in name only. Federal agents were busy throughout the State recruiting for the army. A wealthy land-owner in central Kentucky, near Danville, by the name of Dick Robinson, a strong Unionist, turned his large farm over to the authorities as a recruiting center for the Home Guard. The Home Guard was supposed to be the State forces of Kentucky but the recruiting at Camp Robinson in particular, under the direction of Lieut. William Nelson, of the U. S. Navy, was in effect recruiting for the Federal Army and arms and ammunition were furnished by the Federal Government. Those of Rebel sentiment in Kentucky and Tennessee considered the establishment of this camp a distinct violation of the neutrality agreement and were most bitter about it. It was generally feared that the forces assembled at Camp Dick Robinson were being prepared for an expedition into East Tennessee for the purpose of arming the Union sympathizers there in the same way in which it was being so successfully done in Kentucky.

Opinion was so evenly divided in Kentucky that it is entirely possible that that State might eventually have followed Tennessee's example in seceding except for certain successes of the Federal troops in the State which were to take place early in 1862. The whole affair, however, had the effect of bringing matters more quickly to a showdown than might otherwise have been the case, for men of both Kentucky and Tennessee, feeling that efforts at neutrality would fail, began to display more openly their real sympathies. Volunteers from the whole region poured into Union or into Confederate camps. Guerilla warfare began that fall in earnest along the Kentucky-Tennessee border, where the price of survival for the next four years was to be eternal vigilance. Danger lurked behind each roadside bush and because the merciful were not likely to receive mercy, "No Quarter" was the general rule.

The death of William Frogg was a case at hand.

Esther Ann Frogg, being sworn, testified as follows:

"I am the widow of the late William Frogg, who was killed on the 1st day of November, 1861, eight miles above Albany, in Clinton County, Kentucky.

"Champ Ferguson came to the house, and said, 'How do you do?' I asked him to have a chair. He said he didn't have time. I asked him to have some apples. He said he had been eating apples. He then asked for Mr. Frogg. I told him he was in bed, very sick.

"Ferguson walked in the house to the bed, and said, 'How are you, Mr. Frogg?' My husband told him he was very sick, that he had the measles, and had taken a relapse. Ferguson said, 'I reckon you caught the measles at Camp Dick Robinson.' Mr. Frogg told him he never was there. Ferguson then shot him with a pistol, and I started out of the house, and just as I got out I heard another shot.

"My husband never spoke after the first shot. I didn't hear Ferguson say anything after the first shot. I went about twenty yards from the house, and returned in about fifteen minutes, and saw Ferguson starting towards his horse. When I got into the house, my husband was lying dead. He was shot twice, under the right breast and on the right side. There was no one in the house at that time but Jack Mace and my little child, five months old, lying in a cradle by the bed.

"George Bragg and West Gwinn were with Ferguson, but did not come into the house. They went off with Ferguson. I had known Ferguson all my life, having been raised close by him.

"I have seen Ferguson twice since that. About a month after the murder of my husband, Ferguson came again to my house, at night, and wanted to turn into the yard a yoke of oxen belonging to John Hogin, my father. He left the oxen there. I don't know who, or how many, were with him, but he came to the house alone.

"Last May, a year ago, I met him again in the road near my house. Bill Beson was with him. They were armed, but said nothing. Many others had gone on down the road before them, but I didn't recognize any of them."

On cross-examination, Mrs. Frogg stated that her husband had never gone with any of the home guards or independent companies before his death, but had belonged to the 12th Kentucky Infantry; that he had been with his regiment a while at Albany but was home on leave at the time of his death. She stated that her husband and Ferguson had always been on friendly terms, that he had never made any threats against Ferguson's life nor had ever tried to waylay him or sought to kill him.

A. J. (Jack) Mace also testified for the prosecution, his evidence being substantially the same as that of Mrs. Frogg. He said that he was in the house at the time of Frogg's death and swore to seeing both shots fired by Ferguson.

Much later in the summer of 1865, after the trial was over, Champ Ferguson gave the reporter for the *Dispatch* his own version of some of the killings with which he was charged. The killing of William Frogg was included in this statement:

"The testimony in the case of William Frogg," said Champ, "placed me in a false position. The circumstances are well-known to many in that neighborhood. Frogg was with the Home Guards, and instigated my arrest while I was peaceably pursuing my avocation as a farmer. Not satisfied with this, he laid in wait on the highways to kill me. He even went so far as to make his threat to the neighbors that he intended to kill me.

"On the day that I passed down the road leading to Frogg's house, Mrs. Pleasant Beatty called to me and warned me that Frogg was watching for an opportunity to kill me. I had been cautioned by a number of persons. There were two men with me at the time Mrs. Beatty spoke to us, and I told the boys that I would settle the matter by going direct to Frogg's house and killing him. His wife was at the door peeling apples. I dismounted and went in. He was lying in bed, and on seeing me he pulled the cover over his face. I then shot him twice.

"His wife then ran away, and as I passed out of the house I met Miss Russell, who lived there. She asked me what was the matter? I told her that Frogg was killed, and that she had better go in and look after him.

"No words whatever were passed between Frogg and myself. I consider myself justified in killing him."

Thus the story of the death of William Frogg, the first of a long line of murders laid at the door of Champ Ferguson. Why did he kill William Frogg? Had Frogg previously been seeking Ferguson's life and was his connection with the Union forces and the suspicion of his having been to Camp Dick Robinson sufficient justification in Ferguson's eyes for his death? Or was an even stronger motive necessary in order to cause Champ Ferguson to go into a man's house and, finding this man in bed, shoot him twice, with or without words passing between them? Was William Frogg the first of the eleven men whom, as rumored, Champ Ferguson had sworn to kill with his own hands?

On cross-examination, Mrs. Frogg swore that Ferguson saw Jack Mace while he was in the house. It is worth noting that Mace was neither threatened nor harmed.

It is to be wondered at, too, that, according to her own testimony, Esther Ann Frogg ran away from the house where her five months old baby was lying in a crib beside the bed where her husband was being murdered. Strangely enough, in her rather laconic testimony, she showed no particular bitterness against Champ Ferguson. She and Champ, no doubt, had been friends all their lives, having grown up together in the same neighborhood; in fact, it seems they may have remained on friendly terms even after the death of William Frogg. He came to the house alone some time later, supposedly to see about turning a yoke of oxen into the Frogg barnyard. Ordinarily, mountain women held grudges as well as mountain men, and this would not indicate a deadly feud between these two. Why was this so?

Mrs. Pleasant Beatty, Champ said, also warned him against William Frogg. Were the women of Champ Ferguson's neighborhood more sympathetic to the Southern cause than the men; or were they just sympathetic to Champ himself?

One month and one day after the death of William Frogg occurred the shooting of Reuben Wood. He died two days later.

Reuben Wood was the second of those 53 persons to die with whose murders Champ Ferguson was charged. His daughter, Elizabeth Wood, and son, Robert W. Wood, were in Nashville to testify against the alleged murderer of their father.

Elizabeth Wood, taking the stand first, told the following story:

"I am the daughter of the late Reuben Wood, of Clinton County, Kentucky. He died on the 4th of December, 1861. He was shot at home near Albany, Kentucky, on Monday evening, December 2, 1861, about sunset.

"I heard some persons coming up the road, whooping and hollering as if driving stock. I went to the door to see who it was and saw Champ Ferguson, Rains Philpot, and another man whose name, I think, was Kincaid, coming down the road driving some hogs. I also saw father coming down the road in the opposite direction, and they met just about in front of the house. Ferguson, in a very abrupt manner, ordered father to get out of the road. Father did so, just as soon as he could, and was just coming up to open the front door of the house when Ferguson and Philpot rode up to the fence and ordered him to come back, which he did. Ferguson asked him how he came on, and the usual compliments were passed. Ferguson then, calling father a name, said,

" 'I suppose you have been to Camp Dick Robinson.'

"Father answered,

" 'I have.'

"He then asked what father's business had been there, and before answer could be made, Ferguson, using vile and bitter language, told him nobody but a d—d old Lincolnite would be caught at any such place.

"Ferguson continued in this manner for five or ten minutes. The language I cannot express. Ferguson then drew his pistol and said,

" 'Don't you beg, and don't you dodge.'

"By this time mother was standing in the doorway with me, and she begged Ferguson not to shoot father. I also begged for the sake of God not to shoot him. Father said,

" 'Why, Champ, I nursed you when you were a baby. Has there ever been any misunderstanding between us?'

" 'No,' said Ferguson, 'Reuben, you have always treated me like a gentleman, but you have been to Camp Robinson, and I intend to kill you.'

"Ferguson then shot father, but he didn't fall. He shot again and missed. Father drew his coat around himself as he walked around the house and then in the back door. The first shot took effect in the left side, below the nipple, in the pit of the stomach.

"Ferguson jumped off his horse and went around the other end of the house. Mother and I went to hunt for father, and met Ferguson with his pistol in his hand ready to shoot. He said, 'Where is he? Where is he?' We told him we didn't know. We begged him not to shoot any more, but he paid no attention to us, and went on into the room where father was. I heard another shot, and heard chairs falling over and a desperate noise. Mother and I screamed as loud as we could, alarming the neighborhood. We then went to the Widow Noland's about six hundred yards from our house.

"We returned in a short time, finding father sitting by the fire. We begged him to lie down. He said,

" 'No, I cannot lie down, as you were not present, until I relate the circumstances.'

"I am not sure, but I think he said, 'There will be some hereafter about this. They cannot go on this way. I am bound to die and I want you

to know just how it was.' Father then told us what happened after
he went around the house.

"He said that he went in the back door, picked up a hatchet, and
placed himself in a corner by the front door, supposing Ferguson would
come in that way. Instead of doing so, however, Ferguson came in the
back door, but did not immediately see father, not until he got near the
middle of the floor. Father said he saw Ferguson aiming to shoot again
and that he jumped at him and knocked the pistol down with the hatchet,
when the pistol went off, the bullet going into the wall. Then Ferguson
tried to put his pistol against father's breast to shoot him, and father kept
knocking the pistol off with his hatchet.

"They scuffled around over the floor for some time, and Ferguson at
length threw father on the bed. Again the attempt was made to put
the pistol to father's breast, but he again warded it off with the hatchet,
hitting Ferguson on the side of the head and knocking the pistol out of
his hand into the bed, where it got lost in the covering. Ferguson then
let him loose and started out of the house, with father pursuing him with
the hatchet in his hand. At the door, they met Philpot, who poked his
pistol in father's face, cursing him, and told him if he touched Ferguson
again he would blow his brains out. Father then went upstairs and
remained at the top until both of the men left, holding the hatchet in one
hand and a pitchfork in the other. While there, he heard someone come
into the house and go out again, he supposed to get the pistol off the bed.

"I was with father from that time until his death. To every person
who talked with him, he said he was bound to die. He never had any
other idea. He could hardly sit up to get through with his statement, and
went to bed immediately after he had finished. He would speak a few
words and then stop to rest. He died about eleven o'clock in the forenoon
of Wednesday. I don't know his age exactly but he was nearly sixty
years old at the time. He had no arms about him when shot, and there
were none about the house."

Robert W. Wood was sworn and testified that he came home
the night after his father was shot, that the wound looked very
bad, and that his father's first words to him after he came home
were:

"Robert, I can't stand it long. Ferguson has shot me."

Apparently attempting to show that the ill-feeling was not all on one side, the counsel for the defense asked Robert Wood:

"What is the state of your feelings toward the prisoner? Did you and others attack and shoot at him? If so, state the circumstances."

Robert Wood answered:

"I feel just like I would take his life. He took my father's life without cause, and I feel as if I would take his. I felt then as if I was willing to try it, and I did try it. Myself and others did shoot at him. Before he killed my father, I felt as friendly to him as I did to any man in the world. This attack by me on Ferguson was after my father was killed. I can't give the exact date, though it was in December. Five of us, myself, my two brothers, John Crockett, and Charley Wood, who is a second cousin of mine, went to about three quarters of a mile from our house, where Ferguson was raised. We went there between midnight and day and stayed there until between daylight and sunset.

"We secreted ourselves in the woods, about fifteen or twenty steps apart, along the road. We didn't know how many we were going to attack, as McNairy's battalion of 'Bull Pups' were encamped near there. About daylight we heard horses' feet rattling down the road from us, and I looked round and saw Ferguson and Philpot coming at a full trot, with three other men behind them some twenty or thirty yards, but I didn't know any of them. As the two passed Crockett, he shot with a double barrel shotgun and shot Ferguson's horse in the neck. The horse staggered back just as he got opposite where I was, when I shot. Philpot lay down on his horse, and in a moment Ferguson did likewise. They both went off as fast as possible, and when they were out of sight we left."

Thus was another murder laid at Champ Ferguson's door! Fighting between Union and Confederate troops had not really begun in Kentucky and Tennessee, and yet Champ, it was asserted, had already killed two Unionists in cold blood.

Why did he kill Reuben Wood? Camp Robinson again looms

large in the background of this second death. Was the place such anathema in the eyes of Champ Ferguson and his associates that anyone even suspected of connection therewith must be killed? Had Reuben Wood been seeking the life of Ferguson? Or did his death leave nine alive of the group of eleven who were destined for a violent end at Champ Ferguson's hands?

Whatever the reasons for his death, Reuben Wood was hard to kill! He died like one of the tough old mountain hickories that does not fall immediately after the first stroke of lightning; if those who were to follow in his wake were to be as tough, Champ Ferguson was going to need all the stamina with which nature had endowed him.

Champ also expressed himself on the subject of Reuben Wood to the *Dispatch* reporter after the trial was over:

"The testimony in this case," he said, "was with very few exceptions, false. Reuben Wood and I were always good friends before the War, but after that he was connected with the same company in which my brother, Jim, was operating. I knew that he intended killing me if he ever got a chance. They both hunted me down, and drove me fairly to desperation.

"On the day that he was killed, we met him in the road and he commenced on me, using the most abusive language. I knew his disposition toward me, and I believed he intended to shoot me. The touching story about his piteous appeals to me—that he had nursed me when a babe, and tossed me on his knee—are false, and were gotten up expressly to create sympathy, and set me forth as a heartless wretch. If I had not shot Reuben Wood, I would not likely have been here, for he would have shot me. I never expressed a regret for committing the act, and never will. He was in open war against me."

Here is the only direct statement in the records that a desperate feud existed between Champ and his brother, Jim, during the War, besides Champ's remark that his own family were the first to make war on him after he took sides with the South. In addition to his own blood connections, he was now being hunted by the kith and kin of two more families, the Froggs and the Woods. It was about this time that, considering discretion the better part of valor, Champ moved his wife and daughter across the mountains into Tennessee, near Sparta, in White County.

CHAPTER X

Fount Zachery---Among Others

IN March, 1862, George Wood, Henry Sells, William Allen Edwards, and a man named Robbins were killed by a group of Rebels, of which Ferguson was a member. The formal charges of murder had not included the names of these men among its specifications but Tinker Dave Beatty's testimony, early in the trial, had implicated Ferguson in the deaths of two of them. Later on, the prosecution introduced another witness, John Cobb, whose testimony involved him in the deaths of all four.

By the early spring of 1862, the Confederates had suffered serious reverses in their operations in Kentucky and Tennessee. The defeat at Fishing Creek in January had given the Federals access to Cumberland Gap, the gateway into East Tennessee. The capture of Fort Donelson by General Grant in February, probably the most momentous and decisive battle of the entire War, had forced the Confederates to retreat all the way to northern Mississippi and had allowed the Federals to enter Nashville, Tennessee, the storehouse and munitions depot of the Western armies, possession of which was to be retained for the rest of the War. From that time on, the Confederate Army was to be left facing the North with a strong left arm dangling almost helplessly at its side. Most of the large scale battles were yet to be fought and many spectacular raids were yet to be made by Morgan's Men into Kentucky and even across the Ohio River, but the advantages lost by the Confederates in January and February, 1862, were never to be regained.

Some of Morgan's cavalry were even then operating in the Cumberland foothills, as John Cobb testified:

"One morning in March, 1862, four or five of my neighbors and myself were in the woods near my house in Fentress County, rolling out a log, when all of a sudden a gang of about one hundred Rebels came on us. Part of the company seemed to be Morgan's men, but there were also a number of bushwhackers along and among these I recognized Ferguson, Ben Barton, and John Gregory. They had with them as prisoners, George Woods, Henry Sells, William Allen Edwards, and Robbins.

"They arrested me and my neighbors and took us on with them as prisoners for about three miles. They then released two of my neighbors but took the rest of us along with them. They went by my house and got my mare and then went to several other places and got horses belonging to my neighbors, Mr. Wright's, Mr. Brannon's, and Jerry Woods' horses, among others.

"They had captured us about eight or nine o'clock in the morning and after marching along this way until about two o'clock in the afternoon, we came to Col. Bowles' house just over the line in Overton County. There we met Col. Hughes, who took a paper out of his hat and after looking at it, he and Ferguson and one of Morgan's men made a detail and took Woods, Sells, Edwards, and Robbins out somewhere, and before long we heard some pistol shots. Pretty toon they brought Edwards back and he had a bullet hole in his forehead. Then they brought Woods by and he also seemed to be dead, though I didn't see the bullet hole where he was shot. The same detail then went back again, bringing Sells and Robbins, who had also been shot. That left three of us prisoners still alive.

"After they had brought the bodies of these four men back to the house, Col. Hughes called the rest of the prisoners to come out and when we went to the door he asked us if we saw the road the other four had gone. We told him we had. He then asked which we had rather do, volunteer for the Confederacy or go the same way those men went. We told him we had rather volunteer than go that road. That afternoon, Hughes and Ferguson took us back over into Fentress County, where the next morning they released me and one other, leaving them holding only Young Beatty, a half-brother of Tinker Dave."

In the cross-examination, counsel for the defense attempted to show that the entire expedition was part of Morgan's command

and that Ferguson, as well as Hughes and the others, was taking his orders from one of Morgan's officers, a Colonel Tucker. The witness didn't know the name of the officer in command of Morgan's men and was rather indefinite on this point, but left the impression that the killings described were the acts of Ferguson and Hughes and not of Morgan's command. Counsel also attempted to show that the men who were killed had previously been attempting to waylay Ferguson and kill him, but this the witness did not know or would not admit.

During the winter of 1862 an attempt was made to make a compromise between the Yankee and Rebel factions of the Upper Cumberlands. The prosecution at various times during the trial referred to this compromise.

Not all the residents of that section were as hot-blooded or as vengeful, or perhaps as unprincipled, as most of the characters (on both sides) engaged in the incidents delineated during the trial of Champ Ferguson. Some of them were God-fearing, law-abiding people, such as the Taylors of Fentress County, and even more of them perhaps could see the futility and personal danger involved in the continuing raids upon lives and property between the two factions. It was not the regular armies of the Confederates or the Federals that the people in this region had to fear. It was those who, taking advantage of the conditions of warfare prevailing, indulged in their natural propensity for revenge and greed by taking the lives and property of individuals. Arson, theft, and murder were beginning to run rampant along the Kentucky-Tennessee border.

Sometime during the latter part of March, 1862, therefore, a meeting was arranged between a group of citizens from Overton County, Tennessee, representing the Southern element, and a group of citizens from Fentress County, Tennessee, and Clinton County, Kentucky, representing the Northern element. The purpose of the meeting was to reach an agreement that raiders would not come from Overton County over into Fentress and Clinton counties, and vice versa. Rather strangely, those representing the Rebel element seem to have been reputable citizens of the section, at least persons who so far as is known took no part in the guerilla warfare, while those attending the meeting representing the Yankee element were composed altogether of those actively engaged then or later on the Yankee side. As a matter of fact, of the seven men representing the Northern sympathy who attended the meeting, the murder of four of them was to be charged against Champ Ferguson at his trial.

The compromise was doomed to failure. It really never went into effect. An honest effort was no doubt made to effect a compromise, but probably the wrong representatives attended the meeting or the agreements reached were not properly presented to those involved,—or maybe those directly involved did not want a compromise. It was apparently the intention of the prosecution, however, to show that an agreement was reached by the representatives present at the meeting and that it was immediately violated by Champ Ferguson and the bands with which he was associated.

The main witness with reference to the compromise was Winburn W. Goodpasture, brother of Jefferson Dillard Goodpasture, who was placed on the witness stand by the prosecution although he had represented the Southern sympathizers at the meeting:

"At the request of citizens of Overton County, I went to the meeting arranged to make a compromise between that county and the soldiers and citizens of Fentress County and Clinton County. The Rebels in feeling procured me to go. Col. Lunden Armstrong, Wm. Winston, Jesse Roberts, and myself went to the meeting. We met Capt. David Beatty, of Fentress County, and two of his sons, Mr. Zachery, Mr. Wood, and two Kogiers, Elijah Kogier being the leading man from Fentress County.

"The men from Clinton County agreed not to come into Overton County in arms. It was just before the raid was made into Clinton County by Capt. McHenry's company. On returning home, I told

McHenry's men of the compromise, that no more raids should be made into Clinton County, and that the people of Clinton County should not come into Overton County. I told everybody I saw of the compromise, and advised all to comply with the terms, and quiet would be restored to the country."

The witness was then placed on cross-examination by counsel for the defense:

Question—Previous to the compromise you speak of, and afterwards, were not independent bands coming into Overton County taking property and otherwise maltreating the citizens?

Answer—There had been one company that I remember of. I had not been living in Overton County for some time but I had understood that there had been a company coming into Overton County and taking horses from Alvin Cullom and others.

Question—You say you represented the Southern cause. Now, were those that you compromised with independent bands, and not regularly attached to the service on either side?

Answer—I say I was requested to go by Southern and Union men both, but I suppose I represented the Southern element. I didn't understand that it was a party question. The men with whom I compromised were principally citizens of Clinton County, Kentucky, and Fentress County, Tennessee. There were some that I recognized as Federal soldiers from their dress. Captain Beatty, I suppose, has never been attached to the army; however, I don't know how that is.

Question—Did Kogier, Dalton, and others belong to Tinker Dave's company, as you understood?

Answer—No, sir, I didn't understand that they did. Citizens of Clinton County, Kentucky, I understood them to be.

Question—Did you communicate to Captain McHenry and the leaders of the company who made the raid right after that, anything in regard to this compromise?

Answer—I did not to Captain McHenry. I did to members of his company, but couldn't say they were leaders. I don't recollect of seeing any officers of his company.

Question—As a matter of fact, did not that company go after horses and other property that had been taken from the citizens of Overton County, and bring some back?

Answer—I don't know anything about that—only what I have since heard about it. I lived at Cookeville at the time.

At this point, counsel for the defense discontinued questioning Mr. Goodpasture concerning the compromise, having attempted to show that if a compromise was made, the terms thereof were not communicated to the leaders of the independent bands on the Southern side and that the raids of these bands into the other counties were simply made in order to regain property previously stolen from them.

James M. Beatty, son of Tinker Dave, also testified that he was at the Monroe meeting with his father when the compromise was discussed and that it was his understanding when they left it was agreed by both parties that they would go home, put down their arms, and go to work; and that he and his father acted accordingly.

On the other hand, A. J. Capps, a member of Capt. J. W. McHenry's company but a witness for the prosecution, when asked by the counsel for the defense if they had been informed by Mr. Goodpasture that a compromise had been arranged, said:

"We understood there was a compromise but we got it into our heads to believe that they had not stood by it."

Regardless of whether or not a compromise was arranged and regardless of whether or not the leaders of the Southern faction had been advised thereof, those participating in it had hardly got back to their homes before an expedition was made from Overton County into Fentress and Clinton counties.

It seems that some time during March, the bands of Captains McHenry and Bledsoe had gone on an expedition to Decatur, Alabama, for what reason we do not know, although it was referred to by two or three of the witnesses. Champ Ferguson did not go on this expedition, as he was off on a scout with Morgan's men at the time. This exodus of the organized Southern guerillas left the Rebel element of the section unprotected for the time being and it was testified that the Union guerillas from Fentress County and from over the border in Clinton County came into the Overton County section and made away with a considerable amount of personal property, mainly horses. Horse thieves have never been thought highly of anywhere, either in war or peace. It was rather natural therefore that upon returning from the Decatur expedition the Southern bands should organize another expedition to go into Clinton County in an effort to regain their property, any compromise to the contrary notwithstanding.

According to testimony by A. J. Capps, the prime movers of this expedition were private citizens such as Barry Brannon, Alvin Cullom, Sr., Henry Cox, and A. J. Goodbar, who, as a rule, were not connected with the fighting forces or guerilla bands. The expedition was under the general direction of J. W. McHenry, some of whose men were Capps' brother, Alvin Capps, Ballou Gess, Sam Weaver, Alvin Cullom, Jr., Lafayette Goodbar, James McMullan, John Stone, and John J. Dowdy. McHenry was born and reared in Overton County and had practiced law in the Mountain District. At the end of the War he moved to Nashville where he died shortly after. Captain Hamilton was also along, with his nephews, the Mayfield boys, and one Masters. They all gathered at Dillard Goodpasture's place, about two and one-half miles from Livingston, in Overton County, Tennessee. The first place they stopped was at Eagle Creek, where they waited for Champ Ferguson to join them, which he shortly did, along with Isaac Smith.

Capps stated that David Beatty and a man named Dalton or Woods were the leaders of the bands who had been coming into Overton County and taking the property which this expedition proposed to get back.

Just beyond Rome's Mill, they stopped at the house of an old man by the name of Henry Johnson. Capps testified that Champ Ferguson drew his pistol on the old man and told him that if he didn't bring back some steers and a wagon that had been stolen from him he would kill him. The old man denied having anything to do with taking Champ's steers but promised to do what he could to get them back for him.

It was not far from here, related Capps, that Joseph Stover, William Johnson, Louis Pierce, and Robert Martin were killed, and probably within an hour after they left Henry Johnson's place. Capps did not give much information, however, about the deaths of these men and he was unable to say that Champ Ferguson was responsible for them. Champ Ferguson was charged in the specifications of murder with the deaths of Stover, Johnson, and Pierce but not with that of Martin. Apparently all four men were Federal soldiers, probably home on leave, inasmuch as the witness stated they were dressed in blue uniforms.

Capps stated that he, Captain McHenry, Ballou Gess, and one or two others went to the right after leaving old man Johnson's place and that Champ Ferguson, Captain Hamilton, and the others went on straight ahead. They soon heard firing and then saw a man running with some of the band after him, calling on him to stop. One of the men, he thought it was Ike Smith, shot the man just as he reached a bluff and the man fell over the bluff, which was forty or fifty feet high. A short distance on they found the bodies of three other men, who, he found out, were Stover, Pierce and Martin. He testified they had all been shot and that each of them was stabbed through the heart. He said he did not see the body of Johnson, the man who fell over the bluff.

By the time this testimony was given during the trial, it had become pretty well established that Champ Ferguson was extremely handy with a knife. While the witness was unable to say that Ferguson had killed the men referred to, the prosecution was later on to claim that the knife thrusts through the heart distinguished them as having been murdered at his hands. Champ Ferguson's knife is nearly always alluded to in the reminiscences of the people living near the scenes of his activities.

"They tell me," one old gentleman said, "that Champ would cut men's heads off and roll them down the hill like punkins."

This was no doubt a considerably exaggerated statement, but Champ undoubtedly did find the knife, as had his forefathers who fought the Indians before him, a very effective weapon. Tradition also relates that for some time he would notch the knife handle for each victim, but that finally, when space became exhausted, he was forced to discontinue this practice. Even during the War and at the time of the trial stories were related as to how various ranking Confederate officers, even General Bragg, had personally presented Champ with knives. When asked about this, Champ said that the only person who ever gave him a knife was Captain McHenry.

Champ Ferguson had little to say later on with reference to the deaths of Stover, Johnson, and Pierce, maintaining that they had been killed in the course of ordinary warfare:

"I killed Joseph Stover after he had shot at me twice. He was taking a third aim and I shot him in the mouth, while Fount Frost shot him in the side at the same time. William Johnson was run over a cliff and one of the boys shot him. I shot and killed Pierce as he was running through the woods with a double-barrel shotgun. They were all Home Guards and were out looking for recruits."

Champ gave no reason as to why they were all stabbed through the heart. Were they so stabbed? Was this a finishing touch that Champ gave his victims to make death entirely certain?

On this same expedition and shortly after the happenings just related, occurred the death of young Fount Zachery, a boy of sixteen. It was charged that after Fount had surrendered his gun, Champ Ferguson shot him and then stabbed him as he lay upon the ground. Several days after A. J. Capps had finished his testimony, John A. Capps was called to the stand to testify as a witness for

the prosecution concerning this incident. He must have been the
brother to whom A. J. Capps referred as Alvin Capps.

John A. Capps stated that he was a member of the group of
Rebels who had gone on the expedition from near Livingston,
Tennessee, to Albany, Ky., about April 1, 1862; that Judge Cullom
had come by his house and told him that he must go or he would
be considered a coward; and that while he was not well at the
time he went along.

Judge Alvin Cullom (from the clan MacCullom), it will be
remembered, is the man who had loaned his law books to J. D.
Goodpasture. Born in 1793, Judge Cullom was practicing law at
Livingston, in Overton County, when the War broke out. He was
a well-known lawyer of the Mountain District, having been a
member of Congress from 1843 to 1847, and later a Circuit Judge.

"Along about seven o'clock in the evening on Spring Creek and about 3
miles from Albany," said Capps, "a boy came out of an ivy thicket towards
our company with a gun on his shoulder, and said, 'Boys, you need not
go this way; you won't find them here.' From the way he talked, I suppose he took us for a Federal company.

"George Murphy demanded him to surrender his gun and the lad
handed it to him, and was apparently taking his shot pouch off his
shoulder when someone, Ferguson, I think, asked him his name and he
replied, 'Fount Zachery.' As soon as he had said this, Ferguson shot him.
He fell from his horse, and Ferguson then got off his horse and stabbed
him. I was within ten or fifteen feet of them at the time, and when
Ferguson stabbed him I heard a sort of rough, grating sound that I hardly
know how to describe. We left the body lying there.

"At that time I had known Ferguson about fifteen months or longer,
having become acquainted with him while he was in prison at Livingston
before the War [probably after the killing of Ben Read at the Camp
Meeting fight]. He was in my charge at that time, and I had no trouble
with him."

On cross-examination, the witness admitted that they had orders from Capt. McHenry to shoot on sight anyone who looked suspicious.

On re-examination, the Judge Advocate fairly well scotched any effect this statement may have had by asking:

"You say you had orders to shoot down suspicious persons approaching the column that night. Were you ordered to shoot them after they had surrendered and delivered their arms?"

"No, sir," answered the witness.

Mrs. Esther A. Jackson, the daughter of Squire James Zachery, in her testimony had the following to say with reference to the death of Fount Zachery:

"Fount Zachery was about sixteen years old at the time of his death on April 1, 1862. I last saw him alive about a half hour before sunset that evening. My little brother, Polly Kearny, and I found his body near Mrs. Owens' place, who is Ferguson's mother-in-law, about ten o'clock the next morning. He had been shot through the heart, the ball coming out the back, and a knife had been run through his body."

Champ Ferguson's own version of the death of Fount Zachery as recorded by the *Dispatch* reporter was short and to the point:

"I confess that I shot the lad, Fount Zachery, and stabbed him after he fell to the ground. We were out on a scout and expected a fight that night. Jim McHenry was in command, and had given us orders to shoot down any person who might be seen with guns. As we neared a creek, the lad emerged from a thicket with a gun on his shoulder. I shot him on sight, in obedience to orders."

Fount Zachery was the first of four members of the Zachery family with whose murder Champ Ferguson was charged. The method of their death suggests that they also, at least some of them, might possibly have been members of the group of eleven who had been marked for death by Champ Ferguson.

While on the witness stand, A. J. Capps had been questioned by counsel for the defense regarding his knowledge of Champ Ferguson's company:

Question—You will state if you were present at any time when the defendant was raising his company. If so, by what authority did he raise that company? You will state if the company was organized, who were elected as officers, and in what capacity did the defendant act at the time of raising his company. Did you ever see his commission or authority for raising his company? If so, state it, as well as the time and place.

Answer—I was present on one occasion when the defendant was raising his company. I was then out of the service. I can't give the date exactly, but it was some months after the expedition into Kentucky in April, 1862. It was in Livingston and I saw him endeavoring to get men to subscribe a paper for raising his company. I asked him to show me his authority. He showed me a writing, as I understood it, from the Secretary of War of the Confederacy, authorizing him to raise a company; I don't recollect what kind of a company but understood it to be cavalry. I don't know that I was present when the officers of the company were elected but I heard of it. I was in and out of the house where they had congregated. Ferguson was elected Captain; Henry Sublett, First Lieutenant; Andy Foster, one of the Second Lieutenants; I don't recollect who was the other one. I don't know how many men composed the company. Fifty or sixty men were present, but I don't think when they organized they had a full company. I saw Ferguson after that and my information was that he was acting as Captain.

Captain Scott Bledsoe raised his company before the expedition into Kentucky, and at the time of the expedition, I don't think Ferguson belonged to any company at all. He may have belonged to Bledsoe's company for a while after this expedition. Bledsoe's company was with us at Decatur and Ferguson was not with us then.

The prosecution again examined the witness and questioned him in some detail with reference to the paper purporting to authorize Ferguson to raise a company. He replied that he couldn't say whether it was written or printed or partly both, nor could he say if the signature of the Confederate Secretary of War was attached to the paper. He said he had read it hastily and could tell nothing more, except that it was his impression that the paper was so signed. He didn't think it directed Ferguson to report to anyone for the muster of his men; that the paper was directed to Ferguson on the outside of a large envelope; that he couldn't say if it was so directed on the inside but on reflection it was his best impression that it was.

Question—If you can't tell the date of the paper or who signed it or whether it was signed by the Secretary of War, how can you say that the paper purported to be from the Secretary of War?

Answer—I stated it as my recollection that it was signed by the Secretary of War.

Question—But you say you don't remember whether the words "Secretary of War" followed or preceded the signature, nor the name, nor whether it was signed by the Secretary of War or by some one else by his order. How then did the Secretary of War sign it?

Answer—Well, I don't know.

From A. J. Capps' testimony, it might be assumed that Champ Ferguson's company was raised just about as regularly as a great many other companies of the Confederate Army in the early days of the War. It was not unusual for a group of men to organize and elect their own officers and for this arrangement to be accepted by the Confederate authorities as bona fide. Whether or not Champ Ferguson met later regulations, such as reporting his muster roll and making official reports to his superior officers, was a question that was to be taken up during the examination of General Joe Wheeler later on in the trial. The point at issue at this particular time seemed to be whether or not Capps' testimony should be accepted as satisfactory evidence that Champ had authority from the Confederate War Department to organize a company of cavalry. In view of the contention of the prosecution that the deeds com-

mitted by Ferguson during the War were without the law, regardless of whether he was a regularly enlisted soldier, they went
to considerable pains to cast reflections upon the testimony of their
own witness as to the authenticity of the purported authorization.
Since the written document could not be produced, however, the
advantage of the testimony concerning this particular feature to
either side must be considered as only problematical.

CHAPTER XI

Thirteen Are Dead

BY the Spring of 1862, only two real battles had been fought in Kentucky and Tennessee—at Mill Springs and at Fort Donelson. The War had hardly begun. Yet young Fount Zachery, shot April 1, 1862, was the tenth victim, so testimony at the trial would assert, of Champ Ferguson's gun and knife.

The war in the Cumberlands, especially during its early stages before the sides were well aligned, was fierce and deadly, and old women's tales and malicious gossip and slander caused the innocent to suffer along with the guilty. Common thieves and robbers banded together under the guise of Home Guards to plunder from friend and foe alike. No one could be trusted. Beaten paths were avoided. Men were forced to hide out from their homes by night as well as by day.

Not much wonder, perhaps, that Champ Ferguson considered it a good policy of warfare and even of self-preservation to shoot first and ask questions later, to kill those suspected of being his enemies before they killed him. By June 1st, three more deaths were laid at his door. Before the year 1862 was to end, according to sworn testimony, he was to have killed ten more persons and then three more on New Year's Day, 1863, a total of twenty-three murders in cold blood, according to the prosecution, by January 1, 1863.

The next murder of which Champ Ferguson was accused was that of Alex Huff, committed on May 18, 1862. Six separate witnesses for the prosecution, including his son and daughter, were to testify as to Huff's death.

Preston Huff, the son of Alex Huff, was the first witness examined by the prosecution. While he knew at first hand none of the details of the death of his father, having apparently been away from home at the time, his testimony recounts another event that seems a sort of prelude to the killing of his father:

"I have known Champ Ferguson," testified Preston Huff, "about ten years and lived about fourteen miles from his place when the War broke out. He was some kin to me, as our grandfathers were brothers.

"I met him one day in the road sometime between Christmas and New Year's in December, 1861, in Clinton County, Kentucky, near Given's house. He was down off his horse, with the saddle off. I rode up and spoke to him, and he said, 'Get down off that horse, G—d D—n you.' He then ordered me to ungirth my saddle, and then ordered me to girth it back. He then asked me if there were any clothes in the saddlebags. I told him there was not. He then said, 'D—n you, don't you want a dram?' I told him I would take a dram, and he said, 'Touch it d—n light.'

"About that time two Confederate soldiers came up in an ambulance. He ordered them to stop, and they took a drink. They asked him what he was doing with me. He told them he was going to take my horse,— that my father was a G—d d—d old Lincolnite.

"Champ then turned to me and said, 'If you have anything to say, say it quick, for I'm going to kill you.' He asked me if I didn't want to go to a little place above there they called New Heaven; he said, 'We've got a new government and a New Heaven for all such men as you are.' I begged him not to shoot me. He then asked me if I would go home and stay close to the plantation and not travel about if he let me go. I said that was a hard thing to do, as I had to go out sometimes.

"Champ then said, 'I'll learn my relations something, and you with the balance.' He said that he was going to kill Uncle Louis Huff and others of my relations; that he might as well kill them now as anytime. He asked me again if I could go home and not be caught away, and I told him I would try.

"Champ then told me to turn the bridle over his horse's head for him, which I did. He made me place his feet in the stirrups, and after I had done this, ordered me to start for home, and I turned and went in that direction. He then rode off the opposite way, taking my horse, saddle, and bridle and saddlebags. He had apparently been drinking heavily and was pretty drunk at the time. We had not been intimate before this happened, but had always been friendly. After that, I didn't like him much.

"Up until that time I did not belong to any military organization but in July, 1862, I was appointed a lieutenant in the Federal service in Company E of the Seventh Tennessee, commanded by Colonel Clift. I was mustered out of service in July, 1863, after which time I scouted around with Tinker Dave's command until the end of the War."

The crude acts of a drunken man. So we might dismiss this episode—with a smile at the unconscious irony of understatement of the boy's "After that, I didn't like him much"—were it not for the sequel. The threat made by Champ drunk was to be ruthlessly executed by Champ sober.

William B. Williams was the first witness to testify concerning the killing of Alex Huff:

"I have known the prisoner for about three years. I also knew Alex Huff, who is now dead. My best recollection is that he met his death about the 2nd of May, 1862, in Fentress County, Tennessee, at the old Conrad Piles place, where Jefferson Piles lived at the time.

"I had started to mill that morning but met some pickets, Flem Mc-Ginnis and one of the McDaniel boys, Jonathan, I think it was, and they arrested me and carried me to the Conrad Piles place. After we had been there a short while, a parcel of men brought in Alex Huff, Ferguson being in the group. They sent out some pickets and before long we heard some shooting in the direction the pickets had gone, and at this the soldiers seemed to get scared and, hurrying out of the house, mounted their horses and made up the road in the direction they first came. Ferguson, however, lagged behind and when it was found out that the alarm was caused by a false report that Bill Hildreth had been killed, Ferguson called a halt.

"I was standing on the porch by Huff at the time, and the first thing I knew I heard Ferguson tell me to get out of the way. I was standing between Huff and the edge of the porch and when we looked around, we saw that Ferguson had a pistol in his hand. He said to me again, 'Get out of the way.' Huff sort of raised his hands and said, 'For God's sake, don't shoot me,' and then dashed into the door and through the house. Ferguson took out around the lower end of the house, shouting as he went, 'Shoot him, d—n him, shoot him!' I ran into the house and into a room upstairs, where I stayed for some time, seeing nothing more of the proceedings.

"Presently, I heard the report of a gun and I heard Huff scream out, 'Oh, Lord,' and the guns continued to fire. Huff continued to holler and pray and so on. The firing of the guns lasted for several minutes— I suppose there were twelve or fifteen shots—but the hollering of Huff continued a good while longer. I heard some women begging the men not to shoot him, and thought I recognized the voice of Polly Piles, my sister-in-law, as one of them. Then I heard the sound of another gun, and the noise of Huff was silenced.

"After everything became quiet, I came out and saw Huff lying beyond the end of the house under an old apple tree on a quilt, still struggling and not quite dead. I went to another house nearby and stayed for about a half hour, when a little boy came in and said Huff was dead. I went back and helped pull his coat off and we laid him out. I didn't examine the wounds much but he was horribly bloody.

"Huff had never belonged to the army, but he was a Union man."

In the cross-examination, Williams testified that he also was a Union man and that Ferguson never bothered him at all; that when he would meet him in the road, he would say, "How do you do, Mr. Williams?" or something like that; that while he was being held prisoner along with Huff neither Ferguson nor anyone of his party ever spoke an ill word to him; that he had never heard that Ferguson ever disturbed anybody merely on account of his political principles.

Counsel for the defense then asked the witness:

"Was it not only those men who sought to waylay and kill Ferguson and who sought to involve him in difficulties that he molested or interfered with?"

The Judge Advocate objected to this question:

"This is substantive matter of defense; it is setting up self-defense and making the witness a witness for the prisoner, hence he cannot put leading questions even if he is allowed to make the witness his own."

The counsel for the defense then changed the question:

"You say you never knew of his molesting any man for Union sentiments. You will now state what was the grounds upon which he did molest them. Do you know his general reputation in this respect? If so, what is his general character regarding the matter?"

The Judge Advocate objected again, saying that this was not the way to prove the prisoner's general reputation or character. Tempers were getting short and hot words flew thick and fast between the prosecution and counsel for the defense, until recess was called. Upon reassembling, the following decision was pronounced upon the point at issue:

The accused has the right to show his general character, that is, he may show that he has the general character of a peaceable, quiet man. On a charge of larceny, the accused may show his general character. But this proposition seeks to show by general reputation that through combinations against the prisoner that persons waylaid him and that he attacked and killed only such persons. This would not only prove his reputation but would also prove by hearsay the fact of such circumstances. This, we think, cannot be done.

The counsel for the defense thereupon filed a paper through which they called upon the Commission to compel the Judge Advocate to make election upon which one of the substantive felonies he would try the prisoner, that the proof might be confined to the felony specified. Otherwise it would be impossible, they pointed out, for the accused properly to defend himself against so many distinct felonies.

After deliberating on the questions presented, the Court rendered the following decision:

A single act may not constitute a guerilla. The Judge Advocate cannot be compelled to elect any one of the specifications on which to rest the case for the Government nor can he be allowed to rest the case on proving any one of the acts charged. He must establish as many of the acts alleged as he is able to do by evidence. The defendant has already pleaded generally and it is now too late to plead specially.

The Judge Advocate then put the following question to the witness:

"You stated that you do not know of the prisoner ever disturbing or interfering with anybody on account of his political opinions. Do you know of his ever disturbing anybody besides Alex Huff? State what you know, not what you have heard."

"Well, I don't know that I do," answered the witness.

Thereupon the examination of the witness was closed and the court adjourned.

Alvin C. Piles was the next witness to testify concerning the death of Alexander Huff:

"I belong to the 148th Indiana Volunteer Infantry. Before I joined the army, I lived in Fentress County. I was about six hundred yards from the Conrad Piles place when I heard guns firing that brought about the death of Alex Huff.

"I saw Ferguson twice that day. First, at the house where Huff was shot. I was at the time about 150 yards away on the top of a bluff and could see Ferguson and his men distinctly walking around in the yard and could hear them talking, but couldn't understand what they said. After the firing was over, I saw him again as they were going along the road toward Travisville, Kentucky.

"I also saw Ferguson on the day that Delk, Crabtree, and Williams were killed at my father's house. It was about twelve o'clock. He had a two-edged knife and said he wanted one made the shape of that, only bigger. Some citizens asked him what he was going to do with so many arms and he said he would like to see them catch him without a loaded gun in these times.

"I also saw Ferguson one time in the Fall of 1862 driving out some cattle on the South Fork in Wayne County, Kentucky. Four of the McGinnis boys, John Smith, Abe and Will Hildreth, Fayette Allen, Fount Frost, two of the Poor boys, and others whose names I do not know were along. They were mounted and armed and driving about forty head of cattle and mules and leading some horses. One of the McGinnis boys was riding a very fine horse that belonged to Emanuel Sandusky. I saw two mules and a horse belonging to Dave Beatty. They were going toward Travisville. I also recollect that Henry Sublett, Thomas Ruby, John Gregory, Ephraim Crabtree, Joe Miller, Jonathan Campbell, Titus Page, and Alexander Evans were along."

Marion Johnson, next witness for the prosecution, then testified:

"I have known Champ Ferguson about eight years. I saw him several times during December, 1861, in Clinton County, Kentucky. Some time between Christmas and New Year's of that month I was up in Fentress County, Tennessee, and was halted in the road at night by Ferguson and Philpot and some others who seemed to be regular soldiers belonging to Zollicoffer's army. Ferguson ordered us to get off our horses, which we did, Preston Huff, George Sandusky, and myself. Some others of the men who were with me had made their escape.

"Ferguson asked us who those men were that went off. Told him William Huff, William Delk, and Mr. Gibson's son, I believe it was. We were at Mr. Gibson's house. Ferguson told us that he was going to catch them and ordered us to stay there all night until he came back. Next morning he did not come back and we were taken by some of Bledsoe's men to Zollicoffer's camp, where we were turned loose. On our way from where we left camp, we met Ferguson by himself. A good many rebel soldiers were passing around in sight. Ferguson told Huff to get down, that he wanted his horse, and drew his pistol. Huff got down and told him he could have the horse. Ferguson told Huff he had a notion to kill him or somehow that way.

"I saw Ferguson frequently during that Winter, sometimes by himself and sometimes with others. Sometimes Philpot was with him and Ben Barton. They were always armed and generally had pistols and sometimes guns. In May, 1862, I was collecting some money for Broke Ryan and had been down in the lower part of Fentress County. On my way back, I stopped at the house of a man named Moody, whose note I had, and as I was getting off my horse, two men rode up rapidly and arrested me. One was Titus Page, who belonged to Bledsoe's company, and the other belonged to McHenry's company. We went out to the road where the main command was passing along, and there I saw Ferguson and a good many others whom I knew.

"We went on to Doctor Page's, the father of Titus Page, where they stopped and had dinner and fed their horses. After that we went by the place of a man named Stokely Evans, and when I got up they were leading two horses out of the gate. Cooney Smith was leading one and a man I didn't know the other.

"During this ride, Ferguson, as well as Titus Page and several others, told me they had killed Alex Huff that morning at the old Piles place.

"The crowd had Eli Hatfield's horse that morning. They said they came to the Travis place that morning and took a young man named James Harmon prisoner, and made him tell where his horse and Hatfield's horses were tied out. Also, there was a man in the crowd named Elliott who had on a coat that I knew belonged to Eli Hatfield.

"Shortly before this happened, a compromise had been made between Bledsoe's men, McHenry's men, and the other outside fellows that were with them, on the one side, and Beatty, Kogier, and Beckett's men; and I complained they had taken me prisoner after that compromise. Some of them told me they had seen a notice of the compromise at the place where Alex Huff and Ferguson and the others were all talking together and that Ferguson had seen the advertisement or that he knew it to be there. I was at Monroe when the compromise was made. My understanding of it was that the Home Guards were not to pester the soldiers, and we were to be protected, all faring alike.

"At Ragan's, Captain McHenry and Captain Bledsoe came up and we stayed there all night. We went on to Monroe, where Ferguson and some others went off in another direction. We saw nothing more of Ferguson until we got near Yankeetown, in White County, Tennessee, within five miles of Sparta. We and other prisoners were turned loose there."

On cross-examination, the witness stated that Captain Scott Bledsoe and Captain J. W. McHenry had companies attached to the Southern army in that section of the country during 1861 and 1862; and that Lieutenant McGinnis, of Bledsoe's company, was in charge of the group that had killed Alex Huff and later in the day had taken him prisoner. He stated that so far as he knew, Champ Ferguson belonged to Bledsoe's company, having joined it right after leaving Kentucky, although he often went off on expeditions by himself. He said he knew nothing of the killing of Alex Huff except what they told him; that Titus Page told him that Cooney Smith had shot Huff in the head after he had been shot and could rise no more, and that he didn't know who shot him before that. The witness admitted that he and Preston Huff belonged to the independent company of Eli Hatfield, which operated on the Unionist side.

The prosecution next presented Mrs. Lucinda Hatfield as a witness, with the statement that she was a daughter of Alexander Huff and the widow of Eli Hatfield. Our records do not show how Eli Hatfield met his death, and if he was killed, his was one death at least that was not attributed to Champ Ferguson. Mrs. Hatfield testified concerning the death of her father as follows:

"Champ Ferguson, Galen Elliott, Dock Elliott, Henry Sublett, Cooney Smith, Hamp McGinnis, Janett McGinnis, and Will Hildreth came to our house on the morning of May 2, 1862. My father was sitting in the yard but came into the house when he saw them coming. Some of the men came on in the house. One of them, Janett McGinnis, ordered my father out of the house and then told Cooney Smith to go out and shoot him. Mother and I went out and caught hold of Smith and asked him not to kill father, and Champ Ferguson said he should not be hurt, for us to get back in the house and get to work. They then took father away.

"The next time I saw him was that afternoon at the old Conrad Piles place. Two girls came over home that afternoon and told us he had been killed, and I went over and found my father dead. I saw two wounds on his left arm and one through his ankle, and a bullet had entered the center of his forehead. It had gone through his skull and lodged where I could see the bullet. They said there were more in his back but I could not see them."

Mrs. Nancy Brooks, an eye witness, was the last to testify concerning the death of Alexander Huff:

"I was at my father's house, which is in sight of the old Conrad Piles place, when Alex Huff was killed. I heard the shooting and saw Mr. Huff running down toward the branch, where he fell. I went down there and found him sitting up with his back against a tree, begging for water. His arm was broken and his ankle was broken. I don't know how he was wounded in the body but I do know that afterwards we counted fifteen bullet holes in his coat.

"Ferguson ordered John Smith, (Cooney John), to shoot Huff again. My brother jerked Smith away two or three times, but Ferguson told my brother if he didn't get away, he would shoot him down. Smith then fired the last shot, which hit Mr. Huff in the back of his head. I guess I was standing within three feet of him at the time."

Champ Ferguson, in his private statement later, put a different version on Alex Huff's death:

"I am innocent of the killing of Alex Huff. He was a cousin of my mother and I always liked him. I protested against his being killed, guarding him myself when he was being held prisoner, until he broke and ran when the pickets started firing, when one of Bledsoe's men shot and killed him."

This statement is contradictory, and in the face of the testimony of the six witnesses presented, sounds rather weak. The killing of Alexander Huff must have been a very brutal thing, and one might well venture the guess that he was another one of the group of eleven who so rashly violated Champ Ferguson's home while he was away.

Elijah Kogier was killed about June 1, 1862. Preston Huff, whose father Champ had killed a month earlier, was a witness of the shooting:

"Another time I saw Ferguson and his men was in Clinton County, Kentucky, about the 1st of June, 1862. We had been on the dodge from him and his men and were lying out. Louis Duvall, Jonathan Williams, and Theophilus Williams were with me. Report had come to us the day before that Ferguson and his men were in the County, and several of us were mounted and out scouting around. We heard several guns fire and went out to the road to see what they were shooting at. We heard the women at Elijah Kogier's house screaming and saw some man who was climbing over a fence fall backwards.

"When the men had left Kogier's place, we went up to the house. The man shot turned out to be Elijah Kogier. His little girl was clinging to him and she was very bloody, presenting a horrible sight. We carried the body to the house, but stayed there only a short time as we were afraid to linger about. Kogier was dead at the time. There were about ten in the gang that shot him and probably as many as thirty shots were fired, but I didn't recognize any of the men who killed him.

"Kogier headed a body of men who were scouting the country, but I don't know that he ever waylaid or threatened the life of Ferguson and don't know that they were after Ferguson more than any others. I have seen Williams with Kogier's band, and I also saw Tinker Dave with him once when they were going to Overton County to fix up a peace with citizens of Overton County.

"I heard that Louis and Anthony Huff had taken Ferguson prisoner a few days before Kogier's death and had attempted to kill him, but I don't know it of my own knowledge."

After Preston Huff had finished, Mrs. Nancy Kogier, wife of Elijah Kogier, took the stand to tell about the death of her husband:

"I have known Ferguson all my life. I am the widow of Elijah

Kogier, who was killed the first of June, 1862, on Sunday morning. My husband had got out of bed and was going to the spring, when he was fired on by a band of men who rode up near the house. I didn't recognize any of the men excepting Ferguson and Sublett. I told my husband that the Rebels had come and he must get out of the way. He started but didn't get far, when Ferguson overtook him and shot him. He threw up his arms, and I couldn't hear anything that may have been said for the screams of my children. My husband turned to the right, and they followed, shooting at him until they came to a cross-fence some fifty yards from the house. I saw him fall, and saw Ferguson draw him a few steps from the fence.

"I got to my husband as quick as I could and my little daughter, eleven years old, had her father in her arms. The little girl had run out in the crowd and was among them when he fell. After I got to him, he gasped once but never spoke.

"Ferguson and the gang left the body and went to the house. I stopped by my dead husband about fifteen minutes and then returned to the house. Ferguson was still there with his band, and was sitting down, laughing, while the balance were searching the house.

"I said to Ferguson that it looked like he was going to kill all my friends. He said there were a few more he intended to kill, but did not name them. I returned to the spot where my husband was lying, and after stopping about an hour, the band took one of our horses and went off. They had torn up all our notes that were of any value, and took a shotgun and a pistol.

"Ferguson was at my house in July following, with Morgan's men. He did not take any property, but ordered victuals, and I sent them out to the gate. He didn't stop long, but some two hundred men stayed all night, and ate and destroyed all I had."

Mrs. Kogier's sister, Miss Jane Ellen Walker, then testified:

"I was at the house of Elijah Kogier when he was killed. I cannot tell all of the gang who came there, but Champ Ferguson was one of them. They surrounded the house and commenced firing. Mr. Kogier ran out and tried to escape but they shot and killed him. Ferguson shot twice, and then dragged him along by the arm. When we got up to him, his little daughter had his head in her arms. Her dress was all bloody. I was at the spring when the shooting took place, and the balls flew all around me. I only wonder I was not killed."

Champ Ferguson considered the killing of Elijah Kogier a "good riddance of bad rubbish":

"I killed Elijah Kogier, and done a good trick when I did it. He watched my house day and night, and sometimes until he nearly froze, to get to kill me. He was a treacherous dog and richly merited his fate."

Squire James Zachery, grandfather of young Fount Zachery, was killed on the same day as was Elijah Kogier, June 1, 1862. At the time his daughter, Mrs. Esther A. Jackson, testified concerning the death of Fount Zachery, she had the following to say about the killing of her father:

"I am a daughter of James Zachery, of Fentress County, Tennessee. I was at home at the time my father was killed on June 1, 1862, as it was before I was married.

"About ten o'clock in the morning, a group of about nineteen men came up and surrounded the place. Champ Ferguson and a number of others whom I recognized were in the gang. My father was between the house and the stables, about fifty yards from the house. The first man who shot was Fayette Allen, after which he called out, 'Halt.' Then John Smith shot, and all the others, I think, who were armed. I saw Ferguson run through the orchard, shooting at father and hollering, 'Shoot him, d—n him, shoot him.' They ran on out of the orchard into some woods, and then I heard some person holler out not to shoot a dead man.

"Soon after, they returned to the house and Ferguson came to the door. Our dog was standing on the porch and Ferguson raised his gun to shoot him. I told him not to shoot the dog, that he wouldn't bite, and that I would take him away. Then I took the dog into the house. Ferguson came on into the house and asked for father's navy revolver, saying also, 'We have killed your father.' I asked him if father did not have his revolver with him when he killed him. Ferguson said he had not. I told him that he had it with him when he left the house, and that I didn't know where it was. He searched the house, and not finding it, he went back to the woods and found it.

"Ferguson then came back and set on the porch and loaded his own revolver out of the powder horn that father had with him when he left the house.

"I asked him about Stokeley Evans, whom he had prisoner. He said he was going to send him home, that he was not going to hurt him.

"After they went away, my mother, myself, and a boy named Brock carried my father's body to the house. When I went to my father, he was dead. He was shot in three places, through the head, over the eye, and in the shoulder; the flesh of his hand was on a bush nearby, which I suppose he was holding when he was shot. Miss Carolyn Dixon and Mrs. Dowdy were there also. My father was about fifty years old at the time of his death. He had been a magistrate in Fentress County and was a Union man, although he didn't belong to the army.

"My father hadn't been at home all the time. He had to hide out a good deal on account of Ferguson, who came to our house before the Mill Springs fight and swore he was going to kill him. Ferguson had his pistol in his hand at the time. Two men were with him, and I think one of them was Philpot. We told him my father was at Columbia, Kentucky, the last we heard of him. Then he swore he would go and kill my little brother, William, who was chopping wood. William told him he allowed to join his company. Ferguson said, 'When in h—l do you intend to do it?', and the boy said, 'When I get big enough,' and if he wouldn't shoot him he would do anything he told him to. Ferguson told him to lay down his axe and 'make out,' at the same time pointing his pistol at him.

"My father had been home only about two weeks when he was killed."

Mrs. Sarah Dowdy also testified concerning the death of James Zachery. She said that she lived on Wolf River in Fentress County, at the mouth of Lick Creek, at the time when he was killed and that she heard some firing in the woods about a quarter of a mile from her home; that she went there some time after the firing had stopped and found Mrs. Zachery and a little boy named Francis

Brock with the body; that the three of them carried the body to the house.

Champ Ferguson made the following statement concerning the death of Squire Zachery:

"I suppose that I was responsible for the killing of Squire Zachery, but I was not the man who shot him. I shot at him, but one of my men fired the ball that killed him. He was in command of a company of bushwhackers, and was seeking my life. We went to his house for the purpose of killing him, in order to save my own life. He was a very clever man before the War, but got over it soon after the War broke out, and arrayed himself in deadly hostility to old friends and neighbors."

Thus came Elijah Kogier and James Zachery to their deaths. They did not long survive the "peace compromise" which they were supposed to have helped arrange some two months before. Possibly even then they were in deadly fear of their lives and arranged the compromise as a matter of self-defense; possibly they had reason to know that their lives were not worth a "tinker's damn" so long as Champ Ferguson was alive.

The number of persons whom Champ was bent on killing, or at least the number of his enemies who might kill him, was steadily dwindling.

CHAPTER XII

The Bloody Month

OCTOBER, 1862, was to be a bloody month in the annals of Champ Ferguson. Six men with whose murder he was accused were killed that month.

George D. Thrasher and his brother, William, testified concerning the death of old man Wash Tabor:

"My brother, William, and myself," said George Thrasher, "were captured by Ferguson and his men in October, 1862. There were twenty-two men in Ferguson's group. They were being carried prisoners through Mr. Tabor's farm, when I saw the old man coming up a lane. Ferguson dismounted and went towards him. Tabor was on a horse, but got off when Ferguson got up to him. Ferguson soon brought him up to where we were, and Tabor was pleading for his life. 'Oh, yes,' said Ferguson, 'you oughtn't to die, you have done nothing to die for,' all the while getting his pistol out of his belt, and while the old man was begging for his life, he shot him through the heart and in the body. He fell after the second shot, with his head leaning over a little hill.

"Frank Burchett said, 'D—n him, shoot him in the head,' and at this Ferguson put his pistol down close to the old man's head and again shot him. Ferguson then looked up at me and said, 'I'm not in favor of killing you, Thrasher, you have never been bushwhacking or stealing horses. I have killed old Wash Tabor, a d—d good Christian, and I don't reckon he minds dying.' About this time, Tabor's wife and daughter came up from the house, screaming and crying.

"We left Tabor's body lying in the lane, and had not gone more than a mile further when we were attacked by Elam Huddleston with about eighty of his men. Ferguson had told his men if any skirmish came up to be sure and kill us first, but in the chase I hid behind a tree and got away."

William Thrasher's testimony concerning the killing of Wash Tabor was about the same as that of his brother's, with a few additional remarks that are of interest:

"On the morning on which old Mr. Tabor was killed, while we were taking breakfast, Ferguson sat down by me and asked me what old man Zachery's sons said about their father being killed. I told him they said they intended to kill the fellow who did it. He wanted to know who they thought did it, and I told him, 'Fayette Allen.' He said they need not blame Allen with it, that he was the man that killed him and was responsible for it.

"While I was a prisoner, Ferguson asked me if I didn't think he ought to kill me. I told him I thought it would be hard to kill an unarmed man. Ferguson said no, it wouldn't, and asked me if I didn't think it would bring the War to a close sooner if he killed all he took. I told him I didn't know.

"Ferguson took all the money my brother and I had with us, also some blankets and things we had drawn from the Government. We both belonged to the 18th Kentucky Cavalry. During the excitement after Huddleton's attack, I jumped off my horse and ran, and got away.

"Elam Huddleston and I belonged to the 12th Kentucky Cavalry and to the same company when we went into the service. Later on, Huddleston went off from the regiment and made up a company of his own."

On cross-examination, counsel for the defense asked the witness if Huddleston were in the habit of taking prisoners, but the Judge Advocate objected to the question, saying that the question of who raised the black flag or who did not was not material in the present issue. The Court sustained the objection. The witness did say, however, that one of Ferguson's men, a brother of the Frank Burchett who told Ferguson to shoot Tabor in the head, was killed in the chase but that the others could not be caught up with.

In Champ Ferguson's statement concerning the death of Tabor, he called him "Boswell" Tabor. He inferred that the killing was a good deed well done, and that Tabor's death had been delayed too long as it was:

"I killed Boswell Tabor as a bushwacker; he had killed three of my men a few days previous. He was in front of his house when I shot him. He ought to have been killed sooner."

John Williams, David Delk, and John Crabtree were also killed in October, 1862. According to testimony presented by the prosecution, the murder of these men was particularly brutal, and several witnesses were presented. In his testimony, Preston Huff made the following statement:

"About the 1st of October, 1862, I was at my mother's house in Fentress County, Tennessee. A party of men rode up to the house and called out, 'Pres, G—d d—n you, come out and surrender yourself up.' Then a man whom I took to be Ferguson hollered 'Surround the house.'

"I ran off, with William Huff, through a cornfield and came back on a bluff above the house, where I could hear them talk. The party stopped something like an hour. We could hear them banging about, cursing. I heard one of the men ask if I was in the house, and I heard Champ, (judging the voice his), say, 'No, G—d d—n him, if he was, we would have had him dead before now.'

"Pretty soon, some of them started leaving, carrying with them a lot of bedclothing and a negro girl that belonged to my mother. I heard Mrs. Crabtree cry out as they left, 'Oh, they will kill my son,' and Champ, I took it to be, reply, 'Never mind, we'll leave him down here.' I cut across to get nearer to see if I knew any of them. It was nearly sunrise. I got within fifty or sixty yards of the road when they passed. The prisoners, Crabtree, Williams, and Delk were just going by as I got there.

"I saw Champ Ferguson, Hans Mose, who had the negro girl on his horse behind him, John Gregory, William Latham, Henderson McGinnis, Arch McGinnis, DeWitt McGinnis, and Thomas Riley. There were others, but these, I believe, are all I remember now. On refreshing my memory, though, I can recollect Ephraim Crabtree as another of the party who came to the house. He is a second cousin, I believe, of the Crabtree who was carried off.

"They went straight across the fields toward the William Piles place, which is about a mile from my mother's house, and about a half hour after they left, I heard some gunfire down that way.

"Crabtree, Delk, and Williams were in the Federal service when they were killed, and they belonged to the company of which I was first lieutenant."

Another witness to testify concerning the death of Williams, Delk, and Crabtree was Miss Vina (Lavinia) Piles:

"I am a daughter of William Piles, of Fentress County, Tennessee. I was at my father's house in October, 1862, when Ferguson and his gang came there. It was just about daybreak. I knew some of them. I knew Latham, the McGinnis brothers, Hans Mose, Barton, Riley, and Gregory. They brought John Williams, John Crabtree, and David Delk with them. They were all tied together by their arms.

"I was in the yard with my sister and mother when they came up. They entered the gate, and came into the yard near the stables, taking the prisoners with them. One of them came back and told us to go in the house. We did go in, and then heard three guns fired near the stable. One of them then came back to the house and told us they had killed the prisoners. We then went out, and they passed on out of the gate.

"We found the dead bodies of the boys lying near the stable. Mr. Williams was shot three times,—under his right ear, in his right arm, and in the breast. Delk was stabbed under the right arm. Crabtree was cut to pieces. They were all dead. In one place in Delk's shoulder, a corn stalk was stuck in the wound. His mother took it out. Mrs. Crabtree came to our house about an hour afterward.

"This same gang had come to our house previously on the same night and had taken one of our horses. We were all up from that time until they returned in the early morning. I did not know Ferguson and cannot say whether or not he is one of the gang, of whom there seemed to be about forty.

"The prisoners looked as if they had been cut all to pieces before they were killed."

The next two witnesses were able to give an even more intimate account of the capture and killing of Williams, Delk, and Crabtree.

John Huff, a boy of about sixteen at the time and a son of Mrs.

Patsy Huff, was at home when the three men were captured at his house about one o'clock one night in October, 1862:

"Ferguson, Hans Mose, John Gregory, and Thomas Riley were all I recognized out of the party of thirteen or fourteen who came to the house. They surrounded the house and said for someone to get up and strike a light. I started to do so, and they asked who I was. I told them. Some of them in the house told me if I got up they would kill me, but Hans Mose ordered me to make a light, which I did and went to the door. Then someone in the group asked who was in there. I first told them I didn't know. Then they asked if Preston Huff and Andrew Huff were present, and said they were going to kill them if they were, and again asked me who all were there that night.

"I then told them William Delk, John Crabtree, John Williams, William Huff and Preston Huff were there and that Andy Huff was not there. Then they ordered those in the house to surrender, although they couldn't see them at the time. Then Delk walked out to the crowd and asked what they were going to do with them. They replied that they were going to take them to Albany to headquarters to have them tried. The other boys, Williams and Crabtree, surrendered themselves, and the party all came into the house and went to searching it. [According to Preston Huff, he and William Huff in the meantime had slipped out of the house and got away through the cornfield.]

"Then they took their straps off their guns and tied the prisoners. Delk begged them not to tie him so tight, that it hurt him. Ferguson said, 'D—n you, that's what we want to do—we want to hurt you.' Delk aimed to give my sister some money to give his mother but Thomas Riley grabbed the money. Crabtree started to give his mother a knife, which they grabbed for, but she got it. Champ then got a negro girl, saying she belonged to Eli Hatfield and he had orders to take her. The girl did not belong to Hatfield, who is a brother-in-law of mine, but my mother had raised her.

"They then went to taking things from the house—bed clothing and wearing apparel. Ferguson told the men to take what they pleased when the money was taken from Delk. He told Delk that he would have no further use for money. They took an axe and chopped up the floor and threatened to burn the house.

"Ferguson then told the prisoners he was going to cut their throats. Crabtree's mother said to Ferguson, when they started away, 'You ain't going to kill him, are you?' Ferguson said they were. Then they started and took Crabtree, Delk, Williams, and the negro girl with them. They got about one hundred yards from the house and I saw the light of two or three guns, whereupon I went into the house, and there heard about twelve or thirteen guns. Heard someone say, two or three times, 'Run.'

"About three quarters of an hour after the time they left the house, I went to Piles' place and found Delk, Williams, and Crabtree dead in the horse lot. Williams was shot about the center of the forehead and a piece of his skull was blown off. Delk was shot once through his breast and a bayonet run through his breast—it looked like it might have been a bayonet. Crabtree, I don't think, was shot at all—he was just cut. He was cut all over the breast and in the fore part of his shoulder, between the neck and collar-bone, also in the back under the shoulder-blade. In that wound was a corn stalk stuck in and cut off.

"My sister, Mrs. Lucinda Hatfield, and Crabtree's mother, and Miss Annie Pierce went with me to the Piles' place where we found the bodies. I saw there Winn Piles, Nannie Piles, and William Piles.

"Ferguson gave the orders and had control of this party while they were at my mother's house. They stayed at the house from the time they came until about daylight."

On cross-examination, John Huff stated that he was about sixteen years old at the time and that while at first they threatened to kill him also, John Gregory told them he hadn't been in the army and they let him off. He said he heard Preston Huff and William Huff shooting at the men after they left the house, but that Ferguson and his group shot first. He said that so far as he knew, Williams, Delk, and Crabtree had never belonged to Eli Hatfield's company.

Mrs. Lucinda Hatfield, widow of Eli Hatfield, who had testified concerning the death of her father, Alexander Huff, stated:

"I was at my mother's house at the time Delk, Williams, and Crabtree were taken from there. Champ said that by G—d he intended to burn the house unless I would tell where my brother, Preston Huff, and my cousin, William Huff, were. The men that were with him asked what were the orders next, and he told them to take just whatever they wanted. They took some five or six blankets, four coverlets, some calico, and some other things. They took some of the clothes that my father was killed in, some pants, a hat, and a shirt, and I don't recollect what else. Some of them pulled off their own clothes and put on the stolen clothes in the room. The coat we got back. We found it where Delk, Williams, and Crabtree were killed. We could have sold the blankets for six dollars; the coverlets might have been worth eight dollars apiece. The coat that my father was shot in was shot so that it was not worth much of anything.

"They brought Delk, Williams, and Crabtree into the kitchen. Crabtree's mother begged for her boy, and Champ told her it was too late now, that she ought to have made him do better long ago. His mother said he hadn't done anything. Champ said that, by G—d, he was going to kill them with a knife he drew. He said he never had said yet that he was going to kill a man but what he got to kill him. When he threatened to burn the house if I didn't tell where my brother was, he said if he caught him he intended to unjoint every joint in his body and throw the pieces so far apart that we would never get them to bury them.

"I counted twenty-eight holes cut in Crabtree's coat when we washed it after he was cut up so. I saw two corn stalks driven in his left shoulder.

"I knew Ferguson well. He stayed all night at my father's house about four years before the War."

In the statement made later on by Champ Ferguson concerning these three men, he had the following to say:

"I killed John Crabtree. I went to Piles' house in the night and stabbed him, and did another good job when I did it. He was a murderous villain, and had been to men's houses and shot them to get their money.

"John Williams was shot by Ben Barton, and David Delk was shot by another of our boys, all at the same time."

Specification 15, of the charge of murder, had read:

"Wm. McGlasson, in Cumberland County, Ky., November, 1862. Told him to run, then shot him."

According to this charge, the death of Wm. McGlasson occurred during the month following those of Wash Tabor, John Williams, David Delk, and John Crabtree. No testimony was presented during the trial, however, to support the accusation. In his own statement, though, Champ Ferguson answered the charge as follows:

"I am entirely ignorant of such a man as Dr. McGlasson, and never heard of him until the charges were read to me. He was no doubt in a fight way up the river, in which several were killed on both sides. I recollect of chasing a man to the verge of a bluff, and he ran down the bank to a fence. As he was getting over it, I shot him. He might have been Dr. McGlasson, but I hardly think so, for they say that the doctor was killed several miles from the creek. I know that he never captured my men or was captured by me. The story of my taking him out and telling him to run for his life and then shooting him is a lie manufactured of whole quality. He never fell into my hands and I am innocent if he was killed in a fight, as he no doubt was.

"I am charged with killing many persons who fell in battle, and a good many killed by other commanders are laid at my door."

On the very same day that Williams, Delk, and Crabtree were killed occurred the deaths of Orphe Williams and a negro man. In the specifications of murder, Champ Ferguson was not charged with the killing of Orphe Williams but was charged with the killing of the negro.

"Orphe" Williams, it seems, was the father of "John" Williams, and the two of them were apparently the Theophilus and Jonathan Williams mentioned by Preston Huff as being in his group who were hiding out from Ferguson.

Silas Upchurch was presented as a witness for the prosecution:

"I saw the prisoner with a company in Wayne County, Kentucky, two years ago last October [1862]. I don't know exactly how many men were with him, but I thought there might be fifty-odd. I was a little alarmed. In the group I knew Granville Sandusky, John Gregory, Fount Frost, Ephraim Crabtree, and Benjamin Barton; I don't know that I knew any others. My wife and one of my sons, my brother, and Coleman Craig [some called him Coleman Craig and some called him Coleman Hatfield] were with me.

"This company of men met us and demanded of us to halt. Orphe Williams and a negro man, called Johnson's Granville, had come up with my party and were along when the prisoner's party ordered us to halt. They demanded Williams' arms,—at least I suppose they did. I didn't hear the conversation but saw him give them up. As soon as Williams gave up his arms, they shot and killed him. I didn't know the man who shot him.

"They tied up the negro and marched him off something like a hundred yards. I was not noticing what they did until I heard the report of a pistol. As I heard that, I looked and saw the negro stooping down like, and instantly I heard another report. I was walking toward them and kept going until I got within about thirty steps, and then I saw the same person who did the shooting bending down over the negro cutting him. I couldn't see at the time how often the negro was stabbed, but when we took him away later I saw he was stabbed in three or four places in the breast and neck. When I got up pretty close, I saw the man with the knife quit cutting and wipe the knife on the black man's breeches leg.

"And then the same man who had the knife turned and commenced talking to Craig and accused him of packing mules, or something like that. Then John Gregory spoke up and said, 'Mr. Ferguson, don't hurt that man, for that is the man Dave Travis said not to hurt.' Then the man with the knife said, 'Is this the old man?' Some of the men replied, 'Yes, that's the man David Travis said not to hurt.' This man with the knife then asked Craig what he was doing there and why he was not at home. Craig replied that he had come over to do some work. Then this man told him to go home and stay there and keep his mouth shut and they would protect him. The gang then mounted their horses and rode off.

"I shouldn't have known that there was any man in the crowd by the name of Ferguson if they hadn't called him by name when speaking to him, and have never seen him since then until now. I think that's the gentleman (pointing to the prisoner) that they called Ferguson, and it was him who had the knife.

"They went from there to my home and took seven horses from there and three from my brother, Joe Upchurch."

Question—After Williams was killed, was anything taken from him?

Answer—Yes, I saw them feeling about his pockets. They seemed to take a pocket-book, a knife, his hat, and a comfort.

Question—Please describe the cuts upon the negro.

Answer—One cut was in his right side and one in his left side, and his throat was cut across. I could not say how deep the cuts were as the blood was dry when I went to him. It was about a half an hour from the time that he was shot and stabbed before I went to take charge of the body.

In their cross-examination, counsel for the defense attempted to show that Ferguson was not in command of the group and that it was very questionable as to whether the witness could actually identify the person who did the killing as Ferguson:

Question— Since all this occurred two years ago last October, nearly three years ago now, and you had never seen the defendant previous to that time and had not seen him since until now, how can you identify him as being the same man?

Answer—He has the resemblance, though he is not as fleshy and hearty looking as then.

Question—When you came in this court room, were you told who Ferguson was?

Answer—I was told to look in the company as he came up to see if I would know him.

Question—Was he under guard and handcuffed and in citizen's clothes, —so you would know who the prisoner was,—and did you know from his being guarded that he was the prisoner on trial?

Answer—Yes, sir, you know that I couldn't have thought anything else?

In other words, intimated the defense, it took no particular amount of intelligence for the witness to single out Champ Ferguson, the prisoner on trial.

Question—You say some other men came to your house. How many and who were they? Were they mounted and armed, and what were they doing there?

Answer—Well, there were some five or six came there. This man Williams and the negro stayed, while Preston Huff, John Crabtree, Will Delk, and a couple of the Piles boys, Sherrod and James, went on over on Wolf River, where most of their parents lived. They were mounted and armed when they came to my house, but left their horses with me to feed and rest up. I didn't hear any of them say to what command they belonged, but I heard before that some of them belonged to Clift's company.

Mrs. Nancy Upchurch, wife of Silas Upchurch, was then sworn in as a witness for the prosecution. She stated she was with her husband at the time Orphe Williams and the negro called Johnson's Granville were killed in Wayne County, Kentucky. She repeated her husband's testimony about the killing of the two men, and about the personal belongings being taken from Williams after he was killed.

Mrs. Upchurch also stated that she heard one of the men say they had killed three other men that day, Delk, Crabtree, and John Williams, who was the son of the Williams killed there. She also said that while they were talking to Coleman Hatfield, who was along with her party, she heard some of the men call one of them Ferguson, and that the man so addressed was the same man who stabbed the negro. She stated she didn't know who was in command, but that Ephraim Crabtree asked Capt. Sandusky what to do with Williams' gun and he told him to do as he pleased with it, but that then he asked Capt. Ferguson what to do with it and he said to give it up.

Again the cross-examination attempted to throw some doubt upon the reliability of the witness:

Question—Were you much alarmed and frightened at the time you speak of?

Answer—Yes, sir, right smart.

Question—Could you know or recognize the defendant as being one of the men there that day?

Answer—Yes, sir, I would take him to be the man who was talking to Coleman Hatfield.

Question—This morning, did you not go to the door and look upon Ferguson and say that you did not know or recognize him?

Answer—This morning when I first looked at him, I couldn't reconcile to my mind whether he was the man, but when I sat down and took a good look at him I recognized him. He is a notable man, if you notice, and when I studied awhile he looked natural.

Question—When you went to the door, were you not told or knew that that was the man on trial?

Answer—No, sir, I was not.

Question—Was this man surrounded by the guard and in citizen's clothes that you looked upon?

Answer—I didn't know whether they were guards that were sitting there on that bench or not. I never was caught in such a place as this in my life, and I didn't know who to look for.

It can be imagined that the courtroom got a laugh out of this final statement. Evidently, Mrs. Upchurch was not particularly pleased with the company she was keeping and was somewhat befuddled about the whole affair.

In his statement later on concerning this case, Champ Ferguson intimated that where these two men made their big mistake was in scouting for him, in the first place, and especially, in finding him, in the second place:

"I killed 'Affey' Williams and a negro man in the mountains. I shot and stabbed them. They were scouting after my command, and they found the head of it."

There is a finality about this statement that leaves no doubt in one's mind about the fate reserved for those who crossed Champ Ferguson's purposes or his path.

CHAPTER XIII

New Year's Night, 1863

NEW YEAR'S Night, 1863, was to mark a culmination, with one notable exception, of the murders with which Champ Ferguson was charged in the specifications. The testimony presented at the trial was to involve him in other murders, but the specifications of murder did not include another case in point of time until many months later.

From one point of view this fact seems very strange; from another point of view it is readily understandable.

If Champ Ferguson were out to kill those enlisted in the Union Army and those of Union sympathy indiscriminately, then it would seem strange that New Year's Night, 1863, would mark the beginning of a lapse of almost two years wherein would occur no further deaths with which the prosecution had him definitely charged. Champ Ferguson was still in the full vigor of his manhood, and most certainly his attitude toward the War had in no way changed. The Official Records of the next two years offer plenty of evidence that he was still active against the Yankees and that he had lost none of his zest and fighting ability.

On the other hand, consider the matter from the other viewpoint, namely, that thus far Champ Ferguson in large degree had been avenging an unforgivable insult to his wife and daughter. Then it is not difficult to reach the conclusion that on New Year's Night, 1863, occurred the eighth, ninth, and tenth deaths, or at least the ninth and tenth, of the eleven men who, by their own actions, had laid the mark of death upon themselves. This we shall never know, but this sudden termination of deaths by violence at the hands of Champ Ferguson lends further credibility to the rumor that lasts down to the present day as to why he was so unrelenting in his pursuit of certain individuals through the years of 1861 and 1862.

Ferguson's pursuit of certain individuals, of course, meant that the blood families of these individuals, their whole kith and kin, were included in the resulting warfare. The code of the hills considered avowed warfare upon one member of the family as war upon the whole family, and death of one member required vengeance on the part of all.

If it may be assumed that Champ Ferguson had vowed to kill eleven persons with his own hands, and if he had taken such oath we can be assured it was generally known in the mountains, all this would simply mean that Champ would be forced to kill others in the process of seeking these lives. This would account for the fact that he was to be accused with the murder of twenty men by the end of 1862 and that New Year's Night, 1863, would bring the total to twenty-three. It is not so remarkable that in seeking the lives of eleven men, Champ Ferguson should kill more than double that number as it is amazing that with the whole kith and kin of these eleven men arrayed against him, in addition to the dangers of general warfare itself, he should escape death himself.

On New Year's Night, 1863, were to occur two desperate fights, the second to be the most desperate, according to Champ Ferguson himself, in which he was ever engaged. Considering certain other fights in which he was engaged, no further evidence than this statement is necessary to label the struggle referred to as a desperate one indeed, whatever may be inferred from the testimony given.

The first fight was with Elam Huddleston, one of the strong guerilla leaders on the Union side, whose company after his death was said to have been commanded by Tinker Dave Beatty. It will be remembered that Elam Huddleston figured in the Camp Meeting fight before the War, and he had probably been Champ Ferguson's enemy since, or even before, that fight.

Huddleston had at first joined the regular army, but before long had withdrawn and formed his own guerilla band to operate in the

Cumberlands. Of the Union guerilla band leaders in this section during the War, he and Tinker Dave were probably the strongest and most feared. There can hardly be any question but that it was a war without quarter between these bands and those led by Ferguson, Bledsoe, McHenry, and others. Apparently, Ferguson had been on the trail of Elam Huddleston for some time.

Moses H. Huddleston, brother of Elam Huddleston, was sworn as witness for the prosecution, and examined by the Judge Advocate:

"I have known the accused some ten or twelve years. I was taken prisoner by Ferguson and some of his men on New Year's Night, 1863, at about eleven o'clock at night at the home of my brother, Elam, in Adair County, Kentucky. All the men I can recollect at present as being in Ferguson's band were Henry Sublett, Abe Hildreth, James Singleton, James Holsappel, Ben Barton, Tom Cowen, Alexander Evans, and a man named Burchett, whose given name I don't remember. There were at my brother's house, Elam Huddleston, my cousin David Huddleston, myself, my brother's family, my brother-in-law Braxton Simpson, who was sick in bed at the time, his wife, and my sisters.

"Ferguson came to the window of the room where I was lying on the floor asleep and woke me up. The moon was bright and I could recognize his face. I heard him say, 'D—n you, we've got you now.' My brother, my cousin, and myself immediately went upstairs to fight them. As soon as we got up there, the firing commenced and lasted about an hour, when my brother was shot.

"In the meantime, they had set the house on fire at the backdoor, so my cousin, David Huddleston, and I surrendered. Ferguson ordered us to come outdoors and we went out and gave up our arms, telling him that brother was shot. He ordered us to pack him down the stairs, that d—n him, if he was dead, to pack him down anyhow. He made us bring him out into the yard and lay him down, and just as we laid him down, he turned round with his gun and shot him. My brother was not dead when Ferguson shot him. I know this, because when we were bringing him down the stairs, he moved as if he were trying to catch my arm. When Ferguson shot, he moved and sort of drew himself up. I couldn't see where he was hit but I know the shot did hit him. The moon shone very brightly.

"Then the party plundered our house, my sisters in the meantime having put out the fire. They took some clothing and one of the men, Alexander Evans, pulled off my dead brother's boots and took them away with him. Evans also aimed to make a search of my sister-in-law's person,—Elam's wife—for money and notes, as I supposed, but a Major, who I think, was in command of part of Morgan's forces, stopped that. Ferguson went up to the bed where my brother-in-law, Braxton Simpson, lay and said he believed he wouldn't pester him, for d—n him, he would die anyway. My brother-in-law was very low, not able to help himself, and we were expecting him to die that night.

"We carried my brother, who was dead, into the house, and the gang started for Creelsboro, taking me and my cousin along as prisoners. They went on down as far as Mr. Wheat's store, half or three quarters of a mile. Here they stopped. I was kept back from the house about a hundred and fifty yards and didn't see what occurred there, but saw them bringing some horses out, together with some goods. I couldn't see whether Ferguson went to the house or not. Then Ferguson sent for me and my cousin to come up to the head of the column where he was, and asked us if we knew where Captain Dowdy and Captain Morrison were. Pretty soon they started for Captain Dowdy's place on Crocus Creek. When we got near there, a guard was placed over us, and Ferguson and the rest of the gang went on to the house.

"Soon afterward, we heard some firing. After the firing was over, the guard made me and my cousin go up to the house to see what had happened. When I got inside the gate, I saw Ferguson wiping his knife across the breast of Peter Zachery, who was dead and lying a few steps from the house, his feet towards the door. Ferguson said if it had not been for his knife, the d—n rascal would have killed him. Allen Zachery was lying dead, with his feet just at the doorstep and his head in the yard. The knife that I saw Ferguson wiping was a large bowie knife, with a blade about twelve inches long. At the time Ferguson raised up from wiping his knife, he dropped something from his hand on the breast of Zachery that I took to be an old pocketbook.

"The party then went on to Creelsboro, taking my cousin and me with them. A portion of the band went into the town, leaving us under guard on a hill in sight. Ferguson went with the men. Presently, we prisoners were taken into town too, and I saw them take a horse from little Sherwood Pickens, the small son of Jonathan Pickens. The boy went to Ferguson and tried to get the horse back but did not succeed. I saw Ferguson tell Singleton to saddle the horse up and that I was to ride him.

"From there we started to Burkesville. They took horses from different persons as we went along. When they got to old man Elliot's on Crocus Creek, they halted for breakfast, and Ferguson told Elliot that they had killed three d—d Yankees and told their names, Huddleston and Allen and Peter Zachery, and that he allowed to kill them all alike when he caught them.

"From there they proceeded to Burkesville, where they met a command of Morgan's forces, who carried me along with them that day and night. I did not see Ferguson after we left Burkesville. The next morning I was paroled by some officer of Morgan's command. Ferguson had said on the road to Burkesville that if we were paroled we wouldn't quit fighting, but the Major in command of Morgan's forces said he shouldn't kill us.

"Neither Wheat nor Pickens belonged to the army, but were Union men. Before that, Pickens had lived in Albany, Clinton County, Kentucky, but had left in fear of Ferguson."

The witness, Moses Huddleston, was then cross-examined by counsel for the defense:

"At the time of these occurrences, I was home on 'French leave,' having consent of my captain but not of my colonel. I had my arms with me and had been home perhaps a couple of weeks. I had started back to my command but could not get there. Of course we all had our arms lying handy when Ferguson made his attack, but they were not buckled on. Some of the men told us if we would come down and surrender, they would not hurt us. I heard some of the crowd say that we would be properly paroled, but Ferguson himself made no such promise and said very few words to me.

"My brother, Elam, was leader of an independent band, and on one occasion, a few days before he was killed, I knew of him having been with Tinker Dave's band at his house."

At this point counsel for the defense asked the witness if it were not true that Elam Huddleston and David Beatty had raised the black flag against Ferguson and his band, having sworn to kill him if they ever caught him, and that, knowing this, it was a war of self-defense on Ferguson's part.

The Judge Advocate objected to the question, and there arose an elaborate discussion as to its admissibility. Pending consideration of the question, the Court adjourned until the following morning.

Upon readjournment, the Commission announced the following decision on the question pending:

. . . . the question is clearly inadmissible, on account of its leading character. But the objection goes further and raises the inquiry as to whether a warfare of extermination and an understanding that neither side can give or ask quarter can thus be shown as a matter of defense. To avail himself of any benefit arising from such a state of facts, the accused must first bring himself within the pale of the laws and customs of war and show that *lex talionis* was the law of the land and declared to be so by proper authority. For it is not every man who calls himself captain that can authorize a war of extermination. Nor can the willful killing of a surrendered, disarmed, wounded, and dying prisoner be justified.

Even if the accused had shown or could show himself to be a regular commissioned officer of the opposing army, and recognized by the belligerent power, still he could not avail himself of such a defense. To admit it would be to agree that subordinate officers of opposing armies might at pleasure become butchers. If this last resort is to be allowed, it must be done regularly and it will not do to say that Beatty, Huddleston, and Ferguson could inaugurate a system of indiscriminate slaughter and when called to account for their acts justify them by such a defense as this. Such a doctrine would be to reverse the current of civilization and take us back to the darkest barbarism. It would authorize subordinates to licensed murder. Armies would thus degenerate to murdering mobs and render the profession of arms a disgrace. We cannot recognize such a right in either party; neither can we justify or excuse it in any.

It may be gathered from this opinion that the Court had no particular sympathy for either Ferguson or Huddleston, but that here was a Military Commission, composed of regular officers of the United States Army, that was revolted at the type of warfare carried on by guerilla bands of either side. Moreover, the Court indicated the main blame attached to Ferguson in this incident was the killing of Huddleston after he was wounded and captured, not the fight itself.

The counsel for the defense proceeded with the cross-examination of Moses Huddleston:

"If Ferguson was wounded in the fight at our house, I do not know of it. A corner of his vest was shot off, I believe, at the Zachery fight, but I did not examine to see if he was wounded.

"My brother-in-law, Braxton Simpson, was confined to his bed when the attack was made on our house but was not molested in any way more than the excitement. He died before I got back."

The prosecution then produced its principal witness of the Zachery fight which took place at Captain Dowdy's which Champ Ferguson characterized as the most desperate struggle he ever had. Sarah Dowdy, daughter of Captain Dowdy, testified as follows:

"I was at my father's house on New Year's Night, 1863, in Russell County, Kentucky. Peter Zachery, Allen Zachery, Greenberry Murphy, and Archie Davidson were present. The crowd came to the house between midnight and day. I didn't know anyone among them but Ferguson.

"Some one in the crowd said, 'Open the door.' Mother replied, 'Push it open.' They said they couldn't. Then the door came open and Ferguson came in by himself and walked over between the fire and the bed, while some of the rest of his gang filled the doorway. Ferguson asked who was there, and the crowd at the door repeated the question. Then some of us asked who they were. When we asked that, Ferguson said, 'By G—d, that ain't the question. Get up from there.' Peter Zachery then got up with a pistol in his hand and shot at Ferguson. Mother cried out, 'Don't shoot in the house.'

"Peter Zachery shot only once, when Ferguson caught his pistol and the two got into a struggle over it on the bed. Allen Zachery got up and went to the door, where several shots were fired on him, and he fought on the portico. Then Peter Zachery and Ferguson arose from the bed and went struggling toward the door, Ferguson holding on to Peter's blouse and striking at him with something. After they had gone out, we slapped the door to and mother and I took the children and went to the kitchen. I don't know how long the crowd remained after that, it may have been for some time.

"After they had left, I saw the bodies of Allen and Peter Zachery. Allen lay inside the fencing, close to the portico, with his feet toward the house. Peter was inside the fencing, eight or ten steps from the house. Both were dead."

Miss Dowdy was cross-examined by counsel for the defense:

"My father was not at home on New Year's Night, 1863; he was with his regiment, I suppose, which was at Somerset. All the boys at our house were armed. They were in the habit of coming to my father's house frequently, but they did not belong to my father's company or go with him on his expeditions. The two Zachery boys came armed because they belonged to the First Kentucky Regiment. Murphy was a citizen but he had carried arms for some time."

Counsel for the defense then asked the witness:

"Was Murphy in the habit of watching the woods and shooting at men, Rebel soldiers, passing?"

The Judge Advocate objected, saying:

"This is the same character of testimony that was presented yesterday. It is showing substantive matter of defense and making the witness a witness for the accused, and then putting a leading question."

The objection was sustained by the Court, and the witness continued:

"I never saw Peter and Allen Zachery with any of the home companies. They were on the way to join their regiment, and had stopped at our house to spend the night. The reason I came to see what occurred was because mother and I were in the room where the boys were sleeping. I raised up in bed, and when the door came open the moon was shining in the room bright enough so that I could see several men but could not tell who they were. If Ferguson asked Peter to surrender, I never heard it."

Bromfield L. Ridley, in his *Battles and Sketches of the Army of Tennessee*, gives a somewhat different version of the death of Elam Huddleston and the killing of the Zachery brothers. He says that sometimes the regular armies on both sides would allow detachments of soldiers to accompany the mountain bushwhackers in their war of extermination and that he had a friend in the Confederate Army whose detachment accompanied Champ Ferguson on the night that Elam Huddleston and the Zachery brothers were killed.

According to this story, it seems that Champ Ferguson asked General John H. Morgan, whose men were encamped at Columbia, Kentucky, on the day following Christmas, 1862, for a company of men to scout with him that night, reporting that he had heard that the Union bushwhackers were going to harass Morgan's rear the next day. The narrator states that they first went to a house near Elam Huddleston's house where a Christmas dance was going on and that when he got to Huddleston's house, Huddleston was upstairs shooting at them and that he called out to Huddleston to come down, that he would be given quarter. This Huddleston refused to do, and that he was soon shot and fell between the joists to the floor below; that he was then brought out of the house and Ferguson again shot him. He states that there was only one other person in the house at the time, a man who claimed to be sick, and that Ferguson shot him also.

Then, he related, they went on two or three miles further to a house where two of Ferguson's bitter enemies were in bed in a room by themselves and that Ferguson went into the room, pulled his dirk from his bootleg, jumped in bed with the two men, killed one with his knife and shot the other as he was going out the door.

Assuming that the testimony given at the trial concerning the deaths of Elam Huddleston and the Zachery brothers was fairly accurate, since it was taken within less than two years after they occurred, this statement of Ridley's is to be noted mainly for its inaccuracy. According to Moses Huddleston, Elam Huddleston and the sick man were not the only ones in the house; Elam did not fall through the upstairs floor when shot but was carried downstairs by him and his cousin; moreover, Ferguson did not molest the sick man in the house, Braxton Simpson, Huddleston's brother-in-law. Also, the Zachery brothers were not in a room by themselves by any means, and it is rather doubtful that Champ himself killed both the Zachery boys. It is not known, of course, what became of Murphy and Davidson, who were in the room with them.

The observation to be drawn from this statement in Ridley's book is that old soldiers recounting events of the War thirty or forty years after they happened are not always as accurate as could be desired.

In his statement after the trial was over, Champ Ferguson had the following to say concerning the killing of Huddleston and the Zachery brothers:

"I did not kill Elam. I was along, however. I think Abe Hildreth shot him. I know that Elam shot at me and the ball grazed my clothes.

"I killed Peter Zachery after one of the most desperate struggles that I ever had in my life. We fell to the floor, and he kept shooting, while I would knock the pistol aside. I finally got out my knife and stabbed him a few times, killing him. There were several in the house at the time, and we had ordered them to surrender. Allen Zachery was killed by one of the boys."

Whatever else may be said, it took plenty of raw courage for Ferguson to walk into a room where there were four armed men, with only moonlight to guide him, in addition probably to a faint glow from the fireplace. Sarah Dowdy gives us only a mild description of what must have been a terrific scene, indeed, with the fight going on between Ferguson and Peter Zachery and the shooting by the others, in this room apparently occupied by four men, two women and some children.

According to the seventeenth specification of murder, Peter Zachery was killed while lying sick in bed. From the testimony presented concerning this fight, Peter Zachery could not have been a very sick man. As a strange aside, it may be noted that within the year Champ Ferguson had now killed men from three generations of the Zachery family.

As stated before, it is fairly logical to assume that Elam Huddleston, together with one or maybe both the Zachery boys, made up ten of the eleven men who made the grievous error of insulting the family of Champ Ferguson. There was one more yet to come, but it was to be near the end of the War before he would meet the fate of his ten companions.

These happenings occurred at the time of what is known as Morgan's "Christmas Raid" into Kentucky, another one of his amazing raids into the heart of enemy territory, when he fought four engagements in as many days and seriously disrupted for the time being the railroad communications between Nashville and Louisville. In the meantime, however, General Bragg was not able to maintain his position at Murfreesboro and was forced to fall back to Tullahoma, Tennessee, while General Rosecrans, who had succeeded General Buell, strengthened the position of the Federal forces at Nashville.

The Confederate guerillas of the Upper Cumberlands were again left to their own resources, hemmed in on all sides by the enemy— but still amply able, for the time being at least, to take care of themselves in their own way.

CHAPTER XIV

Hunter and Hunted

IT was shortly after Squire James Zachery was killed on June 1, 1862, that we find the earliest mention of Champ Ferguson in the *Official Records of the Union and Confederate Armies*. While the first few reports that include his name mention him only incidentally, the reports themselves are quite descriptive of the type of guerilla warfare that was carried on in the Cumberland foothills. Champ Ferguson was at that time not yet recognized as a leader of a company and was not so well known to the Union officers as were such guerilla leaders as Hamilton and Bledsoe. It was to be quite different later on.

The first mention of Ferguson in the *Official Records* is by Colonel Edward C. Williams, commanding the Ninth Pennsylvania Cavalry, in a report from Bowling Green, Kentucky, on June 13, 1862, in which he states that according to order he had left Bowling Green on June 6th to proceed to Clinton County, Kentucky, to clear that section of marauding bands. He stated that on his arrival at Glasgow the next morning he learned that the company of Captain McCullough had been attacked by Hamilton and his men near Celina and that Captain McCullough and some of his men had been killed. Colonel Williams then went on to Tompkinsville, where he arrived on the evening of the 7th, and there he was told "that the citizens had driven the marauding band from Clinton County and that a number of Hamilton's and Ferguson's men had been wounded." He was given to understand that the band had taken refuge at Celina and proceeded with his troops to that place, but upon charging into the town found that Hamilton had received thirty minutes notice of his approach and had fled with his men into the hills.

"I, however, succeeded in capturing four of his men," said Colonel Williams, "who gave their names as Samuel Granville, Smith Butler, Tipton T. C. Settle, and William Henry Harrison Peterman. Against the last of these there is an indictment in Monroe County for murder."

Colonel Williams stated that he then sent Major Jordan with three companies to scour the country, while he returned to Tompkinsville. Colonel Williams included in his report another report from Major Jordan, who stated that shortly after reveille on June 9th he was attacked by Colonel Morgan's troops and that he was forced to retreat along the Burkesville road. During the retreat, Major Jordan heard some firing to the rear and upon going back to see about it was surrounded by the enemy.

"I determined," he said, "to try to force my way through them with my pistol answering their shotguns, but soon found that resistance would be madness and surrendered myself a prisoner of war. After I had surrendered, I was fired upon at a distance of but a few feet, the charge, happily for me, missing its mark but blackening the side of my face with powder.

"The forces of Colonel Morgan on that occassion consisted of his own brigade, Colonel Hunt's (Fifth Georgia) regiment of cavalry, a regiment of Alabama cavalry, two squadrons of Texas Rangers, and the independent companies of Captains Bledsoe, Hamilton, McMillen, and Ferguson."

This official report, which of course was not used at the trial of Champ Ferguson after the War was over, bears out in some respects the claim of the defense that Ferguson, sometimes at least, operated as part of Colonel Morgan's command and that he was considered to be a captain of an independent band on the Confederate side. Major Jordan's testimony that he was fired on at close range after having surrendered sounds suspiciously like he was captured by members of these guerilla bands.

It was during this month, June, 1862, that Morgan made his first raid into Kentucky and was joined at Sparta, Tennessee, by Champ

Ferguson, as a guide. Morgan fought swift engagements at Tompkinsville, Kentucky, on the 9th, Lebanon, Kentucky, on the 12th, Cynthiana, Kentucky, on the 17th, and back in Tennessee, at Gallatin, on the 21st. He was feeling out the strength of the enemy and the help of the guerilla bands in the Cumberlands was more than welcome.

The way was being prepared for General Bragg, marching up from Chattanooga, and General Kirby-Smith, coming from Knoxville, who were making a determined effort to regain Middle Tennessee and Central and Eastern Kentucky for the Confederates. After having been driven all the way to Mississippi in the early spring of that year, the Confederates were now back in strength and in good spirits, and the Confederacy was passing through some of its "great days."

In August, 1862, exact day not known, occurred the next death in the series charged against Champ Ferguson,—that of Joseph Beck.

Miss Jane Ellen Walker, the sister-in-law of Elijah Kogier, had the following to say concerning the death of Joseph Beck:

"I went with Mrs. Nancy Kogier, my sister, to find the body of Joseph Beck. I saw Ferguson as he passed the house in the morning, riding along with several others. He asked me if anyone had gone up the road armed. I told him if there had, I didn't know it. He then said, 'We have killed a man up there, and some of the boys said it was Joe Beck. You can find him; his hat and coat are lying by the side of the road in a little drain, and his body is about thirty yards from them.' We found the body in the place described.

"I don't know whether or not Beck belonged to an independent company."

Mrs. Kogier could add very little to this testimony:

"I found Joseph Beck's dead body in company with my sister and Marion Purcell, in the mountains about one mile away from my house.

This was in August, after my husband was killed. Ferguson and his men came down the mountain from the direction in which the body was found."

This evidence, of course, was all circumstantial. In the statement made later by Champ Ferguson, after the trial was over, no mention was made of the death of Joseph Beck.

In August, also, General Kirby-Smith won the Battle of Richmond, Kentucky, and General Bragg left on the 28th on his march from Chattanooga to Kentucky. By mid-September, Bragg was threatening Louisville and Kirby-Smith was at Lexington, living off the fat of the land. Louisville was ripe for the picking.

All this advantage was to be lost, however, when Bragg decided to make his conquest of Kentucky a political rather than a military conquest, and let General Buell, who had paralleled his march from Nashville, bring his Federal army into Louisville while he turned aside to inaugurate a short-lived Confederate Governor at Frankfort on October 4th. The Confederate victory at Perryville, Ky., a few days later, on October 8th, was an empty one. Bragg and Kirby-Smith, divided and outnumbered, could not hold their positions and were forced to retrace their steps back into East Tennessee,—and thus was lost a golden opportunity to strike effectively for the Confederate cause. The tide was now beginning to turn in earnest.

Champ Ferguson is again mentioned in the *Official Records* in a report by Colonel William Clift, of the Seventh Tennessee Infantry, dated October 31, 1862, from Somerset, Kentucky. In this report, Colonel Clift stated that he had been authorized to recruit his regiment during the summer of 1862 from the eastern part of the state and as soon as his command was of sufficient strength to attack the independent bodies operating along the Kentucky border. After some operations during the late summer and early fall, he reported:

"I again sent out a scouting party October 1 and we passed over the counties of Scott and Morgan and a part of Fentress County, Tennessee, capturing some prisoners and a little of the rebel's property.

"I sent out another scouting party about October 15th, which returned on the 29th instant, and reported that they passed over Scott, Morgan, and Fentress Counties, Tennessee, and had a skirmish with Ferguson's guerillas, killing four of them, and among the number was the cruel murderer, Captain Milliken. They also captured some property.

"On October 31st I sent out another scouting party from Somerset, Kentucky, to traverse the country from Monticello to Jamestown, Tennessee, thence from the line of Kentucky and Tennessee to Post Oak Springs, in Roane County, Tennessee, with a view of breaking up several guerilla companies that are roaming in the mountains between the line of Kentucky and Tennessee and the Tennessee River and sometimes in the counties of Clinton and Wayne, Kentucky. . . . .

"I deem it highly indispensable to break up these guerilla companies as speedily as possible, as there can be no safety to the peace of the country while they are permitted to exist. . . . ."

It will be noted that all this scouting took place during that bloody month, for Champ Ferguson, of October, 1862. The skirmish mentioned as having been engaged in sometime between the 15th and 29th of the month may have been the one during which George and William Thrasher escaped from Ferguson and his men. We do know that one of the Burchett boys was killed during this fight, but Colonel Clift's report is the first mention made of a "Captain Milliken."

We also know that Silas Upchurch, in his testimony, said that he had understood Williams, Delk, and Crabtree belonged to Clift's regiment. Preston Huff had testified that he was a lieutenant in Company E in Clift's command. Colonel Clift, therefore, had good reason for urging action against the guerilla bands in the Cumberlands. Champ and his men were making life tough for the Seventh Tennessee.

Champ Ferguson is again mentioned on November 12, 1862, in a

telegram from Brig.-Gen. J. T. Boyle, at Louisville, Kentucky, to
Major-General Wright, at Cincinnati:

Ferguson and Boles in Cumberland County with 200 or 300 men,
devastating it. Can any calvalry be sent there?

This telegram was sent on November 12th. By the middle of
December, 1862, Champ Ferguson was recognized by the Federals
as a dangerous adversary. Convincing official record of this is
found in an exchange of telegrams between Major-General George
H. Thomas and Major-General Rosecrans. General Thomas, located at Gallatin, about thirty miles northeast of Nashville, Tennessee, telegraphed General Rosecrans at Nashville on December
15, 1862, as follows:

Colonel Wolford's scout, returned at 5 P.M. today, reports no rebel cavalry crossing to the north side of the river. Hamilton's and Ferguson's
guerillas crossed the river at Hartsville day before for Lebanon. Colonel
Wolford thinks he can capture Hamilton and Ferguson if permitted to
go after them.

We turn the page to find this very significant answer:

> Headquarters Fourteenth Army Corps
> Nashville, December 15, 1862.
> Major General Thomas, Gallatin:
> Colonel Wolford has permission to pursue and capture Hamilton and
> Ferguson, but let him be careful not to get caught himself.
> By order of Major General Rosecrans.
>
> Charles R. Thompson,
> Captain and Aide-de-Camp.

General Thomas filed the following report from Gallatin to
Nashville on the next day, December 16, 1862:

Nothing has been seen or heard of the enemy north of the Cumberland
since Saturday, when Hamilton and Ferguson crossed the river at

Hartsville going south. My scouts from Lebanon report no force of any consequence in Lebanon, or nearer that place than Baird's Mills, where Morgan has his advanced guards. Morgan's headquarters are still at Black Shop. Kirby-Smith is at Manchester. At McMinnville there are a few, and something like 200 at Alexandria and New Middleton, gathering up forage and conscripts.

Apparently, Champ Ferguson was ranging farther afield and in larger force than had been the case heretofore. By this time, it may be assumed, he was no longer a member of Captain Scott Bledsoe's company but was the recognized leader of an independent company of his own. Working in close liaison with Morgan's men, though probably not actually submitting to his command, Champ and his men were effectively aiding the Confederate cause in the Cumberlands and proving themselves of more than ordinary annoyance to the Federals in that region.

These are the references to Champ Ferguson in the *Official Records* previous to the New Year's Night murders of 1863. After that fateful night, so far as the testimony presented at the trial would indicate, nothing happened during the remainder of 1863. But Champ was not through; he still had some unfinished personal business to take care of. There was at least one more who must be hunted until his lifeblood ebbed, and while he might remove himself from his native haunts so that his trail would be lost in the maelstrom of war—so lost that it was going to take the better part of two years for Champ Ferguson to run his quarry to ground— yet he would not escape. Nothing was more certain in those days than the vengeance of Champ Ferguson.

The *Official Records,* moreover, reveal that Champ was quite active all that year in guerilla warfare. In fact, these guerilla tactics of Ferguson and his men proved so annoying that by December of 1863, in making report to headquarters of the capture of some of Ferguson's men, Brig.-Gen. E. H. Hobson said, "What shall I do with the prisoners? They are the meanest of Ferguson's guerillas. Would it not be well to have them shot?"

It is the usual claim by participants in a fight that the "other fellow started it." It is difficult to say whether the guerilla bands fighting in the Cumberlands during the War made it a practice from the beginning to seldom give quarter, or whether the attitude taken by their adversaries, such as is indicated in the report of Brig.-Gen. Hobson, caused them to form the opinion that no quarter would be given them and that it was therefore a fight to the finish. Regardless of what "started it," it unquestionably became almost a war without quarter in the Cumberlands. No mercy was expected and almost none was given. Very few men in that section whose lives were sought with such deadly intent as was that of Champ Ferguson lived until the end of the War.

Champ Ferguson was now ranging far and wide in Kentucky and Tennessee, like a hound that had lost the trail, during 1863, as the following reports will indicate:

From Brig.-Gen. J. T. Boyle, at Louisville, Ky., on March 25, 1863, to Major-General Rosecrans:

I will detail Second Indiana Cavalry but a few days. I have a cavalry here. Champ Ferguson's gang of rebels reported near Bardstown, 50 miles from here. Suppose Breckinridge's force coming this way from Danville.

The next heard of Champ is in a report from Captain Wendell D. Wiltsie, of the Twentieth Michigan Infantry, from a camp at Green's Ferry on the Cumberland River, in Kentucky. It was dated May 11, 1863, and was addressed to Lieut.-Col. William H. Smith:

Sir: I have the honor to report that, on the 8th instant, I received orders from Colonel Jacob, commanding at this post, to proceed with a force of 200 men to where a band of guerillas, under the notorious (Champ) Ferguson, was supposed to be lurking in the mountains between here and Monticello, and, if possible, to discover and break it up. I accordingly took 25 men of my own company (H), under Lieutenant

McCollum; 30 from companies B, F, G, I and K, all picked men, under Captain Allen; a company of 28 men, under Captain Searcy, of the Ninth Kentucky Cavalry; and a company of Henry rifles (27), under Captain Wilson, Twelfth Kentucky Cavalry, all dismounted, and moved from the river at 9 P.M.

A considerable detachment of Morgan's Men had raided Central Kentucky in March, and some of his men remained in the Cumberlands throughout April and May and June, keeping Federal forces ten times their number on the *qui vive*. With the help of the Confederate guerillas, the Federals throughout that whole section were being kept in a constant state of uncertainty, and the way was being prepared for that most audacious of all raids made throughout the War, the July raid of Morgan into Ohio.

It will be noted that a good percentage of Kentucky soldiers were being included in the detachments being sent out to hunt down the mountain guerillas, but even so they were finding Champ Ferguson and his men veritable will-o'-the-wisps and their method of fighting confusing in the extreme. On May 13, 1863, S. P. Carter, Brig.-Gen. of Volunteers, located at Somerset, Ky., reported to Brig.-Gen. O. B. Willcox, at Lexington:

An examination of a map of Wayne and Clinton Counties will show you how exceedingly difficult it will be to meet the rebels now there on anything like equal terms, if acted against only from this direction. From Monticello there is the righthand road, leading to Albany, another running east, called the "Jacksborough" road, from which a road branches leading to Jamestown, Tenn. Going south from Monticello is the main Jamestown road. One mile out there is another, branching from this to the left, leading to some place. Five miles out on the main Jamestown road there is a fork, the right hand to Albany, and coming into the Albany road first mentioned about 7 miles to south and west of Monticello. If the enemy is unwilling to fight, he can take one of the above mentioned ways, and concentrate at Jamestown or Livingston, or he can fall back to some of the almost impregnable positions on the main Jamestown and Albany roads, and there make a stand.

From the best information I now have of the position of the rebel forces, I have no idea we can do more than come up with their rear guard, if they are unwilling to fight. If a force can cross the river at Burkesville, or better still, at Celina or Martinsburg, and move rapidly on Albany, the main Jamestown and Livingston roads would be closed. If that force would then move in direction, we might cut them off or capture many of them, as the only way by which they could escape would be over the Jacksborough road from Monticello. Should the enemy show a willingness to fight, our two forces could act in concert, so as to lessen, as far as possible, the probability of their making their escape. With regard to the movements you have ordered, from a point some 8 miles south of Monticello the country is broken and poor, until you reach the vicinity of Jamestown. There the country is more open, but still so poor that nothing can be obtained in the way of forage.

I speak now of the main road. This passes a very strong position 9 miles this side of Jamestown, known as "Three Forks of Wolf." There the rebels as early as the Fall of 1861 had troops stationed and threw up some defenses. It can be avoided by taking the left-hand road I have mentioned, and also I believe by going on toward Albany for some distance, and then turning to the left via Traversville. Jamestown is 35 miles south of Monticello, and unless we can drive all the enemy before us, our communications over so long a line will be constantly interrupted. The marauding gangs of Champ Ferguson, numbering about 150, are from Wayne and Clinton Counties, and will in all probability give us much trouble.

On July 9th, Maj.-Gen. George L. Hartsuff, at Stanford, Ky., telegraphed General Burnside:

Just arrived here. News of Wheeler false. (Champ) Ferguson's thieves operating in vicinity of Columbia. Boyle says Morgan is in Indiana, and wants to order up two regiments from Munfordville. Told him to do so if his news is perfectly correct, and also Moore from Lebanon, and put him in command of his regiment. Small party of rebels in Harrodsburg last night, stealing. Will continue to hear of them probably in that way about a week.

For the most of that month of July, 1863, Morgan and his men were riding a thousand miles through Kentucky, across the Ohio River to the "farthest north" the Confederacy ever reached, most of them to death or to prison. The major purpose of this raid was to relieve pressure of the flanking attack which was being carried out by General Rosecrans against General Bragg upon his position at Tullahoma, but without effect, as Bragg fell back on his position at Chattanooga from which he had advanced more than a year before.

The itinerary of the Twenty-third Army Corps (Federal) states that on August 19th the Third Division moved from Stanford to Crab Orchard; that on the 18th, Lieutenant Carr fell in with Champ Ferguson at Albany, killing 2 and wounding 3, among whom was Ferguson himself. This was the first claim that Champ had been wounded; it was to be claimed again the following March. A few days previously, Champ Ferguson and his men, cooperating with the Eighth Tennessee Cavalry (Confederate), had taken part in a lively engagement near Sparta, probably not far from Champ's own home. Report of this fight is given by Colonel George G. Dibrell, commanding the Eighth Tennessee Cavalry, in a dispatch from Sparta on August 18th to Major J. P. Strange, Assistant Adjutant-General:

In obedience to orders from General Forrest, I left Chattanooga on July 27 with the Eighth (Thirteenth) Tennessee Cavalry; moved across Waldrons Ridge and Cumberland Mountains to Sparta, arriving here on the 29th. My instructions were to watch and report the movements of Colonel Rosecrans' army, one corps of which was at McMinnville, 26 miles from this place. I sent scouts into the lines of the enemy, and harassed their scouting and foraging parties, capturing a few prisoners and horses.

On the morning of the 9th instant, my pickets that were 8 miles from camp on the road to Spencer were attacked by the brigade of Colonel Minty and a lively race ensued to camp. Captain (Jefferson) Leftwich, who was in command of the pickets, managed the retreat splendidly, holding the advance of the enemy in check and keeping his men well up until they reached camp. The regiment was encamped upon my own farm, 2 miles north of Sparta. We heard the firing before the courier arrived, just at daylight. Saddled as quickly as possible; sent Captain (Hamilton) McGinnis with his company to meet and check the enemy while we fell back with the regiment across Wild Cat Creek, which, with its deep banks and a mill pond above the bridge, was only passable at the bridge.

The enemy were in full speed, and before we could get into position were pressing our rear, having met and routed McGinnis and his company. I took position in front of the bridge with companies G and K, and sent the balance of the regiment, under D. A. Allison, acting adjutant, to form a line from us to the Calfkiller River, with instructions not to fire a gun till we opened at the bridge. The enemy had to enter an open space between the Wild Cat Creek and a large fence, and pass up some 200 or 300 yards to the bridge.

When their advance reached the bridge, we opened upon them, and then the whole regiment opened. They were yelling and charging at full speed, and the open space above referred to was full of them. Our gallant boys raised the yell as they poured volley after volley into them, until they retreated in great confusion out of the trap into which we had drawn them. They soon rallied and charged us again, said to be by the Fourth Regulars, but we soon repulsed them. They then attempted a charge on foot, but were again repulsed. They then sent a party across the Calfkiller River to gain our rear, but I had anticipated them, and they were soon driven back.

We skirmished awhile, and knowing my force was too small to contend long with a full brigade (we had not over 300 men present), I decided to fall back about a mile to the mouth of Blue Spring Creek, where our position would be strengthened, and did so; but the enemy declined to follow us, when we soon learned they were withdrawing; we gave pursuit, and followed them to the Caney Fork River, a distance of 18 miles, but could not overtake them. The enemy left 20 dead horses and 12 dead men, and had a large number wounded. Our loss was 4 wounded and 8 captured.

During the fight I was enforced by Champ Ferguson with a part of his company, and by several citizens. By the time the fight was over, the

ladies in the neighborhood had cooked and sent to us a breakfast for the
entire regiment, which was highly prized, as we had been driven from our
camps before anything could be prepared. Colonel Minty had four
regiments in his brigade, and was very angry with his Union guides for
bringing him into such a place as we fought him. This caused us
to be cautious.

By this time, Champ Ferguson was being credited in the Official
Reports as commanding quite a large force of guerilla cavalry. On
October 22nd, Major-General Joseph Hooker telegraphed Major-
General Reynolds as follows:

"General Slocum just telegraphs that a force of 600 rebel cavalry
guerillas, under Ferguson, congregated at Rock Island, 14 miles from
McMinnville. He has scouts watching them. General Rosecrans advised
me some days since that a regiment was ordered to McMinnville from
headquarters. I have telegraphed instructions to the commanding officer
at that point, but I am unadvised as to their arrival."

These reports seem to lend some confirmation to certain claims
made by Champ Ferguson during his trial. They would indicate
that he was recognized by the Federals as a commander of Confederate troops during the War; or, they might indicate that a
goodly amount of the leadership and activities ascribed by them to
Ferguson should, in large part, have been credited to other guerilla
leaders. It does seem rather doubtful that Champ, at any time,
had as large a force as 600 cavalry under his direct command. There
is no question, however, but that Champ, regardless of whether
or not he was regularly commissioned in the Confederate Army,
was recognized as a leader of troops to be reckoned with.

Two days later, in a dispatch from Colonel John Coburn at Tullahoma, Tenn., to Major J. S. Fullerton, Assistant Adjutant General,
Ferguson is again credited with having command of 600 men:

Your order of the 17th instant, to send a regiment to McMinnville,
came here on the 22nd instant, and was immediately forwarded to

Colonel Gilbert, Nineteenth Michigan, who will reach McMinnville today. The railroad is not completed to that place, and supplies may have to be drawn from Murfreesboro. There is also now at McMinnville a force of some 300 Tennessee cavalry. The force at Murfreesboro now is weaker than ever before, the Nineteeth Michigan being withdrawn. There are seven companies of the Twenty-second Wisconsin there, three being at Normandy. The Eighty-fifth Indiana has been ordered to Duck River bridge by General Slocum, so that if today the Twelfth Corps moves south there will be no guards from Duck River to Stone's River. There is no cavalry force to patrol the road.

Last night, about 5 miles south of this place, the rebel cavalry, 70 in number, tore up the track, which caused a train with 8 cars to run off; Captain Sligh, of the Michigan Engineers and Mechanics, lost both his legs; the cars all badly smashed. Ferguson threatens with 600 mounted men on the east near McMinnville. I fear much interruption and damage unless cavalry is supplied to chase these fellows away. A rail torn at any point throws off a train.

A negro, captured by the rebels last night, and who escaped this morning, says they say they intend to stop the running of cars on the railroad. He says they told him that General Roddey was some miles west of this place toward Fayetteville.

The Confederates had won the Battle of Chickamauga in September, forcing Rosecrans to bring his army back into Chattanooga. During the latter part of November, however, were fought the battles of Chattanooga, Lookout Mountain, Orchard Knob, and Missionary Ridge, and Bragg was driven off the heights around Chattanooga and into Georgia.

In the meantime, the Federals had left detachments of cavalry in the Upper Cumberlands to dispose of those independent bands of Confederate guerillas who had not gone with Bragg's army into Chattanooga. While the Battle of Missionary Ridge was being fought, these forces were having some rather sharp skirmishes, and the Federal cavalry were not finding it so easy to disperse and subdue the Confederate guerilla bands. On November 25, 1863, Lieut.-Colonel James P. Brownlow, commanding the First Tennessee

Cavalry, with headquarters at Sparta, county seat of Champ Ferguson's home county, sent the following dispatch to Colonel A. P. Campbell:

I entered this place yesterday on three different roads, and had a skirmish on each road. I whipped Colonel Murray's force, killing 1, wounding 2, and capturing 10 men, with them 1 of Champ Ferguson's lieutenants. I have also captured several horses and arms, and destroyed some ammunition. I have sent dispatches to Washington and Pikeville. It will be impossible to hear from Washington before Saturday.

Colonel Murray has sent for the forces under Hughes, Hamilton, Daugherty, Ferguson, and others, who will probably attack me tomorrow night. I will give them hell if they come, although their force is largely superior to my own.

I would like if you would send me 20 men of the Second Michigan with their six-shooters, and the remainder of my own regiment. I can hold my own against any force. Have Major Dyer to send me the ammunition of the dismounted men in camp, as I probably will need it.

If you send me more men have them start early and not stop until they have reached this place, as it will be dangerous for a small force to camp on the road.

I have just learned that Farley is collecting a force of soldiers and citizens to join Hughes.

Six days later, on December 1st, Lieut-Col. Brownlow sent another dispatch from Sparta to Colonel Campbell:

Colonel Hughes' command, consisting of Murray's, Hampton's (Hamilton's?), Bledsoe's, Ferguson's, Daugherty's, and other bands, attacked Lieutenant Bowman while scouting, on yesterday, and after skirmishing for some time, drove him across the river within 2 miles of this place, killing 4, wounding 1, and capturing 5. I went immediately to his assistance, and drove the enemy (numbering 500) 8 miles, killing 9, and wounding between 15 and 20.

I would take no prisoners. One of the Ninth Pennsylvania was mortally wounded (died this morning), and Captain McCahan wounded in the ankle.

Eighteen scouts, of the Second Michigan, got leave last evening. Send Doctor Green to this place. On account of the heavy picket duty I would like to have one more company, unless the brigade is coming soon.

It is rather surprising that the guerilla bands could assemble a force of 500 men. Perhaps Colonel Brownlow was exaggerating, or misled as to the number opposing him. Or, it may be that some considerable detachments of regular Confederate cavalry had been cut off from the main army in its retreat to Chattanooga during the summer and had not been able to regain their commands. These guerilla bands were now completely cut off from the main Confederate armies and were never to regain contact again except as they, themselves, filtered through the ring of steel surrounding them, individually or in small detachments, to join the forces to the south.

For many months yet, however, the fighting in the Cumberlands was to be bitter and, while the Confederate guerillas were to be hunted down relentlessly during the remainder of the War, even its close was to find organized bands operating in the mountains. With the facilities at their command, the nature of the country they had to operate in, and the type of people they had to deal with, it was simply impossible for the Federals to make the complete conquest in this section that they were able to effect throughout the rest of the Confederacy.

On December 12, 1863, Brigadier-General E. H. Hobson, at Munfordville, Ky., sent the following dispatch to Captain A. C. Semple, Assistant Adjutant General, at Louisville, to which reference was made at the beginning of the chapter:

Scouting parties sent across Cumberland into Clinton and other counties returned to Columbia. Had four fights; killed 10 (Ferguson's) men; captured 18 men and 15 horses. What shall I do with prisoners? They are the meanest of Ferguson's guerillas. Would it not be well to have them shot?

The Federal officers were apparently despairing of ever conquering the guerillas by use of the tactics of warfare ordinarily employed, and it seemed were about to come around to Champ Ferguson's way of thinking, that probably the quickest way of winning the war would be to kill everyone on the other side.

Again on December 22nd, Brig.-General Hobson sent a dispatch to Louisville, this time from Columbia, Kentucky:

I have at last succeeded in alarming the rebels, south of the Cumberland River. My orders to scouting parties sent over the river to take no prisoners has had a good effect. Communication from rebel Colonel Hughes complains of my order, and says that I should not hold him responsible for the conduct of Ferguson, Richardson, and Hamilton; and the cause of his now being in Tennessee is that he cannot get out. I think I will demand his surrender.

I have information today that Hughes has issued a proclamation that he would kill every man belonging to guerilla bands who were in the habit of making raids into Kentucky. His command fought some other rebel command killing and wounding 30 of their number. Quite a number of rebel deserters are making application to return to their loyalty. Judge Sam. Bowles, Cy. Hutchison, and others are making application to take the oath, give bond, and remain at home; they seem, from the tone of their letters to be entirely penitent, and are willing to assist in putting an end to disturbances in our State. What shall I do with them? Must citizens and deserters accept terms of the President's proclamation and amnesty? If so, send me instructions, form of oath, and bond, also necessary blanks.

From this report, we find that Ferguson was not the only one of the guerilla leaders who complained that he was being charged with acts properly belonging to others. The people in the Cumberlands were, however, past-masters at dissembling and it is entirely possible that Colonel Hughes was "drawing a red herring across the trail."

CHAPTER XV

Guerilla Warfare, 1864

SHORTLY after the turn of the year, on January 4, 1864, we again hear of Ferguson and his men through a dispatch from Lieut.-Col. A. J. Cropsey, of the 129th Illinois volunteers, located at Nashville, to the Assistant Adjutant General:

From various sources we ascertained that there were no coal barges loaded with coal below the rapids at the mouth of the Big South Fork, and that barges would not come over them with safety except on very high water. Some is being mined and loaded above to come down on the spring floods, but as we could not see the coal men, more definite information can be obtained by a correspondence with them through Governor Bramlette, of Kentucky, who is said to be well acquainted in that region.

There is also a large coal mine on Obed's River, some 50 miles from its mouth, that is at least 150 miles nearer Nashville and much more accessible than that on the Upper Cumberland, as it frequently can be brought out of the Obed on large barges when they cannot come over the rapids at the mouth of Big South Fork. The rebel authorities began working this mine just before their sudden departure from Nashville. That region is now in the possession of the guerillas, and of course no preparation being made for shipping coal.

If the general desires any more definite information concerning this coal mine, it can be had through Maj. Abram E. Ganet, First Tennessee (Union) Guards. He is now stationed at Carthage, and is engaged in raising a battalion for special service in that locality. He lived, before being driven from his home, within 3 miles of the coal mine, and he is especially anxious for permission to move his present command, something over 200 men, into that region, being sanguine that he could make the navigation of the Cumberland, perfectly safe in a few weeks.

The guerilla bands under Hamilton, Hughes, Ferguson, and Richardson number some 200 fighting men, and about twice that number for robbing raids.

The guerillas of the Cumberlands were proving most troublesome. The Federals were finding it possible to drive the Confederate armies out of Tennessee, but were not finding it so easy either to drive out or to subdue the guerillas. So long as these guerillas were able to operate in any force there would be no security in the homes of those loyal to the Union. This situation was aggravating; indeed it was perhaps hard for the Federal commanders to understand. Why couldn't the troops they sent into the Cumberlands restore order? Could these mountain people, even after they had taken the oath, be trusted? Andrew Johnson, an East Tennessean himself and a staunch Unionist, was Military Governor of Tennessee. Surely he could be relied upon to have the best interests of the Union at heart. Evidently there was some question in the mind of General George H. Thomas. Located at Chattanooga, he telegraphed Governor Andrew Johnson, at Nashville, on January 10, 1864:

I believe you can establish civil authority throughout Tennessee, and it is my earnest advice that you do so. Confidence will be restored and many people brought under the Constitution who are afraid at this time to exhibit their real sentiments.

I ordered Colonel Stokes to Nashville some time since to reorganize his regiment; and when his regiment was completely reorganized it was my intention to send it to Sparta to operate against Ferguson and other guerillas. Please do let me know when the reorganization is completed. If you can do so I would advise a separation between Stokes and Galbraith, making two regiments. They will be more efficient than they are at present.

We know, of course, that Andrew Johnson was thoroughly loyal to the Union. Perhaps he, too, was somewhat piqued that his government was unable to restore civil order in his own state—a state which, to all effects and purposes, had been conquered and from which all organized Confederate forces had been driven. Andrew Johnson, however, knew the type of people with whom they had to deal and knew it would be no easy matter to subdue them.

Of all the guerillas fighting on the border, Ferguson was designated by name in General Thomas' telegram. Andrew Johnson, as President of the United States, was to remember this name when it was brought to his attention nearly two years later. For the time being, such military forces as could be spared and as were considered necessary were sent into the Cumberlands to see what they could do.

Colonel Thomas J. Harrison, of the Eighth Indiana Cavalry, reported from Cedar Grove on January 14th:

I have the honor to report that on the 4th instant I proceeded to the other side of the Cumberland Mountains with 200 men, dividing them into four parties. Capt. Thomas Herring was sent down Camp Fork with 60 men; Capt. W. W. DeWitt with 50 men directly on Sparta; Capt. Leavell down the Blue Spring Cove with 30 men; and I headed a party of 60 men that descended the mountain at the head of the Calfkiller. We respectively reached the points indicated at daylight on Tuesday morning. My orders to the various parties were to move in the direction of Sparta and concentrate at that point in the evening, arresting all the men that could be found. The points designated include the localities of Captain Carter's, Capt. Champ Ferguson's, Major Bledsoe's, and Colonel Murray's squads of bushwhackers. Our move resulted in considerable skirmishing.

We remained on the Calfkiller for five days, and in that time we killed 4 of the bushwhackers and wounded 5 or 6, capturing 15, including a captain and a lieutenant, 30 horses, and 20 stand of arms. We visited the farm of Champ Ferguson on two occasions, capturing much of the sutler's goods taken by him from Colonel Brownlow's sutler, and 5 of his horses, with many valuable articles.

We had 2 men captured by straggling, but they were stripped of horses, arms, and valuable clothing, and turned loose. Before we left the valley, these bandits would fly to the mountains on the approach of even a squad of our men.

In making their reports, the Federal officers almost invariably referred to Champ Ferguson as Captain Ferguson. Had these official reports been available to them during Ferguson's trial, counsel for the defense might have made good use of them and might have asked why, if Ferguson were not an officer in the Confederate Army, the Federal officers gave him the title.

The Yankees were now invading Ferguson's backyard, so to speak, but Ferguson himself was never at home to the visitors. He was striking always at unexpected places and in addition to doing considerable damage was, by his very elusiveness, keeping the countryside in a constant state of unrest.

By the end of the month, Colonel William B. Stokes, mentioned in General Thomas' telegram of January 10th, had reorganized his regiment and had moved on from Nashville to take up headquarters at Alexandria, Tenn., on the edge of the Cumberlands. He reported to Nashville on February 7th:

I moved out at 7 A.M. on the 1st of February, crossed Caney Fork at Pin Hook above Sligo, and encamped for the night.

Moved out at daylight the next morning. Upon arriving at Sparta, my advance ran a few rebels out, about 30 in number, some going north, others south from that place. I then turned the command toward Cookeville and up the Calfkiller River, near Yankeetown. I came up with a squad and killed 3. Bivouacked for the night 8 miles from Cookeville.

On the 3rd, at 10 A.M. arrived at Cookeville, and found that Colonel McConnell had left, going in the direction of Livingston. I immediately proceeded over on the Calfkiller, and encamped near the notorious Champ Ferguson's. I found there some 20 or 30 rebels, who fled as usual at first sight.

From Ferguson's we moved down the river to Yankeetown, dividing the command into three squads, we taking the road through Sparta and Rock Island, another on the Nashville road, and the third on the right through Bunker Hill and Falling Waters to Lancaster.

On the following week occurred the deaths of Jackson Garner and Dallas Beatty, son of Tinker Dave. Testimony was presented during the trial concerning these two deaths, indicating that both men were murdered and implicating Champ Ferguson. The killing of these two men was not included in the specifications of the charge of murder against Ferguson, possibly because the information was not at hand at the time and also possibly because no witness could be produced who could definitely say that he was the one who killed them.

Isham Richards, at whose house these killings took place, testified as follows at the trial:

"I knew Dallas Beatty, but only saw Jackson Garner once. That was at my house in Fentress County, Tennessee, about the 13th of February, 1864. A party of 75 or 80 men, under Captain Carter, came to my house that morning. I knew him and Wiley Stickley, but did not know the others."

At this point, the defense raised an objection on the ground that the evidence made no reference to the prisoner. The objection was overruled by the Court, and the witness proceeded:

"Some of the men came on in the house, and shortly afterwards I heard the report of a gun outside but did not see who shot it or what they shot at. A few moments after, I went out to the woodpile and saw Dallas Beatty on the ground, dead. He was shot through the breast and temple. I had not seen Beatty at my house that morning before they came there. His body was lying about thirty yards from the house.

"Garner and my brother-in-law, James Templeton, were in the house. Pretty soon some man came to the door and ordered Garner to come out. He walked out and, as he turned to the right in going out, he got out of my sight. The man who ordered him out raised his gun to shoot, when another man who was in the house stepped out and took hold of the gun, telling him not to kill him, and then later said, 'If you will kill him, take him away from here, for the women don't want to see it.' The man who had the gun, however, pushed the other one off and shot.

The man who had interposed then said, 'I never want to see you do the like of that again, or I'll kill you if you was the best friend I ever had.'

"We then went out and found Garner lying on the porch dead. He was shot twice, in the head. Captain Carter took Templeton aside and told him to get back into the house, that the excitement was great and that they would kill him in five minutes if he did not keep out of the way and that he could not keep them from it. After he came back in the house, Carter came in and took him off to the mountains, after which Carter came back.

"Dallas Beatty was going down that morning to volunteer with Dowdy. He was about 21 or 22 years old. Garner was a member of the 11th Tennessee and his regiment, I think, was at Knoxville. I don't know the name of the man who shot Beatty and Garner, and I can't say that the prisoner was the man, but he was there. It was reported that there was a fight that morning between Tinker Dave's men and Hughes' men."

Daniel W. Garrett was the next witness presented by the prosecution:

"I did not know Champ Ferguson before the War, but have known him during the War. I was at the house of Isham Richards in Fentress County, in February, 1864, when a man named Garner and a man named Templeton were there. Ferguson came to the door and ordered Garner to come out. Garner went out and one of them stepped to one side of the door and the other to the other side. There was a gun fired but I didn't see who shot it, and directly Mr. Ferguson came in sight and fired a second shot but I didn't see who he shot at. His gun was pointing toward Garner, whose dead body I saw about half an hour afterwards lying near the door. Garner had a navy revolver which was taken from him before he was shot.

"I didn't see Beatty until after they had all left. He was out in the woodyard near the gate, dead. When the crowd left, Ferguson left with them."

Ferguson had nothing to say concerning the deaths of Jackson

Garner and Dallas Beatty in the statement he made after the close of the trial.

As the winter of 1864 wore on, there was considerable unrest in the ranks of the Confederacy, especially among those soldiers who had been recruited from the border country that was now in control of the Federals. Confederate soldiers on leave, who lived in this section, naturally made every effort to reach their homes, but the risk was great and even when they did not lose their lives in the attempt, they were often prevented from returning to their commands. These soldiers, on reaching their homes, often found them burned or deserted. They found their people, as they felt at least, being imposed upon, abused, and in every way degraded and insulted by the Federals stationed there. Under such circumstances, it was quite customary for them to band together in guerilla warfare in retaliation against the Federal forces, and the conflict between them was bitter indeed.

They knew that Colonel Stokes had raised the black flag against all known "bushwhackers," and had sent word that he would give no quarter. Here was language they could understand and a threat they could return in kind. Some of the Confederate guerilla leaders who joined forces with Champ Ferguson during this period were George Carter, lately Captain of Company A of the 8th Tennessee Cavalry, commanded by General George C. Dibrell; John M. Hughes, formerly a Colonel in S. S. Stanton's regiment, the 25th Tennessee Infantry; and W. S. Bledsoe, with whose original company of men Champ Ferguson was connected but who had later become a Captain in Stanton's regiment.

Captain George Carter was one of the noted fighters of the Cumberland Mountain section. He was born in Spencer, Van Buren County, Tennessee, the son of Meridity Carter, a blacksmith. He was a man of remarkable strength and the champion fist and skull fighter of his day in that region. It is said that he was a kind and faithful friend but an uncompromising and relentless enemy, and that during the War he became known as one of the most daring men in the Confederate Army. Though he served for part of the War in the regular Confederate forces, he engaged himself mainly in fighting those Unionists on the border known as Home Guards, of whom probably the most notable exponent was Tinker Dave Beatty. Carter was later killed at the Battle of Saltville, Virginia, on October 2, 1864, the engagement in which Champ Ferguson was to take such a sanguine part.

Colonel Hughes was considered by Confederate leaders a gallant and effective officer and seems to have been well respected also by the Federal officers. He was an active, athletic man and was known as one of the best pistol shots in the Confederate Army. He remained in Tennessee after the War and became United States Marshall during the administration of President Cleveland.

W. S. Bledsoe, whose name occurs many times in these annals, was, as we know, one of the earlier leaders of the Confederate forces in the Cumberlands. As we shall note, Colonel Stokes reported on March 28, 1864, that Captain Bledsoe was killed during the earlier part of March by some of his men while they were out foraging. It was the claim of the Confederates, however, that he was captured by Stokes' men and murdered after his surrender.

It was with such men as these, along with Champ Ferguson and Colonel Hamilton, of whom little else is known, that Colonel Stokes, and later Colonel Blackburn, had to deal in their operations in the Cumberlands.

Only a few days after the deaths of Jackson Garner and Dallas Beatty, Colonel Stokes took possession of the town of Sparta—on February 18, 1864—with six companies of the 5th Tennessee Cavalry:

I have occupied all of the deserted houses in the town with my men, barricaded the streets strongly, and fortified around my artillery. Since my arrival I have been engaged in scouring the country and foraging, the forage being very scarce and at some distance from the town. I have ascertained that the country is infested with a great number of rebel soldiers under Colonels Hughes, Hamilton, Ferguson, Carter, and Bledsoe, the whole force being under Colonel Hughes, a brave, vigilant, and energetic officer. There is little or no robbing being done by the guerillas, their attention being directed toward my men. Colonel Hughes' command is well armed, having secured the best of arms while on their raids into Kentucky. They number at least 600 fighting men.

On the 22nd instant, two companies of my command, when returning from a scout on Calfkiller River, were attacked by a portion of Hughes' men, numbering about 300, under command of Hughes, Ferguson, Carter, and Bledsoe. After fighting some time they were surrounded and overwhelmed. The officers (6 in number) with 45 men have come in through the hills.

Yesterday (February 23rd) Carter made a dash on one of my picketposts. He had 6 of his men dressed in Federal uniform. The remainder were dressed in gray, and as those dressed in our uniform approached the vedettes they told them not to shoot, that the rebels were after them; and those in gray appeared a few yards in the rear of those in blue halloing to them to surrender, the story appeared very plausible, and the ones in blue immediately rushed upon the reserve pickets. Four of my pickets were killed—3 after they had surrendered and the other after he had been captured. A great many of the rebels were dressed in our uniform at the time the two companies were attacked, and several of my men were killed after they were captured. Hughes himself does not allow this barbarity, but his subordinate officers practice it.

I have to fight for every ear of corn and blade of fodder I get.

Deserters from the rebel army are constantly joining Hughes. The people are thoroughly and decidedly disloyal, but a great many are taking the oath. The oath of allegiance has been found on the persons of several soldiers we have killed. The country is rocky and mountainous and very hard for cavalry to operate in. I have to fight rebel soldiers and citizens, the former carrying the arms and doing the open fighting; the latter carrying news and ambushing.

Portions of Companies C, F, and H arrived today. The greater part of the Companies remained at Nashville, being without horses. I earnestly urge that they be mounted as soon as possible, and ordered to report to me. Their services are needed very much here, and not in the city of Nashville. Horses are required to mount my men. There are no serviceable ones in the country, the rebels having taken all of them. The rebels are mounted on the fastest horses in the country, and they use them very much to our disadvantage. If all of my regiment were here and mounted I would soon disperse the rebels. I again urge the necessity of mounting my entire regiment and ordering it to the field.

Colonel Stokes was not faring so well in his engagements thus far and felt the need of more men and faster horses. The fight of February 22nd, mentioned by Colonel Stokes as having occurred between two companies of his men and 300 of Hughes' men was the locally noted Battle of the Calfkiller or the Dug Hill Road Fight. The Confederates have their own version of this fight, often related in that section in some detail. It is told that shortly after taking possession of Sparta, Colonel Stokes sent out a scouting party of about 80 of his men to "scour the woods" along the Calfkiller for the guerillas. They were to take the old Kentucky road to Cookeville and return through Dry Valley where the Calfkiller River heads. This force was under the command of Captain E. W. Bass, of Liberty.

Champ Ferguson, as usual, was well informed of this movement and along with the others gathered a force of about 40 men (Colonel Stokes reported 300) and planned an ambush. They selected the precipitous borders of the Dug Hill Road leading out of Dry Valley into the mountains and waited there for the Federals on their return to Sparta. As the Federal scouting command filed into the valley, they were startled by a shot and discovered two men riding rapidly away down the Dug Hill Road. Thinking them alone, they started in pursuit. When most of the command had turned out of the valley into the mountain road, the roadsides blazed and the fight was on. The Federals, being completely surprised, were at a disadvantage and fled wildly in all directions, losing about half their men in the process. It is said that the survivors who fled into Sparta completely demoralized a crowd that had assembled there to hear a February 22nd oration by Colonel Stokes, who found it necessary to file the speech away for more peaceful times.

Captain Carter and another Confederate guerilla, John Gatewood, participated in the most desperate phase of this fight. John Gatewood was known as one of the most reckless daredevils of the mountains. He was only eighteen years old but stood six feet tall and weighed two hundred pounds. His red hair hung in locks below his shoulders, he wore a broad-brimmed hat tilted back from his forehead, and he usually went into a fight with a pistol in each hand. During this particular fight, Gatewood had intercepted five of the Yankees as they were fleeing up the mountain and called on them to surrender. Not thinking him alone, they did so but after seeing he was by himself two of them broke away and ran. Fearing the remaining three would follow their example, Gatewood was in the act of shooting them when Captain Carter appeared on the scene. He called out to Gatewood not to waste his ammunition as it was too hard to get, at the same time picking up some stones. It is related that when Colonel Stokes sent his wagons out the next day for the dead, they found 41 in all and that they were laid side by side in an old store building in Sparta. Thirty-eight of them had been shot to death while the heads of the other three had been crushed by stones.

Gatewood, it might be mentioned, survived the War and then went to the Indian Territory.

While naturally no mention of these fights was made during the trial, we know that Champ Ferguson participated in them. He actively ranged far afield throughout the mountains until his home was burned in August. Then he, along with the remnants of the guerilla bands, found it expedient to retreat southward over the mountains and there join General Joe Wheeler.

A few days after the Battle of the Calfkiller, on February 28th, General Thomas received the following report from Colonel Robert K. Byrd, First Tennessee Infantry, at Loudon, Tennessee:

Champ Ferguson, with 150 men, made a raid on our courier line last night at Washington, in Rhea County, killed the provost marshal at that place, and captured all the couriers from there to Sulphur Springs, killing 1 and wounding 2 others. He carried off 11 horses and 11 repeating rifles.

If this report was correct, it means that Ferguson was traveling faster and farther than usual on his raids. Here again, it will be noted, that of the 150 men on this raid, Champ Ferguson is the only one called by name. It may be there was some basis for Champ's claim that he was blamed for a great many things which were actually done by others than himself. Whoever led the raid, it is obvious that the Confederates too were greatly in need of horses, arms, and ammunition.

On March 28th, Colonel Stokes sent in a report from his headquarters at Sparta claiming that Champ Ferguson had been wounded in a fight with some of his men about March 11th:

On the 11th instant, having heard of the enemy on Calfkiller, I sent out a scout of 80 men, under Captains Blackburn and Waters, in search of them. They met the enemy concentrated, numbering 150 men, 10 miles from this place, and after a stubborn and desperate resistance of one hour they succeeded in dispersing and running them into the mountains. The rebels lost 1 man killed and several wounded, the notorious Champ Ferguson being one of the latter. Our loss was 1 killed and 4 slightly wounded.

The next day I sent out a force of 200 men, but they were unable to find the enemy in any force. While out they succeeded in killing 7 Texas Rangers, men of the most daring and desperate character. Among these was Lieutenant Davis, the leader of the band. These men had been murdering and robbing Union citizens.

On the 15th, this force returned, and after feeding, 150 started in pursuit of Colonel Hughes, who had crossed Caney Fork on the 14th with the larger portion of his command.

On the morning of the 18th, the force attacked Hughes' camp at the foot of the Cumberland Mountains, 2 miles from Beersheba Springs, utterly routing them, succeeding in killing 7 of their number. They were at breakfast and some were sleeping when attacked, and in the rout they threw away saddles, blankets, clothing, and arms. The entire force would have been captured or killed if they had not run up the mountain where it was almost impossible for men to travel. Hughes had visited the railroad near Estill Springs and was returning when attacked. We captured a number of saddles, arms, blankets, and clothing belonging to the Federals, and also Colonel Hughes' portfolio and papers. Our loss was 1 killed and 1 mortally wounded. The rebels at this fight were entirely dispersed, a great many being dismounted.

On the 20th, I sent out a force for the purpose of picking up stragglers and preventing them from again concentrating. They scoured Overton, Putnam, and Jackson counties but were unable to find the enemy in any force. They were out 5 days and killed 5 men, among them Lieutenant Bowman. Captain Loure, of the guerillas, was wounded during this scout. Captain Bledsoe was killed a few days previously by some of my men while foraging. Yesterday, learning that Carter was across Caney Fork, I immediately sent out a force to look after him. They were unable to find him but succeeded in killing 1 of his men. Hughes' command is scattered over the entire country, no 10 of his men being together. They are merely trying to keep out of my way.

There is a story among the Southerners that about the time of the period covered by this report, Colonel Blackburn challenged Colonel Hughes to meet him and seventy-five of his men in a pitched battle; that the challenge was accepted and the place agreed upon was an open field near Yankeetown, a few miles north of Sparta. It is said that forty or fifty guerillas were drawn up on the field to receive them, and that the charge and the succeeding hand to hand fighting was something terrible; that after the battle had lasted for some time, the retreat was sounded and Blackburn's force dashed headlong for Sparta. It is related that when Colonel Blackburn led his men forth to the fight, he wore a large plume in his hat and made a handsome picture of a soldier on his charger, but that when he returned, his hat was gone and his uniform was riddled with bullets. It was reputed that Colonel Blackburn bore a charmed life and that men who ordinarily never missed would take deliberate aim at him and fail to hit him.

This particular story of the fight between the forces led by Colonel Blackburn (or "Captain" Blackburn as he was named in Colonel Stokes' report) and Colonel Hughes' men seems, on the face of it, a little fanciful. The Confederates, nearly always outnumbered, were usually inclined to use their ammunition and their men sparingly. We do know, of course, that Colonel Blackburn played a most important part in Champ Ferguson's career, being directly responsible for his seizure immediately after the War. It might also be mentioned at this point that Colonel Blackburn died at Dowelltown, Tenn., in May, 1913.

Colonel Stokes was probably correct in his report that Champ Ferguson had been wounded in a fight on March 11, 1864. The only mention made during the trial of Champ's activities during 1864, previous to the Battle of Saltville in October, was in connection with the death of Garner and Beatty on February 13th. While he was quite active, according to the *Official Records,* up until March 11th, we find no further mention of him in these records until July 15th. By then, apparently, he had completely recovered from his wounds, if any, as on that date Captain Robert Morrow, at Knoxville, reported to General J. M. Schofield:

The commanding officer at Kingston, Tenn., reports that guerillas, under Champ Ferguson, drove off a few days since 500 U. S. horses that Captain Fry was pasturing within a few miles of that place, and that the mounted force available was inadequate to their pursuit and recapture. General Ammen reports that orders have been given and that efforts will be made to recover the stock and punish the raiders.

This was a daring act and because horses were at a premium, a costly one to the Federals. The report of July 9 of Major Thomas H. Reeves, commanding the Fourth Tennessee Infantry at Kingston, gave a detailed account of the raid:

I have the honor to report that on the 7th instant, about 7 A.M., I was informed that there were some guerillas about Post Oak, seven miles from this place. I immediately went out in person with ten mounted scouts to ascertain the facts. I went out five miles, when I learned correctly that there were about twenty rebels, under the command of Champ Ferguson, at or near that place pressing horses; so I knew my scout was too weak and returned to camp and pressed all the horses I could and mounted fifty more men and went in pursuit of them.

I arrived at Post Oak at 1 P.M. and found that the rebels had taken 113 U. S. horses which were in pasture there and went toward the Cumberland Mountains. They were then eight hours ahead of me. I pressed on as fast as possible all that day and until 8 P.M. when I was compelled to stop and graze my stock, as I had no feed with me. During the night I learned that there were about 400 more U. S. horses on the mountains at one Mr. Meade's sent there by T. W. Fry, Jr., Assistant Quartermaster at this place. This was the first I knew of them being there. So, after grazing and resting my stock, I started out for Crossville about 4 A.M., July 8th, at which place I expected to find them, but there I learned that they (the rebels) had got the U. S. horses on the mountain and had passed that place (Crossville) the evening before, two hours by sun, on quick time, they having then about 500 U. S. horses and mules. So I resolved to follow them again, thinking I might catch them. A portion of my stock was about giving out, so I ordered out thirty of the best horses to follow rapidly and the others to come on slowly and again commenced the pursuit, which was continued until 12 M., July 8th, without overtaking them, though we were close upon them.

They left the road, took into the mountains, and as my stock was very tired I thought it best not to pursue farther. We captured 1 prisoner, retook 2 mules and several horses, 1 gun, etc., and returned as fast as we could to do our stock justice. We returned to Kingston, July 9th, 5 P.M., without any loss in men or stock.

The leaders of the rebel band were Ferguson, Hughes, Clark, and Carter, all present in person. I lost no time in trying to capture them and recover the stock but as they were so much ahead of me and my stock fatigued I could not possibly accomplish the desired end. The information received concerning their plans, etc., will fully compensate me for the trip. I have the honor, most respectfully, to request permission to mount 100 men and prepare myself with rations, forage, etc., to make one other attempt to recover the stock, as I know that I can do it successfully, besides taking a good deal more property which they now have concealed in England Cove. This, I am sure, could be done without much, if any, loss. I went within thirteen miles of Sparta, at which place they left the road, and I followed the mountains. We are all very much fatigued and worn out.

There is a mystery somewhere about them getting the stock, as the man who had it in charge was notified the night before that they were coming, and did not let me know it. I now have him in jail and will investigate the matter.

Major Reeves was vigorously excusing himself for allowing the stock to be taken and for not having been able to retake it. He was "hot under the collar" about it, and apparently most anxious to redeem himself. His request to take up the pursuit again was granted and his report of this expedition, filed from Kingston on July 20th, was as follows:

The expedition ordered out to recapture, if possible, the Government stock stolen by guerillas left this place July 12, 1864, with eighty infantry and twenty mounted men. They traveled in the direction of Sparta, Tenn., fifty-two miles, where they took to the right so as to get into the head of England Cove, at which place the stock was reported to be.

At that point, the advance guard was fired upon by one rebel who made his appearance in the road before them. The guard returned the fire and the rebel fled into the woods. The command moved on til 10 P.M. and halted for the night upon the top of the mountain. At daylight next morning they descended the mountain and reached the head of the Cove, through which the Calfkiller River runs. On reaching that spot they again came upon the bushwhackers and fired some fifty rounds at them, which created quite an excitement in the valley, and all the men fled to the mountains.

It was ascertained then that the stock had been divided among the captors and had been driven into different parts of the mountains and counties. However, some few of the stock were found in out-of-the-way places. The citizens would not give any information about the stock nor against the guerillas, and denied of knowing that any had been brought into that valley. The major commanding found that the citizens were all aiders and abettors to the thieving band. So he commenced to show them the rewards given to such people, and had their stock (private) and everything that his command could consume seized, and plundered every house from there to Sparta, finding in all thirty-three guns, some ammunition, and many articles which could not have been obtained only by theft, and destroyed all that could not be brought away. For a distance of fifteen miles down the valley every house where good stock, arms, or goods of a contraband nature could be found, the most unparalleled plunder was committed.

The command charged into Sparta at 4 P.M., July 15th, but found no armed rebels. Martial law was at once proclaimed and every man in town was arrested; then for two hours the cries of women and children were intense, for they expected the town to be burnt up and all the citizens killed. After plundering the town and examining the citizens they were released, with a few exceptions. The command left that place July 16th, 9 A.M. for Kingston with nine prisoners for various charges and some 25 recaptured Government stock. The progress was uninterrupted from there back.

Champ Ferguson has about twenty men and commands them in person. His range is generally in the Cove. Captain Clark has fourteen men and his range is above Spencer, a small town twelve miles south of Sparta. Camp Kearsy has about thirty men and ranges near Smithville; while one Dunbar, up in Overton County, has about seventy-five, mostly of Morgan's disbanded crew from Kentucky.

These are all the organized bodies now in those mountain ranges, and they are all regular desperadoes, taking no prisoners at all. The command exchanged some few shots with them as they went down the valley but no one was hurt. There is a small force of Federal soldiers at McMinnville, numbering about 200 men. They belong to the Fifth Tennessee Cavalry and owing to the small garrison are afraid to scout out at any distance.

It is thought preparations are being made by the guerillas to concentrate and make a raid upon some point, though they are so sly that nothing reliable could be obtained. The major commanding the expedition expected to find the guerillas as he returned at Crossville trying to cut him off, but as he made a big impression about the number he had, they were afraid to try it. For the good of the service, there should be at least 100 well-mounted men sent into that Cove to stay about one month. They can subsist off the country, as the crops are very good.

After this expedition, during which, Major Reeves naively reported, the Yankees committed "unparalleled plunder," nothing further is heard of Champ Ferguson until the Battle of Saltville, Virginia. It was during the latter part of the next month, August, that Champ Ferguson's home near Sparta was burned by Captain Rufus Dowdy and his Yankee guerillas, and about this time Champ Ferguson and those of his companions who were left marched south over the mountains and joined General Wheeler's cavalry. Champ was not with General Wheeler more than a month before he and his men were ordered to report to General Breckenridge in southwest Virginia. Just why they were a part of the forces detached we do not know.

CHAPTER XVI

The Murder of Lieutenant Smith

THE first specification in the charge of murder against Champ Ferguson was the killing of Lieut. Smith, of the 13th Kentucky Cavalry, who was "shot in the head while a prisoner and lying sick in the hospital at Emory, Virginia." There can be no question but that this was the murder that rankled most in the hearts of the Federal authorities. They listed it first in the charge and they considered it to be the most dastardly of the crimes with which the prisoner was charged.

Here again, no doubt, the Army felt its honor impugned and its principles violated. Most of the other murders with which Ferguson was charged were of persons who were not in the Army or who if they were or had been, were not actively engaged in organized warfare at the time the murder was committed. But this man was a lieutenant in the Union Army who had been wounded at the Battle of Saltville, Virginia, captured by the Confederates, and placed in a Confederate hospital. That this lieutenant was to be murdered while lying on his cot in the hospital was not to be forgiven, certainly not by the Army itself.

The second specification of murder charges the killing of twelve soldiers, names unknown, at Saltville, Virginia. The third specification charges the killing of two negro soldiers, names unknown, while lying wounded in prison at Saltville. The fourth specification charges the murder of nineteen soldiers of the 5th Tennessee Cavalry, names unknown, on February 22, 1865. On this fourth specification, no testimony was submitted, nor is it known why this charge was made. Testimony on the second and third specifications is rather dubious and, since the testimony submitted is closely connected with the events surrounding the death of Lieut. Smith, it will be presented as incident to the testimony concerning the death of this officer.

Many years after the close of the War, the doctor in charge of the hospital where Lieut. Smith was killed, Dr. L. B. Murfree, of Murfreesboro, Tenn., wrote an account of this event, as follows:

During the year 1864 and the early part of 1865 I was stationed at Emory, Virginia, as the surgeon in charge of the Confederate Hospital located at that place.

In the Fall of 1864 a large force of Federal cavalry from Kentucky under command of General Stoneman made a raid through Southwestern Virginia for the purpose of destroying the railroad between Bristol and Lynchburg. They were met by Morgan's command and a fierce and bloody battle was fought near Max Meadow in which the Federals were defeated and driven back into Kentucky. A large number of Federals were taken prisoners, many of them being wounded, some very badly.

The wounded were sent to the General Hospital at Emory and Henry College, of these there were 150 or 200 Federal prisoners. The Hospital was on the railroad, nine miles from Abingdon, beautifully located and in a fine section of country. The college buildings were large and commodious and were occupied by the Confederates as a hospital, containing 350 beds and was under my care as the surgeon in charge. The Federal wounded were placed on the third and fourth floors of the main building which could be only reached by two stairways, one at either end of the building. In order to prevent the escape of any of the Federal prisoners, guards were placed at the foot of each of the stairways.

On a cold and bleak Saturday in November, 1864, Champ Ferguson with twelve or fifteen of his men quietly rode up to the hospital, dismounted, hitched their horses and entered the hospital almost unnoticed. They attempted to ascend one of the stairways to the ward on the third floor where Lieutenant Smith, a wounded Federal prisoner, was confined.

The guard halted them and told them that they could not go up those steps (this guard was an Irishman and as brave as Julius Caesar). Champ Ferguson, followed by his men, advanced on the guard swearing that they would go up the steps in spite of him. But the guard, undaunted

by their threats, raised his gun and leveling it at Champ Ferguson coolly
yet firmly told him that he would shoot him if he came any farther.

Unable to scare this guard, they left him and went to the other stairway
where they overpowered the guard stationed there and ascended the
stairs to the ward where Smith was in bed suffering with a severe wound.
Champ Ferguson went directly to Smith, sat down on his bed, and
patting his gun with his hand, said, "Smith, do you see this? Well, I'm
going to kill you." And without another word, placed the gun at
Smith's head, fired, sending a minnie ball through Smith's head instantly
killing him.

I was busily engaged in the office of the hospital when a nurse came
rushing in saying a lot of soldiers had killed a man in the hospital. I
immediately went to the hospital followed by Major Stringfield, of the
Army of Virginia (who was visiting in that neighborhood). On reaching
the hospital we rapidly ascended the steps to the second floor where we
were halted by one of Ferguson's men with a drawn revolver. I
promptly told him to go down the stairs, to which he replied that, "Captain Ferguson has ordered me to let no one pass up the steps." I pushed
by him going on up the steps, while Major Stringfield remained behind
contending with the guard.

On the next flight of steps I met Champ Ferguson and his men, and I
said to them, "Gentlemen, you must go down from here; this is a place
for the sick and wounded, and you must not disturb them," to which
Champ Ferguson said with an oath, "I will shoot you." Standing within
a few feet of each other, I said to him, "This is a Confederate hospital,
I am in charge of it, I command here, you must go down from here."
Champ Ferguson then advanced to within three feet of me, raised his
cocked pistol and pointed directly at my breast, saying, "I don't care
who you are, damn you, I will kill you."

Realizing the desperate character I had to deal with and being myself
unarmed, yet impelled by a sense of duty, I again said to him, "You must
go down from here and out of this hospital." While we were standing
in this threatening attitude, face to face, with Ferguson's pistol in my
breast and swearing he would kill me, Lieutenant Philpot, of Ferguson's
company stepped in between us, at the same time motioning with his
hand to Ferguson, when they all went down the steps, I going with them,
Ferguson cursing and swearing as he went. They passed out of the

hospital, mounted their horses, and as they rode off shouted, "We have killed the man that killed Hamilton."

Afterwards I was told that Lieutenant Smith, whom Champ Ferguson had just killed, had mistreated Ferguson's family; that he made Ferguson's wife undress and marched her before him along the public road in a nude state.

The killing of Smith was promptly reported to General Breckenridge, at Abingdon, he being in command of the Department of Southwestern Virginia. Champ Ferguson was arrested, a court-martial ordered and held, but it was so near the close of the War that nothing more than this was done with him.

As is so often the case in an old soldier's reminiscences, it is a question as to how accurately Dr. Murfree remembered some of the details of the incident. There is no question but that he was wrong on some points. Lieutenant Smith was killed during the early part of October rather than in November. The raid by the Union cavalry was another of a long line of attempts to destroy, or cut off, the main salt supply of the Confederate army, located at Saltville, Virginia, an objective which was finally achieved in December of that year.

General John H. Morgan had been killed in early September at Greeneville, Tennessee, under questionable circumstances, and while some of the remnants of Morgan's cavalry took part in the Battle of Saltville, the command was in the hands of General Breckenridge. Perhaps the most interesting sidelight which Doctor Murfree throws on this whole case is his statement that as Ferguson and his men left the hospital they stated that they had avenged the death of Captain Hamilton, as another reference is made to this in the testimony of one of the witnesses at the trial. It will also be noted that Doctor Murfree remembers that another reason was later given him as to why Champ killed Lieutenant Smith, that old ghost that would not down, the insult to Champ's family.

At Champ's trial several witnesses were presented by the prosecu-

tion to testify concerning the death of Lieutenant Smith. One of
these was A. J. Watkins:

"I was on duty in the Rebel service about the time of the Saltville fight.
I was quartermaster's sergeant, superintending the quartermaster's depart-
ment of Emory and Henry Hospital. It was called in the Rebel service the
General Hospital of Virginia.

"I saw a Federal officer dead in his bunk. He had a fresh wound.
He was shot through the head, the ball entering the left side of the
forehead and then passing through, tearing off the top of the skull. His
brains were oozing out on the pillow. I heard in the hospital, about half
an hour before I found the body, the report of what I took to be a gun.
This was about the 19th of October last (1864), soon after Burbridge's
fight at the Salt Works."

Another witness presented by the prosecution was George W.
Carter, a second lieutenant in the 11th Michigan Cavalry:

"I was at the Battle of Saltville, Virginia; was taken prisoner there,
and sent to Emory and Henry College. After the fight I saw some
colored soldiers killed, eight or nine of them. All the prisoners were
robbed of everything. My captors took my boots, blankets, blouse, hat,
and spurs, in fact everything but my pants and shirt.

"Three or four days after the first shooting of negroes, I heard five
shots fired in the hospital, the time some negroes were killed there. I also
heard another shot a day or two after. The negroes killed on the field
were shot on the 3rd of October, 1864. They belonged to a regiment of
U. S. Colored Cavalry, either the 5th or 6th. They were all prisoners of
war and none had their arms.

"I couldn't tell whether or not citizens or soldiers did the killing of the
prisoners, as all seemed to be dressed alike. I don't know that anybody
had command. They all appeared to be commanding themselves. At the
Saltville fight, we saw some militia and I think General Breckenridge
was in command of all the troops.

"At the hospital I saw Ferguson as he passed over on his way to Smith's
room. About five minutes afterwards, I heard the shot. I have seen

Ferguson several times, and think the prisoner is the man, but won't be positive. He had a heavier beard than now, and longer hair."

A third witness for the prosecution was Orange Sells:

"I was in the 12th Ohio Cavalry and was in the first Battle of Saltville, where I was wounded and taken to Emory and Henry Hospital, in western Virginia. The battle was on the 2nd of October, 1864, and I saw Champ Ferguson on the 7th.

"At the hospital, I also saw Lieutenant Smith, of the 13th Kentucky Cavalry. He was in my room. He had been wounded in the Battle of Saltville at the same time I was, and was in the hospital for treatment, so badly wounded that he couldn't help himself.

"About four o'clock on the evening of the 7th, we heard a rustling on the stairway. No one was in the room but myself, Captain Dagenfeld, of the 12th Ohio Cavalry, and Lieutenant Smith. All three of us were wounded. Ferguson and another man came in. The prisoner walked to Lieutenant Smith without saying a word, holding a musket in his left hand. The man with him stopped directly in front of my bed near the door.

"Lieutenant Smith recognized Ferguson as he reached the middle of the floor, and exclaimed, 'Champ, is that you?' Ferguson didn't say anything at that, but went to Smith's bed, jerked his gun up in his left hand, hit the breech with his right hand, and said, 'Smith, do you see this?', and pointed it at him. At that, Smith raised his head as much as he could and said, 'Champ, for God's sake, don't shoot me here.' Ferguson put the gun within about a foot of Smith's head and snapped three times before the gun went off. The ball hit Smith about the side of the forehead, going diagonally through the head and coming out just behind the ear.

"Not a word was said after Smith begged Ferguson not to shoot. He didn't live a half minute after he was shot. The man who was standing by my bed spoke and said, 'Champ, be sure your work is well done.' Then both of them went up and examined Smith, and one of them said, 'He is d—d dead,' or something like that. The man who stood by my bed had a revolver in one hand and a carbine in the other.

"The night before the killing, we heard a rustling on the stairway and immediately three men came into the room. One had a lighted candle and the other two had revolvers. They looked into each of our faces and after they got around, one of them remarked, 'There are none of them here,' and went out. They had hardly got out—had not been gone more than half a minute—until we heard firing in the next room to us. Some six shots were fired, and immediately afterward a negro soldier was carried dead out of that room. Another negro soldier ran into our room wrapped in a sheet.

"I didn't know either of the men who came into our room.

"I was also at a log house near the field after the battle and saw a good many negroes killed there. All of them were soldiers and all were wounded but one. I heard firing there all over the place; it was like a skirmish. This was the morning of the 3rd, and the fight ceased on the morning of the 2nd of October. The log house was used for a hospital for those whom our force had carried there wounded."

The witness was then cross-examined by counsel for the defense:

"I never had any acquaintance with the prisoner before that occasion, and knew him at the time only from what Smith said. Smith called him by name. I am not mistaken in the name, but he is a good deal thinner than he was then. Ferguson made no reply when Smith said, 'Champ, is that you?' Lieutenant Smith did not speak after being shot."

Question—If you had not been informed who the prisoner was now on trial, would you have been able to point him out and recognize him in an assembly of men?

Answer—Yes, sir. I wouldn't have known that his name was Ferguson, but I would have known that he was the man who killed Smith.

Question—Do you recollect how the man was dressed?

Answer—Yes, sir. He had on a dark lindsey frock coat, buttoned up in front, and tolerably short waisted. He had on a black plug hat. His hair and beard were both longer than now. His beard was full and made his face look full. He also had a mustache. I can't say how long his hair was, but it was much longer than now and was straight around the back of his neck. I don't think it came down to his shoulders.

Question—He being a stranger to you at the time, did you notice anything peculiar in him which enables you at this distant day to identify him? If so, state it.

Answer—He was a large man, a great deal fleshier than he is now. I know him by his mouth and by his features generally. I would know him on the street or anywhere. We were in so much danger ourselves that I marked the man well.

Question—Was anything said at the time as to why Lieutenant Smith was killed?

Answer—No, sir. There was the next day, though.

The Judge Advocate here objected that what was said the next day was not evidence. The counsel for the accused, however, insisted that the witness be instructed to relate the conversation. The Judge Advocate finally assented and the witness resumed his testimony:

"There were many reports. One was that Smith had gone to Ferguson's house and abused his wife and family. Another was that Smith had run Ferguson out of Kentucky two or three times. That is about all I recollect about it. I didn't hear anything said about Colonel Hamilton at this time, but the day before Smith was killed a man came into our room and had a conversation with Smith and told Smith he had been accused of killing Colonel Hamilton. He pretended to be acquainted with Smith and asked him about the particulars of Hamilton being killed. He asked Smith if he had killed Hamilton and Smith said he did not. He said they had started with Hamilton from Lexington to Camp Nelson, in charge of a guard, and that Hamilton attempted to escape from the guard and was shot by the guard. Smith reasoned with the fellow and they had a long talk. Smith stated that he couldn't help it—that he had done nothing but his duty and what anybody else would have done. Smith said he was in command of the guard."

This brief reference was the first, last, and only time that a statement was made in open court during Champ Ferguson's trial of the insulting act towards Champ's wife, common gossip of which persists down to the present day. So far as the trial is concerned, it

is as if a quietus were purposely placed on all such references. Who
else would have wished such testimony squelched other than Champ
Ferguson himself?

The witness was re-examined by the Judge Advocate:

Question—In these conversations about Smith and Ferguson, was anything said about who killed Smith or where Ferguson was at the time?
State who it was you heard talking about these matters.

Answer—It was the hospital steward I heard telling about it. Burns
was his name. He told me why Smith was killed, and said it was done
by Ferguson and his men; that about fifteen of his men were there and
that three of them came upstairs. But I only saw two come into the
room, as I have stated. The hospital steward didn't say who any of
Ferguson's men were.

Question—Did the prisoner recap his gun when he was aiming at
Smith, and it snapped?

Answer—No, sir.

The last, and probably the most damning, evidence was presented
by the fourth witness for the prosecution, Harry Shocker:

"I belong to the 12th Ohio Cavalry. I saw Champ Ferguson on the
3rd of October, 1864, at the Battle of Saltville, where I was taken prisoner.
My partner and I were lying wounded on the field the morning after
the battle, when I saw the prisoner coming across the field. I saw him
pointing his pistol down at prisoners lying on the ground, and heard the
reports of the pistol and the screams of the men. While Ferguson was
coming toward us, I crawled away about forty feet and stretched myself
out.

"Ferguson came up to my partner, Crawford Hazlewood, and asked
him what he was doing there and why he came up there to fight with the
damned niggers. Champ then took out a piece of paper and wrote
something, after which he pulled out his revolver and asked my partner,
'Where will you have it, in the back or in the face?' My partner said,
'For God's sake, don't kill me, soldier,' and then I heard the report of a
pistol and my partner fell over dead.

"There was no one with Ferguson at the time. He passed on near me, and went over to a log house where they were carrying our wounded. After about fifteen minutes, there were two Rebel soldiers passed me and I asked them to take me to the hospital. They took me to the log cabin, the same one I saw Champ enter. There was a hollow between the battlefield and the cabin, and as we got to the side of the hollow next to the cabin, Champ was coming out with two negro soldiers towards us. The Rebel soldiers with me said, 'Wait, and see what he does with them.' We saw him take them into the hollow about one hundred yards away and shoot them. He fired ten shots with a revolver.

"I asked the Rebel soldiers to hurry me to the hospital, as I was afraid he would overtake and shoot me, and they got me to the log cabin before Ferguson got back. He took two more negroes when he returned and not long afterwards, I heard more pistol shots.

"Ferguson had on something like a butternut suit at the time, and his hair and beard were long.

"I afterwards saw him at Emory and Henry Hospital, where the wounded prisoners of the Saltville fight were taken; it was two days later. He came into my room where I was lying. It was in the morning and he had another man with him. When he entered, he said, 'How are you getting along, boys?'

"There was a wounded boy out of the 11th Michigan Cavalry lying in a bunk nearby. The man with Champ said, 'There is that boy now. I saved his life. He was lying among negroes at the time.' Champ said, 'If I'd seen you lying among the negroes, it would have been all day with you.' The other man asked the boy if he had any money, to which he said, 'No,' and the man pulled out a $10 Confederate note and told him that would keep him in tobacco.

"Champ then said to me, 'Do you know Lieutenant Smith?' I told him, 'No.' He said, 'Yes you do, you d—d Yankee, you know him well enough, but you don't want to know him now. Where is he, then?' I made no reply, and they both got up to leave, and when they got to the door, Champ said, 'I have a begrudge against Smith; we'll find him.' After they were gone about ten minutes, I heard the report of a gun which sounded above me. I was on the second floor of the building. This happened about eight or nine o'clock in the morning."

On cross-examination by the defense, the witness made the following statements:

"The man I saw on the hill and who shot my partner, had on a butternut suit. I had never seen him before that time. His beard was long and dark. I didn't notice whether his mustache was trimmed. He had the appearance of not shaving at all. The battle of Saltville commenced on the 2nd of October, 1864, and ended on the evening of that day. The only man I ever saw with Ferguson was the one that came with him to the Emory and Henry Hospital. I don't know who that man was. I was treated first rate while in the hospital. I was removed from the log cabin between twelve and one o'clock the same day I went there. Ferguson wore no uniform of rank. I have never seen him since, until now.

"The way I knew it was Champ Ferguson was because when he was in the room where I was lying, he asked me what command I belonged to, and after I told him, he said, 'I suppose you have hearn tell of me; I am Champ Ferguson.'"

Thus, according to tradition and folk-lore in the Cumberlands, the eleventh and last man in the group that abused the wife and daughter of Champ Ferguson came to his end. The task to which Champ had set himself some three years before was now finished; his vengeance was now complete.

Who, really, was Lieutenant Smith? Had he fled the wrath of Champ Ferguson for three long years of war, knowing that his ten companions of three years before had met their deaths at his hands? Was this the reason Lieutenant Smith, given name unknown, was shot as he lay on his bunk in the Confederate hospital? We shall never know. Two other reasons were advanced—that Champ had been run out of Kentucky by Smith; and that Smith had killed Captain Hamilton, the Confederate guerilla leader with whom Champ was associated at various times during the War, after he was captured.

One thing stands out rather clearly,—that Lieutenant Smith was not killed just because he was a Yankee and fought in the Union

Army, else the other officer in the room, Captain Dagenfeld, would have been killed and the witness, Orange Sells, would not have lived to tell his tale.

In the statement made by Champ after the trial was over, he said:

"The Saltville Massacre, as it has been termed, was no work of mine. I was not in the fight, and did not kill any negroes as charged. I am charged with killing twelve soldiers at Saltville. I am innocent of the charge. I know they were killed by Hughes' and Bledsoe's commands and they were fairly killed in battle. There were thirty instead of twelve that fell on that day and it was in a regular fight.

"I acknowledge, however, that I killed Lieutenant Smith in Emory and Henry Hospital. I had a motive in committing the act. He captured a number of my men at different times, and always killed the last one of them. I was instigated to kill him, but I will not say by whom, as I do not wish to criminate my friends. Smith belonged to the 13th Kentucky, and operated around Burkesville. I will say this much—he never insulted my wife or daughter, as reported. He was a relative of my first wife and always treated my family with respect. He is the only man I killed at or near Saltville, and I am not sorry for killing him."

This statement ought to be convincing, but it is hardly so. It leaves one with a vague feeling of dissatisfaction,—a feeling that the statement can hardly be accepted at its face value. Ferguson had previously told the reporter that he did not kill Lieutenant Smith, that he had no reason to kill him. Now Champ says he did kill Smith, that he had a motive for killing him. Maybe Smith had killed Champ's friend, the guerilla leader, Hamilton; and maybe Smith was being murdered in revenge. We shall never know.

CHAPTER XVII

The Killings End

AFTER the Battle of Saltville, Champ Ferguson and his men, according to testimony presented by General Wheeler, again joined Wheeler's forces as they were dogging Sherman's footsteps through Georgia and up into South Carolina.

Somebody, however, was bringing pressure to bear back in Southwest Virginia that some action be taken against the murderer of Lieutenant Smith, and once more Champ Ferguson was detached from Wheeler's cavalry and sent to Virginia. Upon arrival there, he was placed under arrest by the Confederate authorities and held in jail at Wytheville, Va., pending trial. For nearly two months Champ was held a prisoner. On April 5th, on an order of General Echols which cited his long imprisonment and the impracticability of obtaining witnesses for a trial, he was released and ordered to rejoin his command.

Five days later, General Lee surrendered. What Champ Ferguson did during these five days we do not know. He probably found it impossible to rejoin Wheeler's command, which was now in North Carolina. On the other hand, it would have been foolhardy, with circumstances as they were, to attempt to return to the Cumberland Mountains. One of Ferguson's witnesses testified that Champ had told him he was with General Williams when Lee surrendered. If so, he did not surrender with General Williams' forces. Apparently he remained for the time being in Virginia. General George Stoneman telegraphed General Thomas from Knoxville on April 28, 1865, stating that he was clearing North Carolina and East Tennessee of all remaining bodies of Confederates and that he had ordered two or three brigades to scout down the Savannah River to learn if possible the whereabouts of Jefferson Davis and his company, with instructions to "follow them to the ends of the earth." His telegram concluded with the strange statement: "Champ Ferguson is in command of Southwest Virginia."

It is likely, however, that Ferguson had left Virginia before that date. If not, he traveled fast for the next two days, for about the 1st of May he and his men killed Van Duvall and John Hurt near Champ's old home in Clinton County, Kentucky. The names of these two men were not mentioned in the charges against Champ Ferguson, but testimony was presented during the trial by the prosecution concerning their deaths.

The first witness presented by the prosecution was L. W. Duvall:

"I was raised with Champ Ferguson and have known him ever since I knew anybody. I also knew Van Duvall and John Hurt. Both are dead. The former was a brother of mine."

Again, the counsel for the defense objected to the testimony, on the ground that the names of Duvall and Hurt were not mentioned in any specification of the charges and specifications, and could not apply to the first charge—that of being a guerilla.

The Judge Advocate referred to the decision in reference to the killing of Woods and Edwards, in the testimony of David Beatty.

"As to whether the proof submitted will apply to the first charge," he said, "the Commission cannot tell whether it will apply or not until they hear it."

The witness then resumed his testimony:

"Hurt and Duvall came to their deaths about the last of April or first of May, 1865, in Clinton County, Kentucky. I saw Ferguson at my father's residence, six miles east of Albany. About fourteen men were along, all mounted and armed, but I didn't know any of them except the accused. It was early in the morning, from half an hour to an hour by sun, when Van, Hurt, and myself were down by the spring, when we saw some men coming down the road that we didn't know.

"Two men came together first and went in to the horse lot; two more came up to the yard fence, and one of them got down and went up on the porch while the other one rode down to where we were standing, and ordered a surrender. The demand was made three times, and the third time the man took his pistol and shot at us. After ordering us to surrender a second time, Van Duvall had said to him, 'We don't know whose men you are.' The man stood there a little longer, and again demanded our surrender, asking for our arms. When we did not comply, it was then he took his pistol and fired at us as we stood there. Then Van Duvall and Hurt drew their pistols and fired at him. He pulled up his horse then and charged up the road a piece, and cried out, 'Hurry up with the command,' or something like that.

"As he did this, the other two boys started up the hill and turned down the branch, and they were soon out of sight. By this time the command passed me, and as it did so, Ferguson, I took it to be him, called out, 'Don't hurt that man,—that's Bug Duvall; I know him.' Bug is a nickname given to me.

"After they passed me, I saw neither them nor the two boys until after the killing was done. I heard several guns fire about five minutes after they passed me. One man was left to guard me. He asked me what command those two men belonged to. I told him they didn't belong to any. He said, 'Don't come here telling me your G—d d—d lies. I'll blow your brains out in a minute,' and he drew his pistol. Then a second man came up and told the man with me to go on, as he would guard me. I think the firing was still going on.

"The man with me then said, 'Let's go back to the house,' which we did, and while we were standing there, Ferguson came back. The first thing he said was to tell the guard to go on, and then I spoke and shook hands with him. The usual compliments were passed between us. Then Ferguson asked, 'Bug, what boys were those?' I told him Van Duvall and John Hurt. He said, 'They were killed up yonder.' Some conversation then took place between him and my sister, but I can't recollect the words. I think Ferguson turned to me and said, 'Bug, they commenced it,' or 'commenced with me,' I am not certain which. Then he turned and went off down the road toward Livingston, in the direction the others had gone.

"A mare belonging to me and a horse belonging to John Hurt were taken from my father's stable. I don't think any other property was taken.

"I helped bring in the bodies of my brother and Hurt just as soon as possible after Ferguson left. Both were dead when we found them. Hurt was shot in the back, the ball entering to the left of the back bone and coming out just below the nipple on the right side. He also had one shot in the head that didn't come out. My brother was shot in the back of the jaw on the right side and it came out about the center of the forehead.

"I am certain all this took place during the last days of April or first of May. I had heard of the fall of Richmond and the surrender of Lee before this took place. I took the papers and had read of it."

The witness was cross-examined by the defense:

"John Hurt was seven miles from where he lived, and Van Duvall was sixty miles from home, as he lived in Taylor County, Kentucky. The cause of his being away so far from home at that time was that my father was lying at the point of death and did die shortly afterwards. Van was there to see him.

"Van was armed with a navy, and Hurt had two. They always were armed when I saw them. We had gone to the spring to wash. They went there armed,—I suppose to be ready if anything occurred. I didn't follow the boys in their retreat up the hill, because I had no arms and saw no chance of defending myself. My brother and I had once belonged to the 12th Kentucky (Federal) Infantry. Hurt had belonged to the 13th Kentucky (Federal) Infantry, and had belonged to his brother's independent company before that, but none of us belonged to any command at that time.

"While talking to Ferguson, I told him my mare had been taken, and he said if I would go with him to the command I should have my mare back. My little boy spoke up and said some old horses had been left there, and I said I would try and get along with them."

Upon reexamination by the Judge Advocate, the witness revealed the circumstances surrounding the capture, or rather arrest, of

Champ Ferguson during the early days of the War, by a group of Union sympathizers, or Home Guard, including himself. Reference to this arrest was often made during the trial. It was undoubtedly an incident which rankled bitterly in the heart of Champ Ferguson, and probably had more than a little to do with his joining the other side:

"My brother moved away from Clinton County, Kentucky, in 1863 because he was afraid of Ferguson, and thought it unsafe to remain there. This came about because he had assisted in the arrest of Ferguson in the Fall of 1861. I and my brother, Van, William and Andy Huff, Ambrose Huddleston, James Padgett, and maybe some others were going down the road one evening about dark in the direction of Jimtown over in Fentress County, when we met Ferguson and a man named Denton. We all spoke, and they rode on. Something was said about stopping them. A portion of us agreed to it, and a portion did not, but finally we agreed to stop Ferguson and take him up.

"We turned round very quick and ordered him to halt and surrender. I think they presented their guns, mostly at Ferguson. Ferguson said, 'Hold on, there,' and my brother said, 'Don't raise your arms, Ferguson,' to which Ferguson replied, 'You'd as soon shoot a man as not.' My brother said, 'Yes, I'll blow your brains out if you move.'

"Then I spoke up and said, 'Boys, hold on, he has given up; don't hurt him.' No guns were fired, but I think they were told to give up their arms, which they did. Before they gave up their arms, they asked if they should have them back after they were tried, and were told they should. Denton had a square barrel navy revolver and a butcher knife. Ferguson had one of those Roland six shooters, commonly called a pepper box.

"We then all turned back and came to John Phillips' place, about ten miles from where we took them prisoners. The intention was to take them to Camp Dick Robinson. I left them at Phillips', and don't know how he got away, but heard later that Ferguson made his escape about the second night after they started for Camp Dick Robinson.

"We were going to Fentress County to get some property belonging to the Huffs when we met Ferguson and Denton. There were some

Rebel soldiers said to be on Wolf River at the time, and we took them prisoners to prevent their going back and telling these soldiers our business."

Evidently, Champ Ferguson had thus early ranged himself on the side of the South or else there was already bad blood between Ferguson and the Duvalls, the Huffs, the Huddlestons, and others. Champ said at one time that he joined the South in return for promise of non-prosecution for the killing of Ben Read at the Camp Meeting fight, but there may have been, and probably were, other reasons as well.

The next day, Martin Hurt, brother of John Hurt, was called to the stand. He said that he was in bed right by the window when he heard Ferguson and his men come up to the house; that he looked out the window and saw ten or fifteen men, some in the horse-lot and some running in the direction of where some firing was going on. He said that very soon he saw Ferguson come down the road about 35 yards from the house and heard him ask Bug Duvall who the two men were that ran away, and after Duvall had told him, heard Ferguson say that they had been killed up on the hill; and that Ferguson added, "I am going to kill all that would kill me, and you know they would kill me."

On cross-examination, Martin Hurt admitted to counsel for the defense that as soon as he heard the shooting begin, he hid himself under the house and saw what happened from his hiding place by looking through an opening where the underpinning had been pulled away. He said that he did not know whether anybody saw him before he hid under the house or not, but that as soon as the men left he also went off through the fields, not even taking time to help bring in the bodies of his brother and Van Duvall. Counsel for the defense asked him if he was not in fact chased from the house and across the fields, but the witness replied that he was not and that if anyone followed him across the fields he did not know it. Neither would the witness admit that he belonged to an independent company which his brother commanded nor that this company had killed some of Ferguson's men.

At least two facts stand out in this testimony: first, that Martin Hurt was in mortal fear of his own life, so afraid that he would not stay to help bring in the body of his dead brother; second, that Champ Ferguson had very definite ideas as to who should be killed —Van Duvall was killed, while his brother, Bug Duvall, who was also a member of the group that had taken Ferguson prisoner in the early Fall of 1861, was left unharmed.

CHAPTER XVIII

Birds of a Feather

THE trial of Champ Ferguson, so far as the prosecution was concerned, was gradually drawing to a close. As it progressed, however, they were by no means overlooking the fact that the first charge against him was that of being a guerilla. They attempted to show that during the early part of the War, at least, he was no more than a "common robber and plunderer."

Several witnesses were presented by the prosecution during the latter days of August whose testimony was solely to the effect that Ferguson was a robber and a thief. D. B. Wright testified that Champ Ferguson and some others robbed his store in Albany, Kentucky, of $1,500 to $2,000 worth of goods in September, 1861. Also Miss Mary L. Rogers stated that Champ and his men robbed their home at Rock Island, Tennessee, of a considerable quantity of goods in October, 1863. Probably the most interesting testimony presented along this line was that of Mrs. Julia Ann Williams and the wife and daughter of Dr. Hale.

Julia Ann Williams testified:

"Captain Ferguson, I mean the prisoner, brought a piano that belonged to Dr. Hale to Yankeetown to be sold. He didn't know what it ought to bring, but thought from three to five hundred dollars. He sold the piano to Mrs. Matt Anderson for two hundred dollars, some time after the Battle of Mill Springs. I can't recollect whether I paid the money over to Captain Ferguson or to his wife; it was paid to one or the other. As well as I can recollect, Ferguson said that Dr. Hale was in the Yankee army, that he held some position in it, and that we need not apprehend any trouble about his coming back and claiming the piano.

"There were a great many soldiers about there around that time. Sometimes they would say they belonged to Captain Ferguson and sometimes they would say they belonged to Captain Bledsoe, just as it happened.

"There were drugs and medicines brought to Yankeetown a little before this time, also some dishes and other wares, and placed at Mr. Bradley's, where they were sold. Mr. Ferguson boarded at Mr. Bradley's at the time.

"The piano was hauled in by a team of oxen, and the oxen were sold by Captain Ferguson to a Mr. Paul, I think."

Counsel for the defense took the witness for cross-examination:

Question—Was not Captain Ferguson generally recognized and believed to be a Confederate soldier?

Answer—So far as I know, I think he was.

Question—Was it not the custom among Confederate officers and soldiers to seize the property of Union men who had abandoned their homes?

Answer—The soldiers as a general thing would take property. I couldn't say what was the custom of the Confederate Army.

Mrs. Hale, wife of the Dr. Hale whose piano Ferguson had sold, related the following incidents:

"At the beginning of the War we lived in Fentress County but moved to Albany, Clinton County, Kentucky, in July, 1861, where we remained until the Spring of 1862. I knew Champ Ferguson by sight before the War started.

"One day after we had moved to Albany, I heard some cursing going on and stepping out in the front yard I saw Ferguson taking the saddle from a bay horse and putting it on a horse that belonged to Daniel Kogier. The horses were hitched in front of the court house. I heard Ferguson call Mr. Kogier a G—d d—d Lincolnite and dare him to come out of the court house.

"I then went around to a neighbor's house and soon afterwards Ferguson came by riding Kogier's horse. After that it was a very common thing to see Ferguson in Albany and generally ten or fifteen armed men were with him.

"About the first of April, 1862, he came to Albany with quite a large company, just about sundown. They came in front of our house, turned down the yard fence, and rode into the yard. One of the men came in and asked me where Dr. Hale was. I told him that I didn't know, I supposed he had gone to Nashville likely. This man then went on into my room, where I followed him, and then Ferguson came in the back door and also came into my room. He asked if there was any ammunition in the house or any guns or any kind of arms or gold or silver or watches; and he went to the mantel piece and took a powder horn that had one or two charges in it. I asked him to leave it but he took it anyway and then said:

" 'We have killed four G—d d—d Lincolnites today and intend to kill some more before we go home.'

"Then they went out of the room and started to leave the house when Ferguson saw a couple of overcoats and spoke to the man, saying:

" 'Here are two coats. By G—d, we must have these; they are worth a hundred dollars apiece.'

"Ferguson took the coats and went out the back way. Ferguson asked the men who were in the yard if they had seen anybody and they replied 'no one but some boys going across the flat.' Ferguson asked why they didn't shoot the boys. The men said they didn't want to be shooting boys. Ferguson then said,

" 'G—d d—n them, take them down as you go—you ought to have shot them.'

"After getting on their horses, they all went up town. They were gone about fifteen or twenty minutes when they came back and went through the yard down into the horse lot. They came back in a few minutes with three horses and two mules belonging to my husband. I went out and asked them if they had left any horses and Ferguson said, 'no.' I said they might have left one small mule that was very gentle as that was the only animal that I or any of the women in town had to go to mill on. A few of the men answered and said,

" 'Your men don't care anything about our women and we are not going to leave you anything.'

"I said I would have the horses back or the worth of them, and they said if we sent anybody after them they would never come back alive."

In answer to a question, Mrs. Hale said that they did not give the names of any of the "four G—d d—d Lincolnites" they said they killed that day, but her daughter, whom the records list as Miss P. A. Hale, said that she heard them mention someone by the name of Johnson as having been one of the four. She said that she was at Mrs. Minor Pickens' house at the time and that Ferguson and his party rode up there and called Allen Elder from the house and talked to him awhile at the front gate.

It is strange that Mrs. Hale made no mention of their piano in her testimony,—the piano which some time that spring took a jolting trip over the mountains in an ox wagon to be sold later to Mrs. Matt Anderson for two hundred dollars. It is also worth noting that Albany and its environs were at the time apparently in full control of the Rebel element; that the women were left in charge for the time being, and needed a gentle mule to go to mill on.

From the testimony of Mrs. Rogers, it seems that the goods taken from the Unionists were taken over the mountains to Yankeetown, a small settlement north of Sparta, where they were sold—mainly at a Mr. Bradley's,—and that Champ Ferguson on these trips stayed at the Bradley house. This was probably the Widow Bradley's place, near Sparta, where Champ Ferguson and his men met Colonel Blackburn after the close of the War to discuss terms of surrender. Something must have happened to Mr. Bradley in the meantime. Miss Hale's testimony indicates that the four men killed by Ferguson and his men that day were Johnson, Stover, Martin and Pierce. It may have been that same evening, within the hour after they left the Hale residence, that young Fount Zachery met his untimely end.

Where was Dr. Hale at the time and where was he during the trial? He did not testify, but Mr. Rogers, of the *Dispatch,* says that Dr. Hale published some pamphlets concerning Champ Ferguson, and that he asked Champ during the first "scoop" interview if he had read the pamphlets. Champ told him that he had seen Dr. Hale's first pamphlet at Squire Gwinn's one day and had read a portion of it; that it could not have been gotten up without a few important facts but that on the whole it was false. Mr. Rogers then reported Champ as making the following statement concerning Dr. Hale:

"I have never had any trouble with him and never gave him any cause to injure me. I think he is my worst enemy and is doing more against me than any other man. I distinctly recollect the last words we had. He and some others got into a row with some Rebels at Jimtown, and at that time the elements were equally divided. I was walking away from the crowd with a friend, when Dr. Hale called to me, 'Champ, come and help me out of this fuss.' I told him that I would not—that I already was under bond and would not engage in any row. This was the last communication that we had."

This incident happened, apparently, while the Hales still lived in Fentress County and was in the early days while men along the border were still taking sides and open hostilities had not started. Champ was out on bond for the killing of the constable, Ben Read, at the Camp Meeting fight. Even then, it seems there was no love lost between Champ Ferguson and Dr. Hale. The Hales were soon to move to Albany, Ky., in Champ's home county but found it necessary to leave there the following spring because, we may assume, Champ and his friends were rapidly relieving them of all their worldly possessions.

On August 25th the prosecution called their last witness to the stand, Captain Rufus Dowdy.

Captain Dowdy proved a most interesting witness but in many ways was probably of as much value to the defense as to the prosecution. Like Tinker Dave Beatty, his own activities during the War were such that any reference to them was of questionable value to the prosecution. His testimony was of a general character, and covered many phases of Ferguson's career—his status as a soldier, his theft of goods as a guerilla, and the circumstances surrounding his final seizure. It tended to show beyond question that the guerilla warfare in the mountains was a war without quarter so far as a good many participants were concerned, and that if Ferguson had ever been caught by the other side he would most certainly have been killed. It was the claim of the witness, as drawn out by the prosecution, however, that the Union guerilla companies were not organized until after Ferguson had terrorized the countryside and had organized his own company. It was again the old claim of "he started it."

Captain Dowdy's testimony also tended to show that Ferguson had organized his company "regularly," insofar as keeping a muster-roll was concerned, but in giving testimony concerning the finding of this muster-roll, he also gave testimony indicating that the charges that Ferguson had stolen a great deal of property were also true.

All in all, the satisfaction that either side might have been able to get out of the testimony of Rufus Dowdy was no doubt offset by features of the testimony tending to favor the opposite side. There can be no question but that Captain Dowdy was in the thick of the guerilla fighting throughout the War.

Question—Were you present at the time of the skirmish between the prisoner and his men and some Union soldiers about the 13th of February, 1864, near the house of Isham Richards, in Fentress County, Tennessee?

Answer—I was at old man Ragan's, near Isham Richards, with some ten or twelve of my men and some eight of Beatty's men. Some men came up that outnumbered us and we retreated. It was early in the morning, about half an hour after sunup. I can't say whether the prisoner was there or not.

Question—Did you see Dallas Beatty that morning? If so, when?

Answer—Dallas Beatty came there between daylight and sunup. Andrew Beatty and James J. Beatty were also along. They promised to volunteer with me. I was then serving as a Second Lieutenant, commanding thirty-five men, and was recruiting a company for the First Tennessee Mounted Infantry. I don't know where Dallas Beatty was at the time we were attacked, but I do know I saw him that morning.

Question—Were you at the prisoner's house in White County, Tennessee, in August, 1864, or about that time? If so, state what property you found there, and give a description of it as far as you can.

Answer—I was there about the last of August or first of September, 1864. We found some bolts of flannel outside of the Ferguson farm, in the woods, also some cashmeres, silk, some coffee, some soda, some shoes, and some sutler's goods. Some sandpaper, some calico, and other articles were found in the house. The goods that we found in the woods were concealed in hollow trees and under logs and under rocks where they could be kept dry.

So far as I know, we didn't see Ferguson at the time, although while we were hunting for the goods among the rocks and logs, I looked up and saw a man's back as he was going away. One of my men went up a little distance and brought down a sorrel horse, which I don't know but think was a horse Ferguson raised. We didn't see anybody else there at all.

Captain Dowdy was asked by counsel for the defense:

Question—Did you ever get possession of the muster-roll of Captain Ferguson's company? If so, when and where?

Answer—I got hold of some blanks in form of a muster-roll and payroll with some names written on it. I got it out there in the woods near Ferguson's house, at the time I got the goods I spoke of. It was in a box packed up in the hollow of a chestnut tree. The box was held up by some poles punched up the hollow of the tree, and when the boys pulled the poles out the box fell down.

The witness was then placed under re-examination by the Judge Advocate:

Question—What orders were you acting under at the time you were at Mrs. Bradley's in May last, and had you anything to do at all with the negotiations for surrender?

Answer—I was ordered to Sparta to escort Judge Goodpasture and bring back General Dibrell to Mrs. Bradley's, and then to go on to Livingston with Judge Goodpasture. I had no orders to take part or participate in the surrender.

At this point, counsel for the defense asked the privilege of introducing General Joe Wheeler as a witness for the defense. It may be presumed that General Wheeler could only be in Nashville for a short while, that he had probably not been subpoenaed as a witness but was merely passing through the city, and counsel wished to take advantage of the opportunity to secure his testimony in behalf of the accused. The Judge Advocate gave his consent, and General Wheeler's testimony will be discussed later.

After the examination of General Wheeler had been completed, Captain Dowdy was again placed on the stand and was examined by the defense, as follows:

Question—You say that you at one time found a muster and payroll purporting to be a roll of Ferguson's company. Is the one here shown you the one you found?

Answer—I found three sheets, or I and some others did, and this I presume to be one of them from the remarks on the roll and the general appearance of the papers. There were two others, but I am not able to say who got them.

Question—Look on the names on that roll. Do you recognize them as belonging to Ferguson's company?

Answer—Here is Sublett, one who was represented as First Lieutenant. Abner Hildreth, 4th Corporal, was one of my neighbors; I understand him to be one of Ferguson's men. Richard Burchett is represented on the roll as being killed in June, 1863, in Wayne County, Kentucky, when, in fact, he was killed in October, 1862, in Clinton County, Kentucky. I was along when he was killed, and seeing that mistake, I remember noting it at the time, which makes me the more confident that this is the paper I got. Burchett was killed before Ferguson appears in the roll as having been mustered, and such is my recollection. I knew J. T. Smith, who is represented on this roll as having been killed about July 12, 1863; I understood him to be one of Ferguson's men. I know A. H. Foster; he was regarded as Second Lieutenant in Ferguson's company. I also know W. R. Latham, who is put down as 3rd Lieutenant; he was regarded as a lieutenant in Ferguson's company. G. W. Twifford told me he was Orderly Sergeant. I knew Philpot; he belonged to Ferguson's company.

Some few of the men I didn't know. Most of them I do know, and they were reported belonging to Ferguson's company.

Question—Did you know Elijah Kogier, Elam Huddleston, John Crabtree, William Johnson, Fount Zachery, James Zachery, William Frogg, B. Tabor, James Stover, Louis Pierce, Alexander Huff, Joseph Beck, Peter and Allen Zachery, John Williams, and David Delk? If so, do you know anything upon the subject of their making threats upon the life of Ferguson and his men, or seeking their lives, or making a war of extermination against them? If so, state it.

Answer—I knew Elijah Kogier. I can't say that I knew Crabtree. I knew William Johnson and Fount Zachery. Tabor, I knew, but didn't know his given name. I didn't know Stover. I knew Alex Huff, Joseph Beck, Peter and Allen Zachery, John Williams, and David Delk. I and Williams and Delk were enlisted together and became soldiers in the Federal Army in June, 1862, and we were sent out to recruit a company or to help do it for the 7th Tennessee. We put on the blue in the morning, and started directly after we ate our dinners. We came into Fentress County, and in coming on, we expected to encounter Ferguson and his men. The general understanding was that if we got hold of Ferguson we would kill him.

As for Alex Huff, I don't know anything about his making any statement against Ferguson in any way. Johnson belonged to a sort of independent company that gathered in February or March after the Mill Springs fight, under Tom Woods. I heard him state he would kill Ferguson if he came across him. He was in search of him when I saw him. I never heard Elijah Kogier make any threats or knew of his making any demonstrations against Ferguson. I heard Huddleston make threats against Ferguson; he said that he would kill him if he came across him.

I can't say anything about Crabtree. Two of the Crabtree boys were with Delk and myself. I don't recollect their names; they were very young, and I think they are both living. I don't suppose Fount Zachery ever made any threats against Ferguson; he was nothing but a boy, and was trying to get away out of the country when he was killed. I saw him the evening before he was killed and advised him to leave the country, and he was trying to get away. I can't so well state whether I ever heard James Zachery make any threats against Ferguson. I don't think I ever did. He was away with the Army, but would come home occasionally to see his folks. He generally had arms, but I don't know that he ever sought Ferguson. He had four boys in the Federal Army, in Wolford's regiment.

William Frogg, I don't know anything about. Tabor was pretty much like Zachery; his boys were in the Army, and he was in and out. I saw him with some soldiers of the 1st Kentucky Cavalry. The soldiers were hunting Ferguson, I suppose; that's the way I understood them. Joseph Stover, I didn't know, nor Louis Pierce. Alexander Huff, I never heard make any threats or saw him going around with any parties. I knew Joseph Beck but I never saw him but once after the War came up. He was then coming out from Nashville and told me he was discharged from the Federal Army.

As for Peter Zachery, I couldn't say that I ever heard him make any threats against Ferguson or knew of his hunting him. He was the father of Fount Zachery. Allen Zachery, I have heard make threats against Ferguson and I knew of his hunting him. Allen and Peter Zachery both belonged to the 1st Kentucky Cavalry and went out in the commencement of the War.

Question—You say that those men made threats and sought the life of Ferguson and his men. Were they to be killed whenever found? Was any quarter given or to be given to them?

Answer—They were going to kill Ferguson whenever they found him, and give no quarter.

Question—Were those independent companies that you spoke of on your previous examination likewise seeking the life of Ferguson and his men, and was quarter to be given them?

Answer—The companies would have given quarter to some of Ferguson's men, and did do it, but they would have killed Ferguson if they had caught him.

Question—You have been asked about independent bands being organized in Clinton County, Kentucky, and Fentress County, Tennessee. State when they were organized and whether it was before or after Ferguson was acting with a company in that region.

Answer—It was after Ferguson was acting with a company. There were no independent Union companies formed there until after the Fishing Creek and Mill Springs fight. Before the Mill Springs fight, Ferguson, Philpot, Moses, and others, sometimes eight or ten, sometimes as high as twenty, were running around that country taking stock, etc., and there were no Union companies then. After the Mill Springs fight, the Union men came back into that country, but some Rebels came back too, and Ferguson's band increased until the Union men had to take to the bushes.

Finally, independent companies were formed, sometime in February or March, 1862. Shortly after that, there was a compromise and the Union men went home and went to work. I was not at the compromise but heard of it, and saw some of our men after they had gone home and they told me about it. Shortly after that, McHenry and his company came in, and then the thing went on again. It was about that time that several men were killed,—Zachery among them. Reuben Woods and William Frogg had been killed before the Mill Springs fight.

Question—You have also been asked about hearing threats against Ferguson and his men, and about what Delk and Williams and yourself said; also about seeing parties in pursuit of Ferguson and what was said. Now state all that was said in connection with those threats and expeditions and why they were made.

Answer—Some of them stated that Ferguson and some of his men had killed their relatives and taken their property, and that he would not take them prisoners if he caught them, or if he did, he would kill them afterwards; and that they would not take him prisoner.

Question—You used the expression all along that you and these men would not take Ferguson and some of his men prisoners, or allow them to surrender. If they were taken prisoners or allowed to surrender, were any threats made to kill them under these circumstances, or do you mean that they would not receive the surrender of or take such men prisoners?

Answer—I mean we wouldn't take them prisoners. I can't tell what would have been done if they had been taken prisoners. I suppose it would have depended upon the power to prevent. There was a man called "Yank"—I don't know his real name—who ran with Ferguson, who was taken prisoner and was killed, but he was killed before I got up. A man named Richardson was also killed, and a man named Evans saved by Elam Huddleston. This was shortly before Huddleston was killed. "Yank" had surrendered to me and I had assured him he shouldn't be killed, but I couldn't help myself. I had received his surrender and gone by Filkin's to get a horse, and before I could get up there they had killed him and Richardson both.

They were killed right close to Mrs. Owens' place, Ferguson's mother-in-law. They were taken at the house of Alexander Evans. Elam Huddleston was rather considered in command, but I was managing partly. Huddleston wanted to save all the prisoners, and prevent any more being killed.

The witness, Captain Rufus Dowdy, was not to receive any rest; he was again cross-examined by the defense:

Question—You will state what company it was that the prisoner joined after he was arrested early in the War, as you have stated.

Answer—It is said that he joined Scott Bledsoe's company. I can't say that he joined it, but I understood that he joined it and I saw him with the company just a few days after he came back after he was arrested.

Question—At the time of the prisoner's arrest, were you not engaged to saw some plank by Ferguson, and was he not coming to see you about that?

Answer—As to his arrest, I knew nothing about it. I only understood that he was arrested. I know nothing of where he was going at the time or what his business was. He had plank at the mill and a few days before that he had hauled a load away.

While they probably realized it was not doing their case much good, the defense was apparently attempting to show that the whole affair was more or less a case of "the pot calling the kettle black." It is fairly apparent that Capt. Dowdy and Champ Ferguson "understood" each other. They were birds of a feather, and now that the War was ended were not averse to doing business with each other. An ironical twist is given the affair by the fact that Capt. Dowdy, who had burned Ferguson's home in August, 1864, was in May, 1865, sawing lumber with which Champ was planning to rebuild!

CHAPTER XIX

For the Defense---General Joe Wheeler and Others

IT must have been a tragically bitter dose for Champ Ferguson and his friends to swallow in that they were able to secure only three or four scattered witnesses to testify in his behalf. Nor were these witnesses anything more than character witnesses. They were not intimately acquainted with the facts of the murders with which Champ Ferguson was charged. They were unable to testify in any respect that Champ Ferguson had not committed these murders. They were unable to prove that Champ Ferguson killed these persons in self-defense. Nor could they prove that Champ Ferguson was a regularly enlisted soldier in the Confederate Army.

Witnesses for the defense were able to indicate, as did the witnesses for the prosecution, that guerilla warfare was about the same on both sides, but from a strictly legal viewpoint, Champ Ferguson's witnesses were of very little use. Counsel for the defense, however, endeavored to make the best possible use of them.

Champ Ferguson had been able to secure one outstanding witness, General Joseph Wheeler of the Confederate Army. General Wheeler was presented not as a witness to rebut any of the charges of murder but in support of the contention that Champ Ferguson and his men had been an integral part of the regular Confederate Army. It was hoped, no doubt, that General Wheeler's rank and reputation would give his testimony considerable weight.

"Little Joe," as General Wheeler was called by his men, was only twenty-four years old at the outbreak of the War. He had graduated from West Point the previous year and had been assigned to duty in New Mexico, but resigned to enlist in the Confederate cause. He was a small man, five feet two inches in height, weighing little more than a hundred pounds. While he lacked the dash and boldness of Morgan and Forrest, yet in the ability to take an order, understand it thoroughly, and carry it through to execution, he excelled them both. His rise was meteoric; as early as July, 1862, he was placed in command of all the cavalry of the Army of Tennessee.

When Jefferson Davis fled south through North Carolina during the latter part of April, 1865, he called upon the cavalry to protect him. With the North in a frenzy over the death of Lincoln, this was a dangerous mission to undertake, but Wheeler, since he had not been present when General Johnston surrendered, felt he could do it without violating any parole. He therefore went to his troops near Greensboro, N. C., and with six hundred men who volunteered for the job, set out for Washington, Ga., where Davis expected to join them.

On May 10, 1865, however, about twelve hours before they were expected to make connection at Washington, Davis and his party were captured by the Federals. Wheeler thereupon separated his force into small groups in an effort to escape, but he and his group were soon captured while they slept and taken to Athens, Ga., where they joined Davis, Alexander H. Stephens, and others as prisoners. Wheeler was sent to prison at Fort Delaware. After being held for about a month he was released early in June. Now, nearly three months later, on August 25, 1865, he was in Nashville to testify in behalf of one of "his men." Champ Ferguson and his command had joined up with Wheeler's command just one year before, in August, 1864. Ferguson was transferred for a period in the fall of 1864 to General Breckenridge, but returned to Wheeler's command right after the Battle of Saltville in October, where he remained until around February 1, 1865, when he was ordered back to western Virginia.

The first questioning of General Wheeler by the defense was an effort to show that, while Champ Ferguson had been arrested by the Confederate authorities themselves for the killing of Lieutenant

Smith, they had been able to produce no proof and accordingly had released him from the charge:

Question—Did you know Brigadier-General Echols, of the Confederate Army? Look upon this order dated April 5, 1865, here shown you, and state whether the same is genuine.

Answer—I have seen General Echols on one occasion. I know J. Stoddard Johnson, whose name appears signed to the order, and have often seen his signature. To the best of my knowledge, that is his signature, and I regard the order as a genuine order.

The following is a copy of the document referred to:

Head Qrs. W. Va. & E. Tenn.
Wytheville, Va., April 5, 1865

Special Orders No. ———

III. In view of the long arrests to which they have been subjected, and the impracticability of procuring witnesses for the trial of their cases, the following officers awaiting trial are relieved from arrest and will report for duty with their command as soon as communication with the same will admit.

J. Stoddard Johnson, A.A.G.
By Command of
Brig.-Gen. E. Echols

Capt. Champ Ferguson
Lieut. William Hildreth

To Capt. Ferguson:

This document revealed the name of the soldier who was with Champ Ferguson when he killed Lieutenant Smith. Indeed Will Hildreth had accompanied Ferguson many times before on his raids of vengeance.

The next questioning of the witness was an attempt to show that Ferguson was a regular officer in the Confederate Army, as was indicated in the document submitted.

Question—You will please state whether the prisoner was received and regarded as a Captain in the Confederate Army.

Answer—1 always heard him spoken of as Captain, but never saw him until January or February, 1865. He was then ordered by Col. Stoddard Johnson to western Virginia and after his arrival there, Col. Johnson wrote to me asking in regard to his status as an officer. On investigation, I was informed that he had been authorized by General Kirby-Smith to raise a company of cavalry for service on the Kentucky border. He was called and regarded as a Captain in the Confederate service. My understanding was that he raised his company in 1862. I am not certain about the date, but it must have been as far back as that. I reported to Col. Johnson that I regarded Ferguson as a Captain in the Confederate service.

Question—What was the custom in the Army in receiving captains, and drawing rations and subjecting them to orders, who had been elected captains of companies under the authority of the Secretary of War, but who had not yet received commissions?

Answer—It was customary when a man was authorized to raise a company, and did so, to regard him as an officer, upon producing his muster roll. I don't know of a single instance of the War Department issuing commissions to line officers in the cavalry service. The War Department declined issuing commissions to line officers, telling them their muster rolls were sufficient.

Question—How long did Captain Ferguson and his company remain under your command, and did they draw rations and obey orders as other companies?

Answer—In August, 1864, I assumed control of the cavalry and ordered it to go to the Army of Tennessee. Captain Ferguson and a portion of his company marched with a portion of my command to Georgia and finally to South Carolina. There was a period of time during which Capt. Ferguson's command was detached from me and ordered to report to General Breckenridge by the War Department. This was about the time of the Battle of Saltville. My understanding and information are that Ferguson and his command remained with General Breckenridge until after the Battle of Saltville. After that he reported back to me. Captain Ferguson remained with me until some time either in January or February, 1865, when I was ordered to send him to western Virginia.

Question—How did he conduct himself while under your command?

Answer—When in Georgia he got into some trouble with the guards, I never knew exactly what it was, and was placed in arrest by General Dibrell, after which he conducted himself with the greatest propriety.

It will be noted that General Wheeler was careful not to state, if indeed he knew, why Ferguson was ordered back to western Virginia during the latter part of January or early February, 1865, to stand trial for the murder of Lieutenant Smith.

The Adjutant General's office in Washington, D. C., states that their records show that Champ Ferguson was arrested and received at Wytheville, Virginia, on February 8, 1865, and that his name appears on a list of prisoners in the guard house at that place February 20, 1865, charged with killing Federal prisoners. Opposite his name, however, appear the words "on parole." The records of this office do not include the order of Col. Stoddard Johnson of April 5, 1865, releasing Ferguson and Hildreth from this charge.

General Wheeler was now to be examined by counsel for the prosecution with the intent of showing that Champ Ferguson and his band had not come into the Army in the regular manner, and that they had committed acts that violated all regular army regulations.

Question—Were you not in command of all the cavalry of the Army of Tennessee during the years 1863 and 1864?

Answer—I was assigned to the command of all the cavalry of the Army of the Mississippi, which afterwards became the Army of the Tennessee, in July, 1862.

Question—Was there not a general order issued in 1862 requiring all the independent companies or partisan rangers authorized by Kirby-Smith to join some regiment and be placed on the same footing as your other cavalry troops?

Answer—The only order on that subject that I recollect was an order issued by me, near Murfreesboro, directing that all such companies should report to me their organization and authority for existence.

Question—Did you ever get such a report from Ferguson, and if so, when?

Here the Prosecution thought they had Wheeler in a corner, but he wiggled out of it:

Answer—I don't recollect. My order did not apply to any troops authorized by General Kirby-Smith. My department was called Department No. 2, and did not include East Tennessee. That part of the country was under the order of Kirby-Smith.

Question—Then prior to July, 1862, the prisoner did not report to you and you don't know officially anything about his company?

Answer—No, sir, prior to August, 1864, he did not report to me.

Question—You say you heard of him as a Captain as far back as 1862. Will you state whether there were any orders issued by you or your government, to your knowledge, authorizing the shooting or killing of men after they had surrendered or when captured and disarmed?

The question was objected to by the defense as impertinent and irrelevant. The objection was overruled.

Answer—No, sir, there were no such orders issued.

Question—In what way did you hear of the prisoner as an officer prior to July, 1864?

Answer—During parts of April and May, 1863, I was at McMinnville. I think I heard of Captain Ferguson being on the Kentucky border, but no orders were issued from any officer to him that I know of and no reports were received from him, or if any such were received, they were received through other parties and not from him.

Question—You speak of his authority coming from Kirby-Smith. Is it not a fact that Jefferson Davis was opposed to the partisan ranger organizations and refused to authorize any such bands; and that all the authority there ever was for such companies emanated alone from Kirby-Smith?

In answering this question, General Wheeler went into some detail concerning the organization and command of the western armies of the Confederacy. He said that at first President Davis was in favor of partisan organizations; that it was the duty of the Department commanders to organize such companies, which they did until orders were issued by the War Department in 1864 prohibiting the forming of new organizations of this type. He then went on to say that General Kirby-Smith was in command of the Department of East Tennessee until he went to the Trans-Mississippi Department in December, 1862, and that after that there was some difficulty among the Confederate officers as to who had control. He stated that after the headquarters of the Department of East Tennessee were moved from Knoxville towards Chattanooga in the fall of 1863, there arose some difference of opinion between General Buckner and General Bragg as to the existence of that Department any longer, General Buckner insisting that he had the right to issue orders for that Department from the vicinity of Chattanooga while General Bragg insisted that he had no such authority, that no such Department existed. General Wheeler mentioned other Confederate generals as having command for a part of the time in that region and that there was some question among them as to just how far the authority of each extended. (He was thereby probably referring publicly for the first time to the differences between the commanding generals of the Army of Tennessee which plagued the western armies of the Confederacy throughout the War.)

Question—You say that Ferguson was sent to Breckenridge about the time of the Battle of Saltville, and after that battle he reported back to you. How long was he absent from your corps, and did he report when he came back that he had obeyed the order and been with Breckenridge?

Answer—The prisoner belonged to General Williams' command and Williams was ordered to report to Breckenridge and did so. I suppose the prisoner went into his command. I never heard anything to the contrary.

The defense had one more question to put to General Wheeler:

Question—Please examine the muster roll produced in court by Captain Dowdy, it being captured from the prisoner. Has it the appearance of the printed muster rolls furnished the captains in the Confederate service?

Answer—It has, to the best of my knowledge and belief.

"Little Joe" Wheeler, having finished his testimony, went on to Alabama to marry the young widow with whom he had fallen in love during the War. He had done the best he could for Champ Ferguson. He had made it clear that whatever doubts the Confederate authorities may have had as to the authenticity of Ferguson's command had been dissipated upon investigation and that so far as they were concerned, Champ Ferguson was a Captain in the Confederate Army.

General Wheeler had been fearless in his testimony as he had been fearless in war. He had told a straightforward story with no attempt at deception even when his testimony might reflect somewhat upon the character of the man he was trying to help. The prosecution intimated that General Wheeler should have determined long before February, 1865, or even August, 1864, the regularity of Ferguson's command. They also attempted to cast a reflection of doubt upon the authenticity of the order from the Headquarters of East Tennessee releasing Champ Ferguson from prison. In reply, General Wheeler freely explained the differences of opinion and the conflict of authority among the Confederate leaders of that section. This might have been a hard thing for a Southern general to do before a military court of the Federal Army. But that was now history and if a Confederate soldier in danger of his life could be helped by the telling, General Wheeler was quick to make his choice. The reputation of Joe Wheeler lost nothing by his attempt to aid a Confederate guerilla of the Cumberland Mountains. He was to go forward to a long life of service to his reunited country.

The next few days were filled with legal squabbles and bitter recriminations. During these days the defense presented its three additional witnesses. In attempting to make the most of the testimony these witnesses were able to give, they incurred the continual objections of the prosecution and several times the Military Commission adjourned court to decide upon the points at issue.

On August 30th, the defense presented Alexander Officer. He stated that he lived in the upper edge of Putnam County, Tennessee, five miles from where Champ Ferguson lived, and that he was acquainted with the general character and standing of the prisoner in the neighborhood. He was asked what Champ's attitude in general had been towards men of Union sentiment, whereupon the Judge Advocate objected that the general character of the prisoner could not be sustained by particular acts nor could the shooting of one man be justified by showing that he used other men entertaining the same sentiments well. This objection was sustained by the court.

After testifying that Champ Ferguson's character was good in the neighborhood in which he lived, the witness was asked:

"State what you may know of his protecting Union citizens against the stealing and raids of men holding themselves out as Southern men."

This question was also objected to by the Judge Advocate, who said:

"How does the fact that the prisoner prevented somebody from stealing at one time and place tend to disprove the killing of a man at another time and place?"

To this objection, the defense replied:

"The prisoner proposes to prove that he, in all cases, protected Union men, and that he punished Southern men who stole their property or committed raids upon them, and, further, that he molested no one on account of his Union sentiments, but he only made war upon those who made war upon him and his men, and who were engaged in seeking his life and the lives of his men. And he further proposes to prove that this was his aim and is his general character."

In order to allow the Judge Advocate time to prepare a written argument, and for the deliberation of the Court upon the point raised, the Court adjourned to meet at eight o'clock the following morning. If one were permitted some second-guessing seventy-five years later, it might be that counsel for the defense made their greatest tactical error of the trial in ever setting up the claim that Champ Ferguson protected Union men and Southern men alike, that it was his general aim and character to protect the oppressed in all cases regardless of their allegiance.

Upon assembling Court the following morning, the Judge Advocate presented a lengthy argument on the objections he had raised and the counter-claims of the defense. He said that the rules of evidence as to character were too well known to admit of much controversy. Also, that as to the proposition of the accused to prove that the parties he slew were hunting him down and threatening his life, if he could prove that by anybody who knew it was so, all right, but that he objected to proving this by proving Ferguson's reputation.

"As to his proving his acts of protecting Union men from the depredations of his co-rebels, if that may be done at all," continued the Judge Advocate, "it would have to be done like any other matter of reputation and be confined to a time anterior to the acts for which he is prosecuted, which takes it back to 1861. If this is to be proven by reputation, it must come in under all the rules pertaining to reputation.

". . . . The argument of the defense is: Ferguson prevented somebody from robbing some Union men. Therefore, he did not rob Wright's store in 1861 and other parties after that; and he did not kill the various parties whom he is proven to have killed. Establish such a rule as the defense contends for, and you license murder. . .. .."

After this argument had been presented by the Judge Advocate, the Commission announced its decision, saying in part:

It is no defense to the crime of murder to prove that the slayer did not kill the neighbor of the slain man.

It being proven that A stole B's horse, how does the fact that he did not steal C's horse, or even that he prevented D from stealing E's horse, tend to disprove the fact that A did steal B's horse?

Does the fact that the strong man, armed, spared some members of a family disprove the fact that the head of that family was murdered?

. . . . He proposes to prove that he only made war upon those who made war upon him. This he may also do, but he must do it by proving the fact that those he made war upon first made war upon him.

. . . . We do not wish to be understood in this opinion as saying that if all the facts here mentioned were proven, it would justify the killing of disarmed and disabled prisoners. But we will hear such testimony when it is presented in legitimate form and consider what bearing it may have on the case and its value as evidence. It is the desire of the Court to hear any testimony which will justify or disprove the acts charged against the prisoner.

The Commission were not leaving any loopholes for use of the testimony that was being offered by witnesses for the defense, and were making a strong case to show that both law and reason supported them in their stand. Counsel for the defense, however, could hardly be blamed for "grasping at straws."

The examination of Alexander Officer by counsel for the defense continued:

Question—Say whether you saw the prisoner and his men on the 24th of May, 1865, on the road leading to Mrs. Bradley's, the place of the surrender. If so, did you have any conversation with the prisoner as to where he was going and the object?

Answer—Yes, sir, I saw them. I asked the prisoner if he was going up with the balance of the boys and his answer was, yes, he was going. I told him I thought it was the best for them all to go up. He didn't tell me anything about his reasons for going up, but from a conversation I had with him about a week before that, I think it was on account of a letter from Colonel Blackburn.

Question—You will please state what were the circumstances of the prisoner up to the time of his capture in regard to property and means of living.

Counsel for the prosecution had been attempting to show that by means of theft of goods and livestock during the War, Champ had accumulated a sizeable amount of property, and this counsel for the defense was trying to rebut.

Answer—His circumstances were just limited.

In answer to further questioning, the witness gave the following information:

"After raising a company in 1862, Champ Ferguson was called the Captain. Opposing him were two independent companies on the Union side, those of Captain David Beatty and Captain Elam Huddleston. I don't know anything about a Union flag being carried to Beatty's house by a group of Rebels. A group of us went to Beatty's house in February or March, 1862, as well as I recollect, but I don't know anything about a Union flag. We were in command of Lieut. McGinnis, of Captain Scott Bledsoe's company. I didn't know Mr. Ferguson at the time."

A further question by the defense, attempting to show that Ferguson did not kill his prisoners, as claimed:

"Do you know if Ferguson was taking prisoners and releasing them?"

This question was objected to by the Judge Advocate, who said:

"Releasing one prisoner doesn't justify or excuse the taking and killing of another prisoner."

The objection, as usual, was sustained by the Court, and the witness was then cross-examined by the Judge Advocate, giving in substance the following answers:

"It is about sixty or seventy miles from where I live to Albany, in Clinton County, Kentucky. I don't know how many times I have been up in there since 1862, but I have talked to several citizens of Clinton County about Ferguson's character since that time. Mr. Harrington was one of the persons I talked to.

"It is about forty or fifty miles from where I live to Dave Beatty's. I wasn't a member of the company that went to Beatty's at the time we have been speaking of. The reason I happened to go was because a man came along and forced me out."

Question—Was that the only expedition you were ever forced to go upon?

Answer—I object to answering the question.

Question—What was the object of going to Beatty's that day?

Answer—The object was to put down robbing and stealing, I was told.

Question—Who was robbing and stealing at Beatty's house?

Answer—No person, as I know of.

The witness for the defense was not doing so well.

It was a claim of the defense that Ferguson and his guerillas were acting under orders and by authority in committing the acts with which they were charged. The prosecution attempted to disprove this claim and, at the same time, probably, reflect somewhat on the good intentions of certain well-known Southerners of the section, including as will be noted later, the senior counsel for the defense, Judge Guild:

Question—State if you know whether inflammatory speeches were ever made in your neighborhood encouraging guerillas or independent bands. If so, who made those speeches and what was the line of remark?

Answer—I don't think there were ever any made.

Question—Were any speeches made by citizens there or anyone coming into the neighborhood?

Answer—If there were, I never heard of it—no speeches of any kind since the rise of the rebellion.

The answers the prosecution was trying to elicit from the witness were to be given a few days later by Captain Rufus Dowdy, when he was called to the stand.

The testimony of the next witness for the defense, Elisha Cameron, was not to take long:

"I live in White County, Tennessee, and have known the prisoner about three years, perhaps a little over. His character has been very good since he has been in our county."

Question—Have you made inquiries in regard to his character previous to the War? And do you think you are acquainted with his character previous to the War? If so, what was it?

Hereupon, the Judge Advocate again objected, saying:

"The witness lives in White County, Tennessee, seventy miles from where the prisoner resided before the War, and this long range swearing ought to be stopped."

The objection was again sustained by the Court.

Question—What property has the prisoner?
Answer—I don't know that he has any property in our county now except his little farm. He has a small chunk of a farm, worth I suppose $500 to $1,000.

The prosecution only asked one question:

Question—How much of the time since 1862 has Ferguson been in White County, and that region of the country?
Answer—I am not able to tell. He has been occasionally away. Up to last Fall, he hardly ever was away long at a time.

The next, and last, witness presented for the defense was Carrol Johnson:

"I have known Champ Ferguson some three years, or longer. His general reputation in our neighborhood is good, and I have never heard anything said against him in that country.

"I was present at the meeting at Mrs. Bradley's on May 24, 1865. Captain Walker told me he had a letter from Col. Blackburn and showed it to me. I told him that under the terms of that letter, he ought to surrender; that there were too few of them to do any good and as all the rest had surrendered, I thought he had better surrender too. He said he would. The letter you have here in court is not the one Walker showed to me."

After some argument back and forth concerning the letter, the court adjourned until the following morning, at which time counsel for the defense presented the following affidavit:

MILITARY COMMISSION ROOM
DISTRICT MIDDLE TENNESSEE
Nashville, Tenn., August 30, 1865.

United States Criminal Action
vs
Champ Ferguson

The prisoner makes oath that the letter of Colonel Blackburn, inviting Captain Walker, and the guerillas generally, to come in, and upon which they should secure protection, is not in his possession or control. He is informed and believes the same is lost. It was captured from Captain Walker by some Union soldiers as he is informed, and cannot now be found. Since the trial he has dispatched a special messenger to procure said letter, and the same cannot be found. This is one of the letters spoken of by Colonel Blackburn before this Court, in his testimony in which he admits he wrote such letter. He asks to be permitted to prove its contents.

(signed) CHAMP FERGUSON

To this affidavit, the Judge Advocate objected:

"The affidavit does not show when nor where the letter was lost. It does not show what search has been made, nor where it was made, nor by whom it was made."

The Court then rendered a lengthy decision, the substance being that counsel for the defense had not tried very hard to produce the proper witnesses or even the letter itself, provided there really was such a letter:

It is urged in the remarks of counsel for the accused that the letter was in Captain Walker's coat pocket, and the coat was lent to a young man to wear, and that this young man had lost the letter. Where is this young man? Who is he? Why cannot he be produced? For aught we are shown, he may be in Nashville. He should be here as a witness or reason shown why he is not here. And if the accused is unable to procure this young man as witness, then Captain Walker should be produced, as he was the proper custodian of the letter.

The Court is of opinion that due diligence, as contemplated by law, has not been made to produce the letter in court, and the motion to produce oral evidence is, therefore, overruled.

Counsel for the defense then resumed questioning of the witness, Carroll Johnson:

Question—You will state, since the commencement of this trial, if you were directed by the prisoner or his counsel to return to White County and make diligent search after the letter inquired about. You will state what search or inquiry you made on the subject and whether the letter is lost or not.

Answer—I was requested to do so by Judge Guild. I went to Captain Walker, who was the man who had the letter, and asked him for the letter. He said Mrs. Ferguson had asked him for it; and he said the letter had been in his coat pocket, that his coat had been worn off by a young man that belonged in his company, that he had searched for the letter for three days, and that it was bound to be lost or it would have been found.

The accused then submitted the following proposal through his counsel:

The prisoner proposes to prove by the witness, Carrol Johnson, that the letter enquired of from Col. Blackburn to Capt. Walker invited the independent bands and bands of guerillas to come in and surrender, and that they should be protected by the Government, and that that letter was shown the prisoner, and that he concluded to accept its terms, and accordingly did come in to surrender to Col. Blackburn on the 24th day of May, 1865, and procure the protection of the Government.

In reply to the proposal of the prisoner, the Judge Advocate
replied:

"He may prove it if he can, but he must prove it by legal evidence."

Question—As you are not permitted to speak of the letter inquired of
you, you may state what you may know of the letter of the 15th of May,
here shown you, signed by Col. Blackburn; and what action did the
prisoner take, or conclusion did he come to, in regard to that letter?

Answer—I didn't see the prisoner at the time I first saw the letter, but
after I saw it I had a talk with the prisoner and I named to him "was he
going to surrender," and he said, yes, if he thought that Col. Blackburn
was in earnest about receiving him and not trying to catch him in a trap,
and I told him I thought Col. Blackburn a high-minded, honorable gentleman,—that whatever he proposed to do he would do. I told Capt.
Walker, at the time I saw the first letter, that I would vouch for Col. Blackburn's doing just what he said and I was at the surrender about the 24th
of May at the Widow Bradley's. Capt. Walker came in and Capt.
Ferguson came in; the men all came up, and the privates stacked their
arms. I heard no private conversation between Capt. Ferguson and Col.
Blackburn. It seemed to me that they were friendly as men could be.
I passed several introductions between the men of Col. Blackburn and
Capt. Ferguson. It seemed to me that they all surrendered.

Question—Previous to his arrest, during the early part of the War,
what was the state and condition of this country? Were the people
secure in their lives and property, or were they endangered by independent
bands, or home guards, throughout that section of country?

This question was also objected to by the Judge Advocate, who
said that it was just as leading as the others, that it suggested the
answers sought, and that putting it in the alternative did not relieve
it of its leading character.

The Court ruled that the witness might answer as to the first
clause of the question.

Answer—I think it was pretty bad; the country was in a bad condition.
You see, there were home guards and independent bands killing citizens

occasionally and taking our stock so that we could not make any support, scarcely. At one time they took every horse I had that was able to plow. I did not consider my life safe at all. The reason why I and other citizens were afraid was that there were home guards around there who had run through the country several times in the absence of these guerillas that I have spoken of, when they were across the mountains with a regular service.

Question—On which side were these guerillas or home guards?

Answer—I don't know. Capt. Beatty was said to be on the Federal side, but I don't know that he belonged to either side. The home guards were on the same side.

The witness was then placed on cross-examination by the Judge Advocate, the questioning apparently attempting to show that he had very little personal knowledge of what he was talking about and that his testimony was, therefore, more or less unreliable.

The gist of the witness' answers was as follows:

"I have never seen Capt. Beatty's company but twice—once in the Fall of 1862 and once this Spring at my house. I didn't know any of the men in the company.

"I don't know anything about the arrest of Capt. Ferguson in the Fall of 1861 except what I have heard, nor do I know anything about his raising a company or how many men he had. I have seen him with as many as twenty-five or thirty men at a time along the Calfkiller River where I live, and where I was born and raised. I had not seen them together for some time before the end of the War because Capt. Ferguson had been over the mountains in the regular service.

"As to my own political views, I was Southern at the beginning of the War. My sympathies were with the South. I took the oath some two years ago, while Col. Stokes was in command at Sparta, on the 26th of February, 1864. I have never been connected with either of the armies in any way. I never had fears of any kind except of Beatty's men, and the home guards of Sequatchie Valley. I never feared the regular soldiers. Some of the regular soldiers stayed with me. They always treated me as well as if they were my own brothers."

Question—You said yesterday that you told Capt. Walker that he had too few men to do any good and, as all the others had surrendered, he had better surrender. What good did you expect him to do if he had more men?

Answer—I didn't know what good he could do. I know that he had been injuring our citizens for some time, and I spoke that to try and get him to surrender. He couldn't do any good without it was to keep out those guerilla bands that I spoke of.

Question—After you took the oath, what steps did you take, if any, to give information to the Federal authorities that these bands which you called guerillas were in your neighborhood, or that they went across the mountains in August, 1864, to join the Rebel army?

Answer—I never took any steps to give any information. The guerillas, Captain Ferguson and his company, told me they were going across the mountains, and I told Col. Stokes what they said, namely, that they were going across the mountains.

Question—Did they tell you what they were going across the mountains for?

Answer—They said they were going to join the regular army. After the return, Ferguson told me, or at least I understood him to say, that he had been with General Williams in Virginia. I don't know whose commander General Williams was. My understanding was that Ferguson with with Williams at the time Lee surrendered to Grant. Williams, I understand, was going to join Lee when he got a dispatch that Lee had surrendered.

CHAPTER XX

A Plea for Mercy

THE testimony of Carrol Johnson had been very good as far as it had gone but it had not gone, and could not go, far enough. Nor was the testimony of the other three witnesses for the defense very pertinent to the charges at hand.

Champ Ferguson needed more witnesses, and especially he needed witnesses who knew that he did not kill the persons he was charged with killing or who knew that he killed them in virtual self-defense.

Judge Guild and Captain Goodwin, therefore, made one more effort to effect a delay in the trial until such witnesses could be secured. They may or may not have had any hopes of securing the witnesses but any delay was in the prisoner's favor. They presented the following affidavit asking for a continuance of the case for ten days:

Military Commission Rooms
District Middle Tennessee
Nashville, Tennessee, August 31, 1865.
United States

vs   Criminal Action.

Champ Ferguson

The defendant makes the oath that Doctor Long, Judge William Van, George Gwinn, Thomas Travis, Pleas Beatty, Mattie Sloan, Amanda Beatty, John Elder, Madison Wheeler, John Sandusky, Isham Beatty, are important and material for him in the defense. They reside in Clinton County, Kentucky, and have all been subpoenaed, except John Elder and Madison Wheeler, and failed to obey the process of the court. They have not appeared or been in attendance at this trial.

He prays postponement of the trial of this cause for ten days, for the purpose of enabling him to have the presence of said witnesses and the benefit of their testimony on this trial. He further asks upon the postponement being granted, a military order be made, detailing a military force to compel the attendance of these witnesses. He has every reasonable expectation that the attendance of these witnesses can be had by the day designated for the postponement. This continuance is asked for justice and not delay.

(signed) CHAMP FERGUSON

Sworn to before me and
subscribed in my presence, this
the 31st day of August, 1865.

(signed) H. C. BLACKMAN, Captain and Judge Advocate

The affidavit was held by the Court as insufficient, as not showing how the witnesses named were material; therefore the following additional affidavit was presented by the Defense:

By Amanda Beatty he expects to prove that Wm. Frogg, whom he has been charged with having killed, was armed, going about the country seeking and threatening to take the life of the defendant and that he was a violent and dangerous man, and that she communicated the same to the defendant. He expects to prove by John Sandusky that Elijah Kogier was armed, and threatened to kill him, and was hunting for him and swore that he intended to kill him on first sight.

He expects to prove by the witnesses named by the affidavit that the defendant's character was good, and that he was peaceably engaged at home, and that he had not taken up arms until after he was arrested and his life threatened, and that he was driven out of Kentucky without cause. He expects to prove other material and important facts by said witnesses. He prays this affidavit be attached to the original affidavit and made a part of it, asking a postponement of the trial.

(signed) CHAMP FERGUSON

The Commission announced that they would consider the application for continuance, whereupon the Court was cleared and pending consideration of the affidavit, the Commission adjourned to meet the next morning, Friday, September 1st, at eight o'clock.

When the Court assembled the next morning, the Judge Advocate made his reply to the arguments and affidavit of the defense counsel for a continuance:

The grounds set forth in the affidavit for the continuance of this cause is that alone which demands the attention of this Court and that alone upon which it may be determined whether they will grant the prayer of the prisoner asking a continuance. . . . .

First, the facts stated in the affidavit would not constitute a defense if proven. The danger is not shown to be so imminent as to render the taking of life, under the circumstances, necessary. In both these cases, the prisoner sought the combat by going to the houses of the deceased; and having pre-meditated the contest and sought the encounter, he is not at liberty now to set up self-defense.

Second, the prisoner has been guilty of gross negligence with reference to these witnesses. Two of the witnesses named have never been sub-poenaed at all. Subpoenas for them have never been asked for. Their names appear now for the first time. For the others, subpoenas were issued on the 17th of July, served on the 31st of July, and returned by our course of communication. The accused knew twenty days ago as well as he knows now that these witnesses have failed to appear.

He could have as well made his application for compulsory process then as now, and the affidavit shows no excuse whatever for not doing so; and besides, I announced in open court two weeks ago last Wednesday that I expected to close the prosecution by the middle of the week then following. Yet, though thus warned that he must get himself ready, he takes no steps to procure these witnesses. To allow this continuance on these grounds is to say that the accused is not required to use any diligence whatever and that the Court will wait indefinitely, and hear the witnesses for the defense whenever it waits his pleasure to produce them.

The Court was then cleared and after an hour's deliberation, the President of the Commission announced their decision:

The grounds upon which reaction is made by the defense for continuance are considered insufficient. In the attempt to show the materiality of witnesses mentioned in the affidavit of the defendant, Ferguson, affidavit alleges that he expects to prove by these witnesses that the parties or persons slain by him were seeking to take his life. Affiant does not allege that he, the defendant, expects to prove by one of the witnesses that the slain parties attacked with intent to kill or that he slew in self-defense, or that he made any effort to evade the conflict. . . . .

To make "homicide" excusable on the grounds of self-defense, the danger must be actual and urgent. No contingent danger will avail; it must be imminent. . . . .

Furthermore, the defendant has had ample time to make ready his defense and to prepare for trial. Summons was issued by the proper authority for the witnesses of the accused, and returned with the endorsement of service except in the case of some of the witnesses who could not be found. The said witnesses having failed to appear within a reasonable time and the Judge Advocate having given notice more than two weeks ago that he was about to close the prosecution, it is strange indeed that the defendant should wait until this late day to ask attachment for forcible process to compel his witnesses to appear. But it is still more strange that the able counsel for the accused should permit their client thus to sleep upon his rights, or that they would allow material witnesses in their cause to remain absent from court until they have consumed nearly a week in their defense, and now, for the first time, ask compulsory process to bring his witnesses into court. . . . .

It also occurs to the Court that at the commencement of this trial the accused allowed two weeks to elapse in the progress before a single summons was asked or any means taken for the procurement of witnesses.

The Court, having carefully considered the circumstances attending this trial and connected with this application, overrule the motion for continuance.

After this decision had been rendered, the Court adjourned until the following morning, Saturday, September 2nd, when it again assembled—fifty-three days after the start of the trial on July 11th. Counsel for the accused announced that they had no further witnesses and requested the Court to adjourn until Monday morning. The Judge Advocate announced that unless the accused appeared with witnesses on Monday, he would insist upon closing the case.

Whereupon, the Commission adjourned to meet at eight o'clock the following Monday morning, September 4, 1865.

"It is almost certain," said the reporter for the *Dispatch* in the Sunday issue of September 3rd, "that this noted trial has at last drawn to a close. Many witnesses for the prisoner have either refused or are unable to attend the trial. He has been ably defended and no effort has been spared on the part of his counsel to bring forward the evidence and make good use of all law points in his favor."

When the Court convened on Monday morning, September 4th, the Judge Advocate announced that no witnesses were on hand for the defense, whereupon Captain Goodwin, junior counsel for the defense, stated that he would formally close the case.

The prosecution, however, decided not to rest the case without recalling Captain Dowdy to the stand and thereby taking an indirect dig at Judge Guild for the part he had taken, as they saw it, in helping to incite the people of the Upper Cumberlands, including the prisoner at bar, to commit such crimes as those for which he was defending Champ Ferguson.

The Judge Advocate questioned Captain Dowdy as follows:

Question—Have you ever known any inflammatory speeches to have been made in your County?

Answer—I have. Judge Guild made speeches in the County. He said that all who were not for us were against us, that the Union men would all have to be hung, and that they might as well commence the good work at once. This was in Overton County, just before the election of June, 1861, on separation or no separation. There was considerable excitement over the speech. Alvin Collum and McHenry made speeches afterwards, in which they quoted from Judge Guild as an eminent man, and were guided by his speech.

Question—What was the object of that speech? Was it to promote rebellion, or excite the people?

Answer—It was calculated to excite and intimidate the people. The general drift of it was that if they did not go with them, they would have to leave the country,—meaning the Union men.

Question—Did you ever hear any others make speeches in that part?

Answer—Yes, I heard Judge Gardenhire make a speech at Jimtown in the same strain but not so inflammatory.

Judge Gardenhire, who was noted for committing long passages of scriptures, Shakespeare, etc., to memory as he rode over the mountain trails, was one of the most prominent jurists of the Mountain District. He was Circuit Judge when the War broke out, and was later a member of the Confederate Congress. It was in his law office that J. D. Goodpasture began law practice in 1845.

Question—Do you know of Judge Bramlette making speeches in that section?

Answer—I have understood that he did, but never heard him.

After this brief re-examination of Captain Dowdy, it was agreed upon by counsel that the closing argument should be made on Monday, September 11th. Captain Goodwin, still hoping, asked the privilege of introducing additional witnesses for the defense in case they appeared during the interim of preparing the argument. None came, however.

The Court assembled on Monday morning, September 11, 1865, at ten o'clock, two months to a day after the trial had started, to hear the closing argument for the defense. Wrote Mr. Rogers, of the *Dispatch*:

The prisoner, Champ Ferguson, was brought in court by ten guards with loaded guns and bayonets fixed. He is looking much better in health and appears more cheerful. He converses freely with the guards, and wears a pleading smile at times that leaves the visitors at the court-room to form a mild opinion of his *personale*. The handcuffs are not used in taking him to and from the courtroom, which apparently gratifies him, as he has a deadly horror of manacles.

During the interval previous to the opening of the Court, Champ was furnished a piece of watermelon, which he seemed to relish. A large number of ladies were present to hear the eloquent argument of the defense, and when the Court adjourned, one of the ladies kindly asked permission to furnish Champ with shirts and the request was granted.

Champ is still provided with an ambulance in coming and returning from the Court, being too weak to walk such a distance on foot. His demeanor in the courtroom, and at all times since his arrest, has been genteel and modest. He is often amused at the curiosity manifested by visitors to have him pointed out to them, and has heartily enjoyed the pranks of the guards in pointing out others as the noted Champ Ferguson, and particularly the expression of opinion after a long look at some innocent citizen who is just as anxious to get a glimpse at the prisoner as the one to whom he is pointed out.

The Court and all present listened to the eloquent and touching appeal delivered by Captain Goodwin with breathless attention, and in the latter part of the argument when the eloquent counsel alluded to the helpless family of the prisoner, his iron nerve bent for the first time during his trial and Champ Ferguson bowed his head and wept bitterly.

Indeed, all present were deeply affected by this matchless effort and the glowing manner in which the eloquent young orator made the appeal for his client reached the hearts and struck a tender chord in the affections of the audience. We are gratified to be able to lay the argument complete before our readers. It is brief, but full of wisdom, and one of the ablest efforts of the age.

Preparing the closing argument for the defense must have indeed presented a problem for Judge Guild and Captain Goodwin. Regardless of their own beliefs and those of the others who sympathized with Champ Ferguson, the arguments before the Court must rest upon the testimony presented during the trial. But the witnesses for the defense had been few and their testimony of little positive value. No effective rebuttal testimony had been presented. Consequently there was little basis in fact for logical and reasoned arguments in the summing up for the defense.

But they did not feel that the case was hopeless. There was

always left the appeal to sentiment, the appeal to emotion. Cases had been won before by such methods, and would be as long as human beings sat in judgment. But would a military commission composed of Yankee officers react favorably to such an appeal? That was a risk they had to take, for no other course was available.

In view of the final thrust at Judge Guild as an inciter, counsel for the defense decided that the appeal in behalf of Champ Ferguson would carry more weight if it came from the lips of Captain Goodwin. Captain Goodwin's effort to justify this decision follows:

By permission of the honorable President of the Commission and the members comprising it, we as attorneys for the defendant, Champ Ferguson, beg leave to submit the following review and argument for the defendant:

There are times in the lives of all men when they doubt what is the best step to be taken to secure a certain object or to promote or cause to be promoted a certain principle or right.

All men have an idea of right and wrong and it is a well established law that the Almighty has set forth that man does right so far as his weak mind will permit him, unless that mind is poisoned by undue influence over which he has no control,—or at least, if he have control, he has not been endowed with a moral courage to resist.

This statement is so nearly an axiom that it is unnecessary to demonstrate or illustrate. The assertion or truth above set forth will apply equally to the prisoner at bar and the honorable Commission. We, therefore, acknowledge that a doubt has arisen how we should proceed to accomplish the object we so much desire and so honestly believe should be obtained.

How easy it would be for a man to live with his fellow men, correcting all evils and promoting all good, had we remained as created. If our reason were always, as in our first ancestors before the transgression, clear and perfect, unruffled by passion, unclouded by prejudice, unimpaired by disease or intemperance, the task would be pleasant and easy; we should need no other guide but this.

But every man finds a contrary to this in his own experience—that his reason is corrupt and his understanding full of ignorance and error. We, therefore, in the blindness of human reason, must resort humbly to a Divine Power for advice and direction. Our mediator is our conscience, which is an original faculty of our nature, a faculty or power or principle within us which decides on the lawfulness or unlawfulness of our own actions and affection, and instantly approves or condemns them.

We ask that this case may be so considered by the Commission that all prejudice may be thrown aside, all undue public opinion may be ignored, and that after a cool, impassionate reasoning as to the facts has been undergone, a quiet spirit may counsel them as to justification or mercy.

This case has occupied the time of the Court for a period of nearly two months. The amount of testimony collected is immense, too great to attempt to recall to the Court in this argument,—nor would it be necessary, as they have so patiently listened to every syllable uttered by each witness.

The Court will remember that the universal tenor of the evidence is that, in all cases where the defendant was proven to have committed a wrong, it was against those who had wronged him, or threatened to do so. It is not necessary to mention the names of the persons who suffered the wrongs or who sought to wrong the defendant. It has been fully shown, both by the prosecution and the defense, that the state of the section in which the acts alleged to have been unlawful were committed was that of perfect chaos. No law prevailed, no order could be restored. The military of either side permitted it to remain unprotected and, therefore, personal feuds arose which were adjudicated by personal force. That this has been mutual is shown in the testimony of the first and other witnesses for the prosecution, as well as witnesses for the defense.

Why, therefore, should one individual be punished and others equally guilty of the same offense be held blameless?

It appears by the testimony of at least two witnesses that the defendant was a commissioned officer of the Rebel forces and such acts as he committed were under the direction of superior officers of the Confederate States. That the commanding officer should be responsible, and not the individual who was compelled so to act, is plain. (See Halleck's International Law and Laws of War, p. 346 following.)

But even admit, for sake of argument, that all falls to the ground, that the prisoner's commission does not protect him, that he should be pun ished for the acts committed under positive directions from his superior officers, that he had no right to defend himself, that his organization of a company was illegitimate, that his command had done violence—yet is not the letter of Major-General Geo. H. Thomas to Major-General Lovell H. Rousseau a complete pardon for all past sins, provided the conditions therein contained were complied with? Was not that letter founded on good judgment and cool reasoning; does it not show that the precepts of the Holy Book had been studied and regarded? Is it not plain that the Pardon there offered was like that offered for the sin com- mitted in the garden of Holy History? Can anyone claim that the con- ditions set forth in that amnesty were refused by the prisoner at bar? The proof was plainly to show that immediately on reception of the in- formation therein contained, the prisoner accepted the same and was anxious to lay down the bloody swords so long wielded with the blood stained swords of his opponents. He willingly gave up his followers and directed them to sacredly swear, in the presence of their Divine Creator, that hereafter the blood of their fellowman should no longer attach to their garments.

All this was done. Yet, of all the band within his own section of country; of all within the noble Department of the Cumberland; of all within the sacred lands of the Potomac; of all within the bounds of the United States of America who had identified themselves with similar independent bands—he alone was refused pardon.

Why is it that all others are permitted to go free and he punished? Why is it that the high officers who commanded this almost unknown man are free and he arraigned for his life? Why is it that the man who issued him his commission and the many civil officers of the rebellious government are free while he remains in a dungeon?

These are serious questions; these are questions of right; these are ques- tions that will be asked by our children, and children's children, and they will wonder if they should commit a crime whether they should suffer for it or arise higher in the scale of sin and be pardoned. We also call the minds of the honorable Commission to the pleas in bar that were offered by the defense at the beginning of the trial. We hold them to be good in law,—and how fervently mercy will plead them!

When due deliberation has been taken, the evidence and law properly considered,—should it be adverse to the prisoner, should your minds be so affected by any circumstance that you decide that there is no reasonable doubt (remembering that the prisoner has advantage of all reasonable doubts) that the prisoner should be punished—we beg you for mercy. We beg you to follow the precepts so plainly laid down in the Book of Holy Writ. We beg you to remember his helpless family—the helpmate, passing into old age; the daughter just budding into womanhood—knowing that you can stay the gray hairs of the one and prevent a miserable, blasted, unhappy, guideless life of the other.

Remember how cold and heartless this world is—even a man must be strong to withstand the turbulent waves.

We leave this case with you, and hope and have reason to believe your verdict will be such as to relieve the prisoner from further incarceration.

The prisoner wishes to thank the Court for the kindness they have shown him during the protracted and laborious trial.

At the conclusion of the argument by Captain Goodwin, Judge Advocate Blackman stated that he had hoped to be ready to reply immediately but the great volume of testimony to collect and consider, together with his duty as Acting Judge Advocate of the District, precluded him; that he considered it his duty to make a full reply to the argument of the defense. He gave notice that he would endeavor to make his argument for the prosecution on Thursday or Saturday, to which time the Court granted him.

The Commission then adjourned.

CHAPTER XXI

A Life in the Balance

IF counsel for the defense had any expectations of mercy at the hands of Judge Advocate Blackman, they were soon to be disillusioned. When the Court assembled on Saturday morning, September 16, 1865, to hear the closing argument by the prosecution, they heard a typical prosecuting attorney's speech. Major Blackman reviewed the case at length, and he, too, appealed to the emotions. But in addition, he was also able to support the charges with the sworn testimony of witnesses, testimony which the defense had not been able to rebut. And while making a case against Champ Ferguson, he also indicted the leaders who fomented the rebellion in that section; he indicted those citizens of Nashville, including the women, who evinced what he considered unseemly sympathy for the prisoner; he, in effect, indicted the whole Confederacy. If mercy was to be looked for, it must come at the hands of the Military Commission who sat in judgment on the case.

At ten o'clock that Saturday morning, Judge Advocate Blackman, in the presence of the prisoner and his counsel, the Military Commission, and a number of interested spectators, both ladies and gentlemen, arose to deliver the following reply to the speech of the counsel for the accused:

The case to which you have listened so patiently for nearly two months is but an incident of the great crime of rebellion.

Though the evidence discloses a series of crimes at which humanity shudders and good men stand aghast, those scenes are but as the trickling rivulet to the great sea of blood which has deluged the land. Rivulets make the ocean, and the aggregate acts of man made the great time of rebellion; and Champ Ferguson, today, ignorant, vicious, a creature of impulse and brutish passions, is less a criminal than those who incited him to the crimes he has committed. If ex-members of Congress and men who are pleased to style themselves the governing classes, who advised and by their appeals to local prejudices and passions, and false representations, brought about the horrors of the last four years, can live and look back upon the results of their labors and desire to live, let them live! If they have souls, if there are any of the tender impulses of human nature left in their breasts, life to them may be the worst punishment that could be inflicted.

This much in reply to what the counsel for the prisoner has said in regard to letting great criminals go, while Ferguson be punished. Our business, however, is now with this prisoner.

His counsel has appealed to you for mercy. They say they beg your mercy. Mercy! What have you to do with mercy? You are sworn to try this case according to the law and evidence. Upon your oath you must answer simply, is the prisoner guilty of the crimes set forth in this specification. If specifications are true, you must say so; if they are not true, under your oath you must say, not guilty. You are asked, are those charges and specifications true? Did the prisoner do the deeds here charged? Upon your oath you must answer.

To this inquiry, then, let us address ourselves.

You are first to decide, was the prisoner a guerilla. And the second charge is murder. To this second charge, there are twenty-three specifications. Upon each of these you must pass. Of each of these specifications you must say that the prisoner is guilty or not guilty.

For the purposes of convenience in the collation of the testimony, I choose to consider first in order the specifications to the charge of murder. After that we will inquire as to the first charge.

First, then, did the prisoner murder Lieutenant Smith, 13th Kentucky Cavalry, while he was lying wounded in the hospital, after the Battle of Saltville, in the month of October, 1864?

The first witness on this specification was young Shocker, a private of the 12th Ohio Cavalry. You saw that young man; he was highly intelligent and his face spoke honesty in every glance. He was just the man that either of you would have picked out to go upon the skirmish line with you or you would have trusted him with any order or message in the greatest of emergency. He told his tale in a plain, simple, and honest way. . . .

Lieut. Carter is a wounded prisoner. He sees the party that killed Lieutenant Smith. He saw them as they passed the door of his room. He thinks the prisoner is the man, and he is certain that the man whom he saw going toward Smith's room is the man who killed the negroes.

Allow that he is mistaken. Captain Sells testifies positively. He saw the prisoner and recognizes him now. He describes the scene. Ferguson enters the room and says, "Smith, do you know me?" "Champ, is that you?" "Yes, it is me; and do you see this?", raising his gun. There lays Smith, wounded, just able to raise on his elbow, and in that condition, begging for his life, he is shot.

Gentlemen, there can be no doubt as to who did this deed. But if there was a doubt in your minds, the counsel for the accused has taken care to remove it. They produced witnesses here whom I could not have called. They draw from Captain Sells that Burns, the hospital steward, said it was Ferguson and his men who committed these murders. And then, to drive the nail home, General Wheeler swore that Ferguson was at Saltville. He swears that Ferguson was detached and sent to Breckenridge and that his command went there—was there—and reported back after the fight was over. Gentlemen, this settles it. If Champ Ferguson's command was at the Battle of Saltville, he is the man who did those deeds. His command was there, for General Wheeler swears it was. This makes the murder of Smith so clear that if you would, you cannot doubt.

Specification second charges the killing of twelve Federal soldiers at the Battle of Saltville.

Gentlemen, it is for you to say how many were killed. The partner of Shocker was killed. The two negroes whom Carter saw led out of Emory and Henry Hospital were killed. The two negroes taken from the log house were killed, and Captain Sells tells you the firing was like the firing of the skirmish line. I cannot say how many were killed, but it is certain that that specification is sustained.

The third specification charges the killing of two colored soldiers at Saltville. That is well proven. He killed two at the Hospital; he killed two at the log house.

The fourth specification charges the killing of nineteen soldiers of the 5th Tennessee Cavalry. Upon that specification there is no proof.

The fifth specification charges the killing of Reuben Wood. To this you have the evidence of Miss Wood who saw the deed, and you hear a voice from that bloody grave telling you that it was Champ Ferguson, the man whom he had dandled upon his knee, who had grown up to manhood under the eyes of that old man—Reuben Wood, with his dying breath, tells you it was Champ Ferguson who killed him. And why? Champ, why did you kill that old man? He had been at Camp Dick Robinson. He had followed the old flag; therefore, he must die. "Don't dodge—don't stir—stand still"—and in the presence of his aged wife and young daughter, he is shot down.

Gentlemen, the prisoner's counsel has said that Ferguson only slew those who sought his life. Will you tell me where is the evidence that Reuben Wood ever sought Ferguson's life? But I must not dwell.

The sixth specification charges the killing of Wm. Frogg. Mrs. Frogg and young Mace both swear that Ferguson killed him. Words cannot add to that scene. There is a wife—there is a sleeping babe—and there is the prisoner. Why was Frogg murdered in his bed?

The seventh, eighth, and ninth specifications charged the killing of Stover, Johnson, and Pierce. I do not say that the evidence makes it certain that Ferguson killed these men. But he was along and was the leading spirit and they all are stabbed. Bloody Nathan, in the "nick of the woods," always left his bloody mark upon his victims. Champ Ferguson's victims are just as certainly marked by that knife that was given him by the honorable McHenry.

And, gentlemen, right here just remember when it was that this raid was got up. A compromise had been effected. The Union companies had all disbanded. And now came forward the Honorable Alvin Cullom, and inaugurates a carnival of blood. Champ Ferguson today is a better man, more honorable, than such men as Alvin Cullom and James W. McHenry.

The tenth murder is the killing of Master Fount Zachery, a mere boy, shot after he had surrendered. And then why does the prisoner dismount from his horse and stab the dead body? The heart sickens at the contemplation of the scene.

Then comes Elijah Kogier, then old James Zachery, and then old Alex Huff.

Gentlemen, what have these old men done?

The killing of Joseph Beck is proven so plain that none doubts who is the murderer. Mrs. Kogier and Mrs. Walker are told by the prisoner first where to find his clothes and his body. They do find him, just where Ferguson said he would be found.

There is no proof as to who killed McGlasson.

Elam Huddleston was killed after he had been wounded and surrendered. Lying in the agonies of death, he is brutally murdered by the prisoner.

Now Peter and Allen Zachery are murdered. You remember the testimony of Miss Dowdy, and you remember how the prisoner hacked Allen Zachery to pieces with that fatal knife.

As to the killing of Williams, Delk, and Crabtree, Preston Huff was at his mother's house in October, 1862. Williams, Delk, and Crabtree were there. A party rode up in the night, and someone said, "Press, G—d D—n you, come out here and surrender." A voice which he took to be Ferguson's called out, "Surround the house." The witness and William Huff made their escape. About daylight, they came down near the road and saw the party coming from his mother's house, and saw that they had Williams, Delk, and Crabtree prisoners. He saw Ferguson, Moles, the McGinnises, Latham, and others. The party was going in the direction of Wm. Piles', about a mile from his mother's. About half an hour after they passed, he heard three guns fire that sounded as if they were in the vicinity of Piles' place. They had a negro girl along. She was riding with Hans Moles. They had some bed clothes taken from his mother's.

Miss Vina Piles is a daughter of William Piles and was at her father's house in October, 1862. The morning of the 3rd, a party of men came there with Williams, Crabtree, and Delk; don't know the prisoner; identifies Moles and others of the party that Preston Huff identifies, also the negro girl riding with Moles, and the bedding of Mrs. Huff. The prisoners, Williams, Delk, and Crabtree, were tied together when they came in. The crowd went through the gate into the yard about fifty yards from the house. A man then ordered witness and her mother into the house; heard three shots; and shortly after, the same man came to the house and told her they had killed three men. Witness and her mother then went out and the crowd went off. The witness, with her mother, then found the bodies. Williams was shot three times. Delk was cut under the right arm. Crabtree was cut all to pieces; couldn't tell how often he was cut, and in one wound in the right shoulder a corn stalk was sharpened and stuck into the wound. They were all dead when witness and her mother went to them.

Alvin C. Piles, son of William Piles, and brother of Vina Piles, saw Ferguson on the day that Williams, Delk, and Crabtree were killed. It was after they were killed, about noon. The same men were along with him as those named by Vina Piles and Preston Huff. Saw them on the main road, leaving from his father's house. Saw Ferguson pull out a large bowie knife, and could tell that he was talking about it, but couldn't understand all he said. Could hear him say "knife."

Specification twenty-two is the killing of the negro that old man Upchurch and his wife swear to.

Specification twenty-three is the killing of old man Tabor. This is proven by the evidence of the two Thrashers.

Now, gentlemen, he murdered:

Woods, Edwards, Sells, Garner, Dallas Beatty, Williams, Delk, Crabtree, Alexander Huff, Elam Huddleston, old man Tabor, Peter and Allen Zachery, James Zachery, Fount Zachery, Lieut. Smith, Beck, Kogier, and Frogg, and old Reuben Woods. These men were his neighbors and he killed them because they were Union men and for no other reason.

To all this the prisoner, by his counsel, answers that Ferguson is an officer of the Rebel Army, and that he surrendered to Col. Blackburn.

Gentlemen, if he was an officer, why did he not surrender with the army of Lee and Johnston? And right here, let me say, if the prisoner belonged regularly to the Rebel Army, why has he not surrendered with it? The testimony of Wheeler shows that he must have been there at the time of the surrender; and the declaration of the prisoner to his own witness, Carrol Johnson, and others shows that he was there.

Now, why did he not surrender with the balance of the army if he was regularly in Rebel services? Or was he surrendered and paroled there with the balance of General Williams' command? And did he, in violation of that surrender and parole, return armed and in hostile attitude, with an armed band, to Tennessee? If he failed to surrender according to the terms of that cartel and returned armed and in a hostile attitude, he grossly violated his obligations as a soldier and cannot now come here and ask the benefit of that cartel. If he did surrender—accept the parole according to the terms of the cartel—and afterwards joined this armed band and come home armed and hostile, committing acts of murder and outrage—then he has violated his parole and is not entitled to demand the rights of a prisoner of war.

Now, the prisoner cannot be permitted to escape the position in which he has placed himself. He has shown that he was with General Williams, a part of General Wheeler's command, at the time of the surrender. He was bound by that surrender. I care not for what purpose or view he got with Wheeler,—if he was a part of Wheeler's command, he violated his faith in failing to regard the terms of that cartel. He cannot play fast and loose here. This is too serious a matter. Neither he nor his counsel will be permitted to say that it was not his duty to surrender with General Williams' command. It is this testimony which damns him. Will his counsel tell this Court, will they tell our Generals, who they say are trying this man improperly, why he did not come to Col. Blackburn and say, "I was with General Williams, a part of General Wheeler's command, when it surrendered. I was surrendered and paroled with that command and here is my parole. I demand the rights of a paroled prisoner of war."

Tell us, gentlemen of the defense, why you did not surrender as you were bound to do with General Wheeler, or if you did surrender why do you not have your parole? And in either view, is it not sublimated impudence to come in here and talk about that affair between Captain Walker and Col. Blackburn up here at Widow Bradley's?

Now, gentlemen, is the prisoner a guerilla? If he was ever an officer, there is no proof of it, prior to August, 1864. Before this, he had been a common robber. He commenced in 1861 by the robbery of Wright's store, in Albany. He was a general plunderer in all that region. He stole Dr. Hale's property, and sold his piano and appropriated the money to his own use. He robbed the residence of John B. Rogers. And then take Captain Dowdy's testimony of the finding of the goods concealed about Ferguson's premises. It won't do, gentlemen, for the soldiers to deny that he had charge of those goods. This remarkable muster-roll is found with the other property. If the roll is Ferguson's, the goods are

Ferguson's. If those goods were concealed there in the woods, on Ferguson's premises, he was a guerilla.

And now, as to his surrender. I have already said that if this man had any rights as a prisoner of war, he was bound to have surrendered with General Wheeler's command, and he cannot be permitted to be a regular officer and guerilla at the same time. My friend, Captain Goodwin, has been too long an officer, and been too familiar with prisoners, not to know all this talk about Ferguson's surrendering to Col. Blackburn is mere gammon. He did not surrender. He was not allowed to surrender. Col. Blackburn had absolute orders not to receive the surrender. He could not have surrendered if he would. And he was notified by Col. Blackburn that he cannot surrender, and more than that, Blackburn tells him that if he remains in that country that he will capture him in less than five days—and he makes his word good and does capture him.

Besides all that, what is the use talking about Ferguson's men surrendering. Walker and his men surrendered. The correspondence is with Walker; there is not a word in all this evidence showing that Ferguson had any men there. It was Walker's company. All the correspondence was with Walker, and Ferguson is not known in the matter.

It is sheer nonsense to talk about this man being a prisoner of war.

I will not take your time by arguing the question of jurisdiction. That matter has been sufficiently considered in the beginning of this case. If this man is to be punished for all these crimes, he must be punished by such tribunal as this.

The evidence adduced in this case must convince all that a trial by jury of this man for his many enormities, in the counties where they were committed, would be impossible. And it cannot have escaped the observation of the Commission that even here in Nashville he has the warm sympathy of every one of Rebel proclivities—so strong, indeed, that some have found it difficult to keep their admiration and sympathy within the bounds of decency. Were he a philanthropist and benefactor of mankind, surrounded on all sides with evidence of good deeds, instead of a man covered all over with human gore—had he filled his country with joy instead of wailing, lamentation, and sorrow—the evidence of the sympathy and admiration of certain parties could not have been more plain or marked. The daughter of Judah weeping by the waters of

Babylon over the sorrows of Israel were not more sorrowful than the daughter of Dixie weeping over the misfortunes of Champ Ferguson.

I cannot say that I disapprove the evidences of sympathy shown by the women. It was they who, by their smiles and frowns, incited and drove the men of the South to deeds that the world admires; and it is eminently proper that they should show here that they are brave enough to console the victims of their wiles; and I admire the openness of their conduct and honor them more, far more, than I do the men who were equally active in inciting men to deeds like this, and who now leave their dupes to believe, while many sneak away shielding themselves from the consequences of their crimes of amnesty oath.

Gentlemen, take this case. Answer by your finding whether the proof shows the prisoner guilty or innocent. Pronounce your decision without fear or favor, and answer now as you must answer at the Great Bar, where all secrets shall be known, and where all the deeds of our lives will be laid bare. The case is in your hands.

CHAPTER XXII

The Execution

THE Nashville *Dispatch* of Tuesday, September 26, 1865, reported that the decision of the Military Commission would first be transmitted to the General Commander of the District of Middle Tennessee, who would publish it in General Orders. Two weeks later, on October 10, General Orders were received from the Headquarters at Murfreesboro, stating that the findings and the sentence of the Commission were approved and confirmed.

Champ Ferguson was to be hanged.

Immediately upon receipt of the General Orders, the Post Commandant, Colonel W. R. Shafter, who was later to distinguish himself during the Spanish American War, proceeded to the Military Prison and read the sentence to Ferguson:

"The Court do therefore find the said Champ Ferguson guilty and sentence him to hang by the neck until he is dead at the time and place as the General Commander may order, two-thirds of the members of the Commission concurring in the sentence."

The General Commander had decreed that the sentence of death was to be carried into effect ten days later, on the 20th of October, 1865, between the hours of ten o'clock A.M. and four o'clock P.M., at Nashville. Col. Shafter stated that the execution would be within the walls of the prison and would not be open to the public in general, although some passes would be issued.

On Wednesday, October 18th, Mr. Rogers, of the *Dispatch*, had the interview during which Champ "confessed," or gave his side of the many killings with which he was charged and concerning which testimony was given during the trial. There can be no question but that to the very end Champ Ferguson felt he was fully justified in all the acts he committed. The statements he made during this interview with reference to the various charges of murder have been previously given during this account in connection with each of the cases referred to.

On this Wednesday afternoon, Mr. Rogers, in company with Lieut. A. M. Coddington, Adjutant on Colonel Shafter's staff, visited the prison and found Champ sitting by the stove in the hallway that surrounded the cells. They found him much concerned that the members of his family had not arrived. Apparently they had been notified of the result of the trial and were expected at any time.

Champ had previously told the reporter that if the trial went against him he "would tell all." Mr. Rogers reminded Champ of this statement, but before making the "confession," Champ exacted a promise from him that he would not publish it until after his execution. He thereupon proceeded to make the statements which have been quoted at various times during this account, and which were given to the public on the Sunday following the execution.

Champ Ferguson was now once more in good health, and his courage and firm spirits had not been weakened by his sentence of death. A certain calm, or resignation, seemed to have come over him. He said that he slept well and was not disturbed by dreams; that he was reconciled to his fate. He said that he was not surprised at the death sentence and that he only grieved for his wife and daughter, as they would have no support after he was gone since the War had left him penniless, and he regretted leaving them in an unfriendly world.

Champ asked Lieut. Coddington to get him a bottle of pure brandy to drink on the morning he was to be hanged. He also asked that a raised cherry coffin be furnished to receive his body. In answer to a question, he remarked that he was considered one of the best shots in his part of the country and said he rarely aimed at anything but Tinker Dave but what he brought it down.

Mr. Rogers had another interview with Champ on the next day, Thursday, the day before he was to be hanged. He appeared in even more lively spirits than he had the day before, apparently being greatly relieved by the arrival of his wife and daughter, who, by permission of Col. Shafter, were allowed to spend most of the day with him. Both wife and daughter, the reporter noticed, manifested in their pale faces the anguish they were suffering. Champ endeavored to cheer them at intervals by a few words lightly spoken, as though he had no thought of his doom. He reiterated the statement that, except for his desire not to incriminate any of his friends, he might say a great deal that he was not saying. It had been promised him, he said, that his remains would be given to his wife, who would take his body to be buried in the pure soil of White County a few miles north of Sparta.

On the very morning of the execution, upon being asked by the newspaper reporters present if he had any last statement for the press, Champ requested that he be allowed to make one final statement to Mr. Rogers alone. It was his one last attempt to justify his actions in the eyes of the people and a recrimination of the method by which he was brought to trial—a statement which he swore before God to be true:

"I surrendered to General Thomas on the letter or order sent to all armed bands, me with the rest. I did not think they would treat me as they have done. I am the same man I was before the War and will be till the last minute of my life. I don't know what men in high office can think of in sending out such men as Colonel Blackburn and others for the purpose of inducing me to come for the sake of hanging me. He told me I was no worse than the rest and that I should be protected and that he was glad to see me.

"I was a Southern man at the start. I am yet, and will die a Rebel. I believe I was right in all I did. I don't think I have done anything wrong at any time. I committed my deeds in a cool and deliberate manner. I killed a good many men, of course; I don't deny that, but I never killed a man whom I did not know was seeking my life. It is false that I never took any prisoners. I took a great many and after keeping them awhile paroled them. I tried to prove this during my trial but they would not give me time to do it. I had always heard that the Federals would not take me prisoner, but would shoot me down, wherever found. That is what made me kill more than I would otherwise have done. They never got a man that belonged to my company or Bledsoe's company but that they killed him, and of course they might expect that I would not miss doing the same thing with their men.

"I repeat that I die a Rebel out and out, and my last request is that my body be removed to White County, Tennessee, and be buried in good Rebel soil."

It was between ten and eleven o'clock on Friday morning that Champ Ferguson made this final statement to the press in his cell in the penitentiary. On emerging from the cell, Col. Shafter requested Mrs. Ferguson and her daughter, who had been with Champ during the morning, to take their final leave of their husband and father. It was a painful scene and brought tears to the eyes of the reporter and the officers who witnessed it.

Martha Ferguson did not embrace her husband, but grasped his hand firmly and gave him a loving, farewell look—then turned away and surrendered herself to the terrible anguish of her heart. Ann Ferguson, a lovely girl of sixteen, then approached her father, who opened wide his arms to receive her, and her head fell on his chest. They stood thus without speaking, and when the last bitter word of command to part was given, the girl shrieked, "Farewell, my poor, poor papa!" Mother and daughter then retired to a brick building adjoining the prison.

On Wednesday and Thursday, before Champ Ferguson was executed on Friday, rumors were rife in Nashville that a reprieve had arrived, and that Champ had either been pardoned or his sentence changed to life imprisonment. "Criminal as the man is," said the *Daily Press and Times*, "he has adherents to his fortunes who are ready to spare neither effort nor expense to secure his release." It was known that the necessary papers in the case had been dispatched to Washington by a trusty messenger and strong hopes were entertained by Champ's sympathizers that a power higher than General Stoneman, then in command of the District of Middle Tennessee, would stay the execution.

What slight hope may have lingered in their breasts, however, was doomed to disappointment. Andrew Johnson was having troubles of his own, troubles that might cost him the position of President of the United States. More than that, as Military Governor of Tennessee, his own attempts to curb the activities of the then active Champ Ferguson had been without avail. Champ Ferguson was to receive no sympathy from that source, the only authority with power to stay his sentence of death.

Friday morning dawned clear and bright, "as if," stated the hostile *Daily Press and Times,* "the very insensate elements were glowing with exultation over the approaching exit from life of that guerilla chieftain whose murders, outrages, and cruelties had made the name of Champ Ferguson a by-word of reproach to human nature."

Detachments from the 15th United States Colored Infantry were on duty before the entrance of the penitentiary, a fact which must have irritated the Rebels of the city no little. A large crowd of persons had gathered before the entrance by ten o'clock, endeavoring to secure passes to witness the execution, but most of them were refused. Only three hundred passes were issued. A wagon stood at the entrance, waiting to receive the coffin containing Champ Ferguson's body, as soon as the execution had taken place.

Within the stockade of the prison stood a gallows which had been used for the purpose at other times during the past few years, although several workmen were kept busy for some time on Friday morning making certain repairs to the scaffold and testing the hangman's rope. The scaffold, standing six steps off the ground, was about eight feet square and contained a trap door in the center about four feet square. The latter could be released by chopping the rope tied over the edge of the flooring.

After bidding final adieux to his wife and daughter, Champ turned to the executioner who had the ropes, and asked if he must be tied. On being informed that it was required, he calmly folded his hands behind his back and was tied at the elbows and wrists. He was asked if the rope was too tight, or painful, to which he replied, after moving himself, that he was very comfortable. The guards then formed on either side of him. With the Reverend Mr. R. F. Bunting, lately of Virginia, and pastor of the First Presbyterian Church, in front, and Captain Dykeman, Post Provost Marshal, on one side, and Col. Shafter, Post Commandant on the other, Champ entered the prison yard with a firm step and walked with head erect some one hundred fifty yards to the scaffold, which was surrounded by a hollow square of soldiers from the Sixteenth Infantry. Without the least sign of fear and with entire outward composure, Champ passed by the coffin which was placed near the scaffold and ascended the steps to the platform, where he took his position upon the drop. Standing there, he deliberately surveyed the audience and nodded to several familiar faces he saw in the throng.

"He appeared," said Mr. Rogers, "like a man who was about to make a speech on some leading topic, and had simply paused to refresh his memory."

It was somewhat ironic, perhaps, that Champ was now dressed in a new black cloth frock coat, with vest and pants of the same material, and a neat, white shirt—furnished, no doubt, by the "ladies of the South" whom Judge Advocate Blackman had referred to rather sarcastically in his final charge. Standing there, thus neatly dressed and apparently in excellent health, Champ Ferguson made a fine picture of a man as he listened rather impatiently to Colonel Shafter proceed with a re-reading of the charges and specifications upon which he was tried and the sentence of the Court approved by General Stoneman.

This procedure occupied about twenty minutes and during the reading Champ looked about restlessly as if he considered the procedure entirely unnecessary. As the different charges were read, he either bowed in acknowledgment of their truth or shook his head in denial. When the name of Elam Huddleston was read, he remarked in a firm voice, "I can tell it better than that." At the conclusion of the reading of the sentence, Colonel Shafter said, "In accordance with the sentence I have read you, Champ Ferguson, I am going to have you executed." Without evincing a single emotion, and with iron nerve and countenance firm and determined, Champ replied, "I am ready to die."

The Reverend Mr. Bunting thereupon offered up an appropriate prayer, invoking the blessings of Almighty God upon the man who was about to die. It was evident that Champ was deeply affected by the words of the minister for tears glistened on his cheeks, and at the conclusion, he asked Col. Shafter to take his handkerchief from his side pocket and wipe his face. The Colonel complied, meantime conversing with Champ in an undertone, his words evidently being of some cheer, as Champ's features lighted up noticeably. Colonel Shafter then expressed the hope to Champ that he had no hard feelings toward the officers or any others who were performing the painful duty imposed upon them, to which Champ replied that he had none in the world and thanked them for their kindness.

Colonel Shafter then asked Champ if he had any remarks to make, to which Champ replied that he had plenty to say if he only knew how to say it. But he merely requested that his remains be placed in "that box" nodding toward the coffin, and turned over to his wife to be taken to White County. "I do not want to be buried in such soil as this," said Champ.

The white cap was then drawn over his face, and Colonel Shafter once more asked, "Have you anything further to say?" Champ replied that he had not. The Colonel then motioned to the executioner to take his post, when Champ exclaimed in a clear and loud voice, "Lord, have mercy on my soul!" As these words fell from his lips, the executioner, with one blow of the hatchet, severed the rope which held the drop, and the trap fell.

Postlude

YEARS later, Captain S. J. Johnston, wrote to his fellow Confederate officer, Bromfield L. Ridley:

"My farm and home were once owned by Champ Ferguson. He is buried near my home, in White County, Tennessee, on the Calfkiller. I can stand on my front piazza and see the tall gray tombstone that was cut from rock in the mountain not over a mile from his grave."

We know, of course, that Champ's last request as he stood on the scaffold was that his body be placed in the nearby coffin and turned over to his wife, in order that she might take him back home to White County where he would be surrounded by his family and buried in good Rebel soil. Colonel Shafter had promised that this would be done.

Other than this last request, the statement of Captain Johnston was the only reference I found as to the approximate location of Ferguson's grave. Correspondence with acquaintances in Sparta, the county seat of White County, failed to produce anyone who knew just where the grave was located. The only recourse left was to attempt to find it myself.

Sparta is about ninety miles northeast of Nashville, an easy two hours drive by automobile. But what a tedious journey it must have been to Martha and Ann Ferguson, as they drove a wagon those ninety miles over rough roads in October, 1865, carrying their husband and father to his grave! They were heartsick and weary, and after performing this last sad duty, were to go on to what is now Oklahoma, where they might find in a new country the peace and opportunity for happiness which had not been theirs for so long.

There was no trouble getting directions out of Sparta on the